Marco Bagli
Tastes We Live By

Applications of
Cognitive Linguistics

Editors
Gitte Kristiansen
Francisco J. Ruiz de Mendoza Ibáñez

Honorary editor
René Dirven

Volume 50

Marco Bagli

Tastes We Live By

The Linguistic Conceptualisation of Taste in English

ISBN 978-3-11-125576-7
e-ISBN (PDF) 978-3-11-063040-4
e-ISBN (EPUB) 978-3-11-062686-5
ISSN 1861-4078

Library of Congress Control Number: 2021944317

Bibliographic information published by the Deutsche Nationalbibliothek
The Deutsche Nationalbibliothek lists this publication in the Deutsche Nationalbibliografie;
detailed bibliographic data are available on the Internet at http://dnb.dnb.de.

© 2023 Walter de Gruyter GmbH, Berlin/Boston
This volume is text- and page-identical with the hardback published in 2021.
Typesetting: Integra Software Services Pvt. Ltd.
Printing and binding: CPI books GmbH, Leck

www.degruyter.com

per Jodi

Preface

When I talk to my friends and colleagues about my research, they typically think that I am an expert taster and, as such, I can describe the taste of food stuffs with the most appropriate vocabulary. They assume that I know every aspect of flavour, and that I can effortlessly choose the most appropriate wine for dinner. Other people instead need clarification on the meaning of "taste": following the academic and sociological tradition by Bourdieu, some people think that I deal with "social" taste – the set of cultural and aesthetic choices that an individual may make according to their preferences.

These topics, albeit fascinating, are only tangentially related to the core of this book. I am not interested in food description *per se*, nor in wine description. Furthermore, the discipline of interest is linguistics (not sociology), and to me, the confusion that arises in conversation between *physical* taste and *social* taste is a metaphor that enables us to understand an abstract concept such as personal preferences in terms of a more concrete concept such as the sense of taste. This book is about the words that describe taste, and their metaphorical and metonymic elaborations. Ultimately, this is a book about our capacity to create meaning out of physical perception and sensations. This often happens in a creative way, but perhaps even more often the words of taste follow predictable and nonarbitrary paths of meaning expansion.

One of the crucial assumptions in linguistic theories from Saussure onwards is the arbitrariness of meaning. Signs denote concepts, and the association between a sign and its meaning is thought to be arbitrary. According to his view, the sequence of sounds that constitutes the word *crunchy* is nothing more than a convention adopted by a community of speakers to describe a quality of food, and there is nothing in the word *crunchy* that resembles what it means. I want to emphasise that a century worth of linguistic investigation has shown that this is not always the case. Languages show some traces of *iconicity* (an icon is a type of sign that resembles its meaning), and *crunchy* is an example of this relationship between a sign and its meaning. Moreover, the extended meaning of concepts (i.e., the non-literal meaning) is motivated by the architecture of our brains and the nature of our bodies. The words that an individual utters daily are not (totally) arbitrary: rather, today general consensus in Cognitive Linguistics maintains that linguistic choices are constrained and dictated by a number of factors. Some of these might be external to language, such as frequency of use, entrenchment, attention, cultural factors, and perceptual qualities, to name but a few. The words we utter have come down to us through centuries of nonarbitrary dynamic patterns of sense relations.

Cognitive Linguistics is the branch of linguistic studies that integrates different approaches to language description and recognises the role of external factors on language production, recognition, and use. Scholars in this tradition have largely investigated the lexicon and semantic processes of meaning-making. For instance, a fruitful area of investigation in Cognitive Linguistics (and anthropology) is colour and vision studies. The cross-cultural investigation of the spectrum of colour and visual perception partitioning has inspired many researchers and has led to the formulation of a theory of categorisation that is still valid and continually supported by empirical data. According to this theory, a representative concept of a category occupies a central spot (i.e., a prototype), while other members are distributed around the prototype in a radial network. As a result, the different *reds* that a person may experience are judged against a prototype of *redness*, instantiated by a central and prototypical concept of RED,[1] which arises from the combination of everyday experiences and language use.

Unfortunately, the sense of taste has not been given the same scientific attention as vision. There are only scattered and incomplete accounts about the words of taste used by different cultures and languages around the world. These contributions are dated (they date back to the early years of the 20th century), and the methodology with which data have been collected is often inconsistent and doubtful. Following this, taste had been forgotten for years, and no solid investigation solely dedicated to this sense has been published until (1994) when Backhouse published his book on the "lexical field of taste in Japanese". Information on the words of taste in Indo-European languages and in English is however scattered in several papers working with different foci of attention and in different traditions. The major impetus towards a reconsideration of the lexicon of the senses has arisen mainly within Cognitive Linguistics, as a consequence of the centrality of the theory of embodiment. According to this theoretical stance, our mental processes (including language) are motivated by the information obtained through our bodies.

Why would taste be less represented in linguistic studies than other senses? The reasons for this disparagement are manifold. Hints of this scientific and intellectual neglect may be traced back to ancient Greek philosophy, where philosophers in the Socratic school partitioned the senses in different categories and considered taste to be in one of the lowest positions. A meager consideration of the bodily sensations associated with taste and smell has crossed the centuries and academic investigations until recently and has been reinforced by

---

[1] In the book I use SMALL CAPS when referring to conceptual domains in keeping with the typographical conventions of Cognitive Linguistics literature.

the observation that the lexical items to describe taste and smell are less numerous than those that describe other perception modalities. Nonetheless, recent data in cross-linguistic literature show that this is not true for every language, and that comparing different systems of conceptualisation of perception may help us better understand our bodies, our minds, and our cultures.

Culture plays a crucial role in the conceptualisation of perception. On one hand, cultural practices license or block specific linguistic realisations: despite its embodied and biological basis, the lexicon of perception varies among different linguistic systems. On the other hand, the meaning of this lexicon is elaborated in different manners across cultures, and it mirrors specific practices. In the case of English, the language under scrutiny in this book, this elaboration has been brought about over centuries through literature and usage, and over a considerable geographical area of diffusion. This boils down to thousands of generations of individuals using English to communicate and exchange information, resulting in wide linguistic variation and semantic change. This terrific wealth of information has been stored in linguistic units and described by lexicographers in dictionaries encompassing the possible meanings and realisations. Furthermore, English boasts one of the largest corpora available for a researcher to test hypotheses and verify usage. This represents a valuable tool for the investigation and description of linguistic phenomena in linguistic research, especially for researchers working within the descriptive approach sponsored by the Cognitive Linguistics tradition.

Three books have been sitting on my desk while working on the final revision of this book: Sensory linguistics (2019a), by Bodo Winter; Perception metaphors (2019), edited by Laura Speed, Carolyn O'Meara, Lila San Roque and Asifa Majid, and my Ph.D. dissertation. Sensory linguistics represents the first attempt to unify several strands of research working on the interface between perception, cognition, and language, and sets a theoretical and methodological standard for linguists interested in this area of research. Perception metaphors collects contributions on the elaboration of perception language, thus exploring the range of possibilities of human meaning creation. Lastly, Tastes We Live By represents an improved version of my Ph.D. dissertation. This was mainly written in Perugia, Italy, but it largely benefitted from a period that I spent at the University of Glasgow. There, I became acquainted with the Mapping Metaphor with the Historical Thesaurus Project, a monumental effort to map the role of metaphor throughout the history of English. Furthermore, many other inputs and insights came from the conferences I have attended, and the fruitful debates that followed. This book adopts various methodologies, sometimes borrowed from neighbouring disciplines, in order to account for the linguistic elaboration of taste in English and its representation. The interdisciplinarity of this approach mirrors the interdisciplinary approach of Cognitive Linguistics. It integrates multiple perspectives and tools with the aim of exploring the representation of taste in English: philosophy, evolutionary anthropology, psychology, psycholinguistics, biology, cultural anthropology, corpus analysis, and lexicographic analysis contribute to the identification of the words of taste, and to how and why we use these words to communicate.

This book represents in many ways the sum of years of research dedicated to the topic of the language of perception and taste more specifically. It is primarily addressed to scholars in linguistics, as well as in cognitive science and psycholinguistics. Furthermore, scholars in disciplines such as anthropology, psychology, philosophy, and even advertisement and food sciences may find it beneficial. The variety of approaches and the array of linguistic phenomena described should be of interest across a diverse audience. As such, it provides a brief introduction to central topics in Cognitive Linguistics, and it discusses at length only the core theoretical concepts that are applied to the description of taste. The interested reader is able to find references to further their understanding of the subject, while the expert reader may benefit from detailed exposition of specific topics. Information coming from other disciplines integrates the discussion to give an exhaustive account of the conceptualisation of taste.

The contributions of this book to the scientific debate are manifold. Firstly, it fills a gap in scientific literature about the language of taste in English, thus representing a first attempt towards the description of the role of this sensory modality in the creation of meaning through language. Secondly, it showcases the application of methods and tools that are only tangentially adopted in Cognitive Linguistics, such as the Cognitive Salience Index and Sorting tasks. The choice of these methodologies, involving native speakers either directly or indirectly, were dictated and influenced by my identity as an *outsider* to the language I am describing. I am not a native speaker of English, and I learned the language through schooling and many years spent living in the countries and working with people whose native language is English. The approach of the outsider enabled me to have an external eye, since my intention in writing this book is that of an ethnologist who decides to describe a culture to which they don't belong. As opposed to representing a drawback for my investigation, this has given me the opportunity to verify my intuitions through dictionaries and corpora, which is also in keeping with the Cognitive Linguistics approach. To complete the picture, this book also adopts standard methodologies such as corpus and lexicographic analysis. Again, both methods allow for a usage-based description of language. Particularly, the lexicographic analysis with the data of the Mapping Metaphor Project presents a methodology for the diachronic investigation of semantic change in the English language of perception. This perspective has been sporadically investigated in previous literature, and it offers a promising area of analysis. The rich and well-documented history of English offers a great opportunity for tracing the lexical and semantic development of perceptual language. The linguistic phenomena explored in this book are located at the intersection of language, culture, cognition, and perception, thus posing questions on the nature of our minds and the constraints operated by our bodies on our conceptual organisation. The data discussed in the following pages are restricted to English gustatory words, and therefore are specific to this linguistic system. These data may however be further elaborated and compared with (hopefully) homologous data coming from other languages, to gain a better and more general idea of the role of taste in human cognition. Moreover, the empirical data and their theoretical interpretations contribute to the current debate in sensory linguistics on the nature and the internal structure of the lexicon of the senses. The usage of gustatory lexical items to describe other sensory domains, and the motivation that underlies these linguistic realisations both confirm and partially question recent theoretical proposals on the conceptual organisation of the lexicon of the senses.

As I stated, the main objective of the research reported in this book is a description of the lexical domain of taste in English. In the lexical semantics tradition, there are two main approaches to the description of meaning: onomasiology and semasiology.[2] The onomasiological perspective is concerned with the elicitation of all the different *lexical items* that may be used to refer to the same concept. This approach structures the first section of the book, which answers the question "what are the words of taste in English?". Whereas a semasiological approach investigates the different *meanings* associated to the same lexical item, dealt with in the second section of the book, which answers the question "what are the conceptual mechanisms that drive the figurative usage of taste words?".

The physical experience of taste starts in the womb, and gustatory stimuli accompany us in our daily lives. Our physiological responses to specific tastes are shared with other members in the order of Primates, thus testifying to its biological origins. Information coming from this sense guides our dietary preferences and behavioural responses daily, yet our linguistic understanding of this sense is still fragmentary. Considering the scientific scenario in which this book is nestled, and the research questions that shape the enquiry, we may start our journey into the discovery of the tastes we live by.

---

[2] The distinction between onomasiology and semasiology is most commonly used in continental, European lexicology, less so in the Anglo-Saxon tradition (Geeraerts 2000: 82; Groendelaers, Speelman, and Geeraerts 2007: 988). Nonetheless, it is useful to illustrate the double scope of this book.

Acknowledgements

This book represents an expanded and improved version of my PhD dissertation, defended at the University of Perugia (Italy) under the guidance of Jodi Sandford. The years of fruitful discussions spent together have consistently shaped the information contained in the book. She also carefully assisted me during the revision process and proofread the entire book even when it was just a draft. She witnessed the entire development of this effort – from its birth to the final round of revisions. This book is dedicated to her, her passion, her patience, and enthusiasm. Faculty members at the University of Perugia also contributed to its realisation. Carla Vergaro, Roberta Mastrofini and Yhara Formisano have provided insights, support and inspiration throughout the process of writing. Furthermore, Vergaro proofread the book before submission, providing detailed comments and suggestions. Her commitment and professionalism truly are a source of inspiration.

I spent most of my PhD in Perugia, working on my project and working at the Umbra Institute, an American Study Abroad program to which I am profoundly indebted. There I had access to linguistic data coming from native speakers, and my colleagues contributed to a friendly and stimulating environment. They coped with my frenzied and fragmented schedules, and never lamented my grumpiness. Moreover, the original idea of researching taste was conceived for a presentation held there during a Conference in 2014, organised by the Faculty members of the Food Studies Program: thank you for the opportunity of working there, and for the inspiration. Particularly, I want to honour the memory of Anna Girolimetti. She supported me and sponsored my academic efforts. She was an example of dedication and endurance. Thank you, Anna: *sit tibi terra levis*.

The months spent at the University of Glasgow were crucial for the development of my research. The Semantics reading group enriched my knowledge of the subject, and the discussions with the other researchers deeply inspired me. Special thanks go to the Mapping Metaphor with the Historical Thesaurus team: Wendy Anderson, Ellen Bramwell and Rachael Hamilton for having welcomed me and having showed me the MMP and the terrific effort they put in creating it.

Although much of the research was carried out during my PhD, a small but significant part of the research was carried out while working at the University of Genova, to which I am currently affiliated. Particularly, the funding system of UniGe provided financial support for the realisation of research discussed in chapter 6. Although the final months of writing and revision were spent under lockdown measures and in smart-working, I could count on the assistance and support of Annalisa Baicchi and Cristiano Broccias, whose precious insights and encouragement contributed significantly to the final version of the manuscript.

The final version of the book benefitted tremendously from the contribution of an anonymous reviewer recruited by De Gruyter, who provided extremely useful comments and feedback to earlier drafts of the manuscript. Furthermore, many of the ideas contained in this book have been discussed around Europe at conferences and seminars with leading scientists in sensory linguistics: I want to thank Rémi Digonnet, Nina Julich, Marcin Trojszczak, and Francesca Strik Lievers, for the discussions and the inspiration. Bodo Winter deserves a special mention for having invited me to conduct the *Figurativity in Perception language workshop* at the University of Birmingham during the UK Cognitive Linguistics Conference in 2020, and for having written his programmatic book *Sensory linguistics*, to which the current book is largely indebted both theoretically and methodologically.

Finally, a huge thank you is for my friends and family – you know who you are. Cristiano provided feedback on early versions of the book. Marco Cherin proofread the evolutionary chapters. Adrian S. Hoch proofread the final round of drafts. Giulia assisted me with the table of contents. Daniele spent an entire afternoon numbering tables, before concluding that "life may be sweet, sometimes spicy, and definitely bitter". I'd say: it's more *sweet* than *bitter*.

Contents

Preface —— VII

Acknowledgements —— XIII

1 Introduction and theoretical tenets —— 1
1.1 Cognitive linguistics —— 1
1.2 Embodiment —— 5
1.3 Ineffability —— 10
1.4 Perception in cognitive linguistics —— 11
1.5 Tastes we live by —— 13

2 Taste —— 16
2.1 Taste in philosophy —— 16
2.2 How many senses? —— 19
2.3 Physiology of taste —— 20
2.4 The evolutionary value of different tastes —— 23
2.5 The linguistic representation of taste: A brief literary review —— 28

3 The words of taste —— 33
3.1 Introduction —— 33
3.2 Methodological tenets: Usage-based approach —— 34
3.3 Basic level terms —— 36
3.4 Basic taste terms —— 40
3.5 Salience and entrenchment —— 42
3.6 Freelistings and salience —— 44
3.7 Comparison to other methodologies —— 46
3.7.1 Before Cognitive Linguistics —— 46
3.7.2 Corpora-based lists —— 47
3.7.3 Lexicographic analysis —— 48
3.7.4 Norm-based lists —— 49

4 The semantic domain of TASTE in English —— 51
4.1 The Cognitive Salience Index —— 51
4.1.1 Specific methodology —— 52
4.1.2 Results —— 53
4.2 Basic taste terms reassessed —— 57
4.2.1 Application of the criteria —— 58

4.2.2	Discussion —— 60	
4.3	Source-based language —— 62	
4.3.1	Which sources? —— 64	
4.4	What are the most salient words of taste that correspond to the basic taste terms in English? —— 66	

5	**The multisensory lexicon of taste —— 68**	
5.1	Introduction —— 68	
5.2	Norming taste —— 69	
5.2.1	Gustatory terms —— 70	
5.2.2	Haptic terms —— 72	
5.2.3	Olfactory terms —— 73	
5.2.4	Visual terms —— 74	
5.2.5	Auditory terms —— 75	
5.3	The dark side of norms —— 76	
5.4	Which modalities do we use to elaborate the sense of taste? —— 77	

6	**Categorisation patterns —— 78**	
6.1	Naming tastes —— 78	
6.2	Conflation patterns: A cross-cultural perspective —— 79	
6.3	Taste association and confusion in English words —— 80	
6.4	Free sorting task —— 83	
6.4.1	Methodology —— 83	
6.4.2	Items —— 83	
6.4.3	Participants and instructions —— 84	
6.4.4	Results —— 84	
6.4.5	Discussion —— 86	
6.5	Closed sorting task —— 88	
6.5.1	Methodology —— 88	
6.5.2	Items and categories —— 88	
6.5.3	Results —— 90	
6.5.4	Discussion —— 93	
6.5.5	A brief comparison with the pilot tests —— 96	
6.6	What are the semantic relationships and network that structure the internal organisation of the category of taste? —— 97	
6.7	What are the words of taste? —— 98	

7	**The taste of words** —— 99
7.1	Introduction —— 99
7.2	Conceptual metaphors and polysemy —— 100
7.3	Novel, conventional, live, dead, and sleeping metaphors —— 102
7.4	Polysemy and sensory linguistics —— 105
7.5	Primary metaphors and culture —— 106
7.6	Mapping taste metaphors with the English thesaurus —— 108
7.6.1	Methodology —— 109
7.6.2	CHARACTER IS TASTE —— 110
7.6.3	KNOWING IS TASTING —— 113
7.6.4	INTELLECTUAL ABILITY IS TASTE —— 116
7.6.5	EMOTIONAL FEELINGS ARE TASTE —— 117
7.6.6	AESTHETICS IS TASTE —— 120
7.6.7	VALUE IS SWEET —— 121
7.6.8	HARMONY IS SWEET —— 122
7.6.9	MITIGATING IS SWEETENING —— 123
7.7	What are the conceptual mechanisms that drive gustatory semantic change in English? —— 126
8	**The taste of words today** —— 128
8.1	Introduction —— 128
8.2	Methodology —— 129
8.3	Sweet —— 130
8.4	Bitter —— 137
8.5	Sour —— 142
8.6	Salty —— 146
8.7	Spicy —— 149
8.8	Savoury —— 150
8.9	What do taste words mean when they are used figuratively? —— 151
9	**Intrafield metaphors** —— 154
9.1	Introduction —— 154
9.2	The hierarchy of the senses —— 155
9.3	The sensory linguistics account of "synaesthetic metaphors" —— 158
9.3.1	Are they synaesthetic? —— 158
9.3.2	Are they metaphorical? —— 160
9.3.3	Are they literal? —— 162
9.4	A different proposal —— 163

9.5	Intrafield expressions with taste as source domain —— 167	
9.5.1	Sweet —— 167	
9.5.2	Bitter —— 170	
9.5.3	Sour —— 172	
9.5.4	Spicy —— 173	
9.6	How do we conceptualise taste to talk about the other senses? —— 173	
10	Conclusions —— 176	
10.1	The words of taste —— 177	
10.2	What are the conceptual mechanisms that drive the figurative usage of taste words? —— 180	
10.3	Intrafield metaphors reassessed —— 184	
10.4	What can gustatory perceptions tell us about the nature of our minds and conceptual systems? —— 186	

References —— 191

Index —— 215

1 Introduction and theoretical tenets

1.1 Cognitive linguistics

There are many animal species that show signs of communication, some of them even display signs of sophisticated and refined exchange of information between individuals. Among them, only humans "speak". The complexity of our communicative strategies has developed over millennia of physical and cultural evolution. This dynamic development has involved not only humans, but also other life forms that share our environment, including non-human animals, bacteria, and plants. Currently, each human being is an individual belonging to the species *Homo sapiens*, the only extant species in the genus *Homo*. This has not always been true: there have been moments in the past when more than one species of humans coexisted and even interbred, as testified by our DNA (e.g., Vernot and Akey 2014; Browning et al. 2018).

According to recent estimates, *Homo sapiens* developed in Africa around 100,000 years ago. In this relatively short span of time, we have reached unimaginable achievements thanks to our capacity to cooperate and exchange information. One of the most outstanding accomplishments is the diversity of human languages around the globe. Despite the recent threats to linguistic diversity, there are more than 6000 different languages with which individuals communicate daily about the most different topics. The variety of these languages is overwhelming at different levels: syntactic, phonetic, and lexical. Some of these languages even defy the prototypical definition of language: for example, Sign Languages lack a sound and oral component, while others developed to communicate across long distances, like whistled languages (e.g., Meyer 2008). These are languages – a code with which a species communicates – nonetheless, and all of them share some basic cognitive mechanisms that are wired in *Homo sapiens'* brains.

According to Cognitive Linguistics, the neural underpinnings of language perception and production are not unique to language, which "is not an autonomous cognitive faculty" (Croft and Cruse 2004: 1). The human ability to rely on language has evolved and has been built upon previous mechanisms of non-linguistic reasoning and cognitive processing (Tomasello 2008; Orians 2018), and as such, it relies on these mechanisms to function. Moreover, cognitive linguists have turned to the study and insights provided by other disciplines (such as cognitive psychology, artificial intelligence, anthropology, philosophy, biology) to account for mechanisms observed at a linguistic level. Despite being originally focused on semantics and meaning creation, Cognitive Linguistics and its interdisciplinary nature account for a wide array of linguistic phenomena, e.g., syntactic variation, phonetic realisations, socio-linguistic descriptions, and lexicography. As such, Cognitive Linguistics is best described as a dynamic approach to the study of language, and it originated as a reaction to previously widespread theories of language.

The recognition that language relies on other more general cognitive faculties implies that in order to describe language and linguistic phenomena one should look into general mechanisms that may also be independent of language. The units that constitute our linguistic system are thought to represent concepts in our minds, although the nature of this relationship is a matter of debate (for a comprehensive discussion, see Speed, Vinson, and Vigliocco 2015). A linguist who wishes to describe language in the cognitive framework should take into account the conceptual structure that underlies the linguistic phenomena under scrutiny, and this should be done in keeping with knowledge of the cognitive architecture of the human mind (e.g., Dąbrowska and Divjak 2015).

A second crucial aspect of the Cognitive Linguistic approach is the hypothesis that "knowledge of language emerges from language use" (Croft and Cruse 2004: 1). Any thoughts and theories about different languages, about their structures and their grammars should emerge from linguistic data observed in their "natural" occurrence. This means that cognitive linguists collect and analyse linguistic data produced by native speakers, in what is often referred to as a usage-based approach. Linguistic data may come either from elicited tests, or from large collections of text such as corpora.

Lastly, Cognitive Linguistics argues that language evolved to convey meaning. Any component of the linguistic systems deployed by the meaning-making ape (Evans 2015) conveys meaning, from grammatical structures to phonetic units. According to cognitive linguists, meaning is created through construal operations (Croft and Cruse 2004: 40–73), it is structured by our encyclopaedic knowledge of the world, and it is embodied. Construal operations are cognitive mechanisms that intervene also in other cognitive skills, such as our capacity for attention, memory, perception, and reasoning. Construal operations are dynamic, and they may occur together in our processing of language. As a consequence, different linguists may concentrate on different aspects of the same meaning-making structure. For instance, consider the example in (1):

(1) Our relationship went **sour**.

In order to understand the meaning of the utterance in (1), our minds and conceptual systems need to perform a number of cognitive operations and rely on language-independent resources. The consensus in Cognitive Linguistics is to regard (1) as *figurative*, an umbrella term that is used in contemporary discussion to refer to all the types of conceptualisations that are *not literal*, thus involving metaphors, metonymies, and/ or a combination or continuum across the two. The labelling of these phenomena as figurative should not be mistaken with previous accounts of metaphors as a figure of speech or rhetorical device in language and in literary critique. After the seminal book by Lakoff and Johnson (1980) *Metaphors We Live By*, conceptual metaphors within the Cognitive Linguistics tradition are understood as cognitive mechanisms and not purely as linguistic devices. They are a fundamental mechanism through which our minds create meaning. Therefore, in order to understand the meaning in (1), our brains need to activate a metaphorical mechanism with which our conceptual systems are endowed. Nonetheless, it is legit to ask: what is metaphorical about (1)?

There are at least two possible answers. The usage of the verb *went* in the construction in (1) is an instantiation of the event-frame, according to which CHANGE IS MOTION. This means that our understanding of both concrete and abstract CHANGE may be conceptualised as MOVEMENT from one state to another. A non-figurative rephrasing of (1) could therefore be:

(2) Our relationship changed to **sour**.

Although sentence (2) has been reformulated to avoid the metaphorical conceptualisation of CHANGE AS MOTION, we still need some figurative mechanisms to understand it. If we understood (2) as literal, it would not make much sense: how could a relationship possibly be *sour*?

In the English linguistic system, *sour* is an adjective that describes one of the basic taste sensations, alongside *sweet, bitter,* and *salty*. Prototypically, it is elicited by unripe fruit and vinegar; the by-products of fermentation may also elicit a sour taste (such as yeast: ever wondered why sourdough is *sour*?); and most notably spoiled foods taste sour, for instance milk (as in *sour cream*). Although *sour cream* is appreciated for its culinary qualities, spoilage of milk may have represented a considerable and frequent problem in ancient societies. It represents a potential threat for our bodies and a loss of valuable food products. Luckily, our senses evolved to avoid this type of threat. Furthermore, our conceptual systems store information of the danger of sour milk in our encyclopaedic knowledge, which is what enables us to understand the second layer of conceptual meaning in (1), namely SPOILAGE IS SOUR. Considering this information, we are able to interpret the meaning of (1) correctly, and to infer that the relationship in question is spoiled and no longer pleasant.

In Conceptual Metaphor Theory, the mappings across two domains that arise directly in correlation of experience are frequently referred to as *primary metaphors* (e.g., Grady 1997a). A good example is MORE IS UP, where more is not always up, yet the experience of something piling vertically is correlated to the experience of an increase in volume, resulting in the conceptual projection of quantity with verticality. This is confirmed also in experience as we pour a liquid in a container and see the level rise. Hence, the relationship between SPOILAGE and SOUR may be considered a primary metaphor given their direct correlation in everyday experience and encyclopaedic knowledge; thus this type of repeated experience becomes *entrenched* (see Paragraph 3.5)

We may further extend the reasoning onto the relationship that holds between the concepts of SPOILAGE and SOUR and consider the two as part of the same event structure. In Chapter 8, I argue that the relationship between the two concepts is not only metaphorical – as much as it is metonymic. In this case, we can say that (1) is motivated by the metonymy SOUR FOR SPOILAGE. In conceptual metonymy phrasing, I understand FOR as an abbreviation of STANDS FOR. This in turn is in alternative phrasing to the current definition of metonymy, which is precisely A PROVIDES MENTAL ACCESS TO B (Barcelona 2003: 32–33; Kövecses 2010: 176; Sandford 2021). What is the metonymic construal of utterance (1)? If we understand perception as a Gestalt, a unified account of a sensory event (see e.g., Lakoff 1987 on ICMs[3]) we may think of *sour* as the vehicle to access a larger concept, namely that of SPOILAGE. Our embodied correlation of experience informs our encyclopaedic knowledge, according to which *sour* is the prototypical property of spoilt foods (such as milk). The relationship between SOUR and SPOILAGE therefore may also be described as metonymic, thus giving rise to a different account of the processes involved in (1).

The difference between metaphors and metonymies is subtle, but substantial. Barcelona (2003) proposes an account according to which metaphors may be based on metonymic relationships, and metonymies may spring out of metaphorical relationships, thus suggesting a high level of dynamic, conceptual interplay and integration between the two construal operations. Pérez-Sobrino (2017: 7–8) exemplifies the difference between conceptual metaphors and metonymy by equating metaphors to bridges, and metonymies to icebergs. A conceptual metaphor connects two distinct semantic domains, typically enabling us to understand a more abstract domain in terms of a more concrete one (e.g., Dancygier and Sweetser 2014). For instance, an utterance such as *Look how far I've come* conceptualises achievements in life as distance covered,

---

[3] The notion of Idealised Cognitive Model (ICM) is central to many theories and models of meaning creation in Cognitive linguistics. By ICM I mean a mental model of reality, which arises from experience, and it is structured around a central prototype. A thorough discussion however exceeds the scope of this book.

thus licensing our usage of the verb *to come* in a seemingly unrelated topic. Thus, a conceptual metaphor is a bridge between two concepts on the basis of a perceived similarity between them.

Conceptual metonymies instead are better imagined as an iceberg, "whose tip makes us think of the rest of the ice hidden below the level of the sea" (Pérez-Sobrino 2017: 8). For instance, an utterance such as *Rome did not intervene in time* is analysed as metonymic because the word *Rome* (more precisely called the *vehicle*) is used to refer to Italy, the nation of which Rome is the capital city. Thus, the relationship between the concept Rome and the concept Italy is of contiguity: the two concepts are part of the same whole, as much as the tip of an iceberg is *a part of* the whole iceberg. The theoretical relationship between metaphor and metonymy ignites passionate debates in Cognitive Linguistic literature, with remarkable theoretical and empirical contributions. Rather than further elaborating on the distinction between metaphor and metonymy, the aim of this book is to investigate how these conceptual mechanisms intervene in our representation and elaboration of gustatory experience in English. I apply Cognitive Linguistics to the study of the gustatory lexicon and endorse a dynamic construal of meaning, by considering alternative explanations and cognitive operations involved in the same utterance. The ultimate objective of the book is an investigation of the relationship between language and perception through the exquisitely human ability to create meaning on the basis of gustatory perception.

1.2 Embodiment

I argue that the relationship between bodily perception and conceptual processes may be evidenced through language. This is consistent with a *modal* view of semantic representation, according to which our bodies play a crucial role in the creation of meaning. In linguistic tradition there are two opposing views of meaning, which occupy the opposite ends of a spectrum: the modal view contrasts sharply with the *amodal* view of meaning.

According to the amodal view, words have an abstract and symbolic meaning with no direct grounding or evident connection to the world. In such theories, a physical stimulus is thought to be transduced in amodal representations, such as a frame, a semantic network or feature list. Thus, for instance, a car may be represented by the following feature list: [+physical object], [+machine], [+engine], [+wheels], it may be part of the semantic network VEHICLE together with concepts such as BOAT or AIRPLANE; and it may be part of a frame that includes concepts such as FOUR WHEELS, RED COLOUR, and FOUR DOORS (Speed, Vinson, and Vigliocco 2015: 194). The amodal view of meaning however needs to face both theoretical and empirical criticism. From a theoretical perspective, such an approach does not explain how language refers to the world, a problem more commonly referred to as the *symbol grounding problem* (Harnad 1990). From an empirical point of view, such theories do not account for the wealth of data that in turn support the competing view of meaning.

According to proponents of the modal view of semantic representation, meaning is represented in the mind of speakers through a mental representation: the same neural circuits that activate sensorimotor processes are also activated when processing the semantic content of words. This mechanism is often referred to as *neural reuse* (e.g., Barsalou 2016: 1130), which offers an account of *mental simulation* (e.g., Barsalou 1999, 2003, 2009; Zwaan and Pecher 2012). According to this view, the word *asparagus* is processed by reusing the same neural pathways that were activated when confronted with the experience of an asparagus, such as those to process its shape, colour, and taste.

The modal view of meaning fits particularly well with the theory of embodiment. It occupies a central role in the theoretical models developed within Cognitive Linguistics, and it is often invoked to analyse and motivate a wealth of data collected with numerous methodologies. The contributions to the scientific debate issued in this approach are manifold, and so are the definitions of embodiment (Bergen 2015: 10). In a philosophical perspective, the theory of embodiment is largely indebted to Marcel Merleau-Ponty, who worked in the phenomenological tradition and was largely influenced by the theories of Husserl. The historical link between Merleau-Ponty and embodiment has not always been fully acknowledged, thus prompting scholars such as Sambre (2009), Zlatev (2010) among others, to re-establish such a philosophical link between the two traditions.

In Cognitive Linguistics, language is conceived of as a set of symbolic units that refer to parts of knowledge stored in our memory, that are informed by our real-world experiences, which form our encyclopaedic knowledge (e.g., Croft and Cruse 2004: 30). As such, language plays an important role in our understanding of the human mind and provides access to the nature and structure of concepts. Language has been credited as a "window on the mind" (Evans 2015: 18), and a "window on the senses" (Majid and Levinson 2011: 7). Linguistic description however is not a sufficient line of evidence for a detailed understanding of the human mind, and it is often backed by other lines of research, such as behavioural experiments, fMRI scans, and electrophysiological studies, which provide an image of the brain in action. Coupled together, these efforts provide evidence and support for the embodied nature of the human mind.

According to cognitive scientists, embodiment may be seen as existing on three levels: the neural level, the phenomenological conscious experience, and the cognitive unconscious. The three levels are not independent of each other but must be considered as interdependent and functioning simultaneously (Lakoff and Johnson 1999; Gibbs 2005: 39–40). The positions within the broad spectrum of embodiment vary, thus it is useful to give a definition of embodiment adopted in this book:

> The human mind and conceptual organisation are a function of the way in which our species-specific bodies interact with the environment we inhabit. In other words, the nature of concepts and the way they are structured and organised is constrained by the nature of our embodied experience. (Evans 2007: 78)

This definition fits particularly well with the present discussion for a number of reasons. Firstly, it explicitly makes reference to "our species-specific bodies", thus evoking a biological frame to our understanding of cognitive and semantic processes that motivate the conceptual elaboration of physical, gustatory experience. This is especially evident in the case of perception: the type of stimuli we perceive as a species have been shaped and selected by millennia of evolutionary history. For instance, exclusive carnivores seem to have lost their appreciation of sweetness (see Paragraph 2.4), which in turn shapes primates' diets quite consistently. Secondly, the definition provided by Evans mentions the "environment we inhabit", thus including external factors in the array of evolutionary pressure that shapes language as we know it. These include the ecological niches we populate (or have populated as a species), which in turn are also a function of the different cultures that *Homo sapiens* has developed, and the type of dietary habits that humans have. Some scholars have even argued that "the environment and the organism actively co-determine each other" (Levins and Lewontin 1985: 89, in Gibbs 2005: 5; Orians 2018; Maturana 1980, in Gibbs 2005).

What evidence is there that our brains simulate the meaning of gustatory words? In the neuroimaging line of research, Barrós-Loscertales et al. (2012) show that passively reading food-related words (e.g., Sp. *sal*, 'salt') on a screen activated both primary (the anterior insula and frontal operculum) and secondary gustatory cortices (the orbitofrontal cortex, OFC), more than other words with no specific gustatory association. Although the authors claim that this represents proof of automatic semantic activation in gustatory regions of the brain, Speed and Majid (2019: 13) in reviewing this evidence suggest that it is not as unequivocal. They state this mainly because the OFC is activated also by tasks involving other modalities. Furthermore, the specific design of the study (2 seconds between each word) could lead to deliberate imagination of the food qualities, which in turn activates the sensory system (Kikuchi et al. 2005, Kobayashi et al. 2011, Si and Jiang 2017). Similarly, in the fMRI line of inquiry Citron and Goldberg (2014) notice the activation of taste related areas in the brain (primary and secondary cortex) during semantic processing of sentences involving taste metaphorical expressions, as opposed to non-metaphorical sentences (e.g., *She is a sweet girl* vs. *She is a nice girl*). Furthermore, Citron et al. (2016), find that metaphorical sentences of this type elicit a reaction in the amygdala, thus suggesting that their emotional engagement is higher than literal texts.

According to Conceptual Metaphor Theory, conceptual metaphors are the main cognitive mechanism through which abstract concepts are grounded into more concrete concepts, thus licensing for our understanding and manipulation (e.g., Lakoff and Johnson 1980, 1999; Sweetser 1990; Kövecses 2010; Feldman 2006; Dancygier and Sweetser 2014). As a consequence, conceptual metaphors have a behavioural effect on speakers. For instance, the linguistic metaphorical links existing between INTIMACY and WARMTH (e.g., *Paul is a warm person*) were explored by Williams and Bargh (2009), who report that participants who were drinking warm drinks were more sociable towards strangers than participants who were given cold drinks. Gibbs (2005) explored TIME through physical SPACE suggesting a change in embodied construal according to where the participants were situated in relation to their final goal. Schubert (2005) assessed the metaphorical link between POWER and VERTICALITY in a non-linguistic task; Schneider et al. (2011) explored the embodied links between IMPORTANCE and WEIGHT. These are just a few examples of the neural basis of conceptual metaphors; for a review see Casasanto (2017); Landau, Meier and Keefer (2010); Winter and Matlock (2017).

Similar behavioural effects have been observed in relation to metaphors involving gustatory experience. Meier et al. (2012) report that exposure to a sweet tastant positively impacts people's attitudes towards others and judgement towards themselves. Ren et al. (2015) found that the same condition influences judgement of a relationship. Notably, the influence of gustatory metaphors on behaviour shows signs of bidirectionality of transfer, so that thinking about love, affection, and a romantic relationship may influence taste perception. Gray (2012) reported these results observing an increased sensibility to sweet taste and pain inhibition in individuals who were addressed in a more loving manner than others in the control group. Chan et al. (2013) found that induced simulation of love led participants to sweeter ratings of different foodstuffs, including tasteless distilled water. Participants in the study who were asked to recall and describe love scenes and situations consistently found that the taste of the substances they were exposed to was sweeter than peer participants who instead were asked to recall jealousy scenes or neutral scenes. These behavioural effects instantiate the LOVE IS SWEET metaphor, one of the most frequent and evident metaphorical realisations associated to sweetness (see Chapter 8). More recently, Ahn and Min (2019) investigated the role of perceiving a sweet tastant (both physically and through imagination) in decision-making and evaluation processes related to food. Their results suggest that exposure to sweetness influences consumer behaviour, by making an advertisement more attractive. Finally, Schaefer et al. (2020) replicated earlier results, showing that exposure to sweet taste (as opposed to salty) enhances pro-social behaviour and influences the rating of attractiveness of faces, but not of paintings.

The conceptual link between LOVE and SWEETNESS is not the only metaphorical, gustatory link investigated in behavioural research. In keeping with the metaphor VARIETY IS THE SPICE OF LIFE, Mukherjee et al. (2017) find that exposure to spicy tastes (as opposed to mild potato chips) enhances variety-seeking in candy bars. Crucially, while participants display no difference in variety-seeking between those who tasted a spicy candy and those who were primed with the metaphor, those who tasted a mild candy displayed a lower level of variety-seeking, thus suggesting a direct involvement of the metaphorical realisation. In a similar study, Wang et al. (2016) observe that exposure to spicy tastants led participants to more risk-taking.

The conceptual elaborations of taste types may vary cross-culturally, and the behavioural effects elicited by these metaphors reflect such changes. For instance, Gilead et al. (2015) report that in Hebrew SWEETNESS is used in metaphorical expressions that conceptualise an inauthentic person or behaviour, while SPICINESS conceptualises INTELLIGENCE. Such metaphorical realisations contradict what they call the "preverbal response" (Gilead et al. 2015: 168) to these stimuli: sweetness is associated to sugars and it elicits a positive hedonic reaction, while spiciness is shown to increase pain sensitivity and rejection responses in rats and humans (e.g., Gilchrist, Allard, and Simone 1996; Klein et al. 2013). In line with these observations, the authors investigate whether participants' behaviours would be predicted by the preverbal value of the taste types, or if in turn this was influenced by the metaphorical elaboration, in keeping with embodiment theory. Their results show that participants' behaviour could be predicted on the basis of the metaphorical elaboration, and not on the basis of the hedonic response triggered by sweet (or spicy) tastants. Similar results were reported by Xu (2017), who investigates the behavioural response of participants exposed to bitterness perception, which in Chinese takes on the metaphorical value of ENDURANCE IN HARDSHIP.

The view of meaning representation endorsed in this book is fully modal and embodied. This position is based on evidence coming from brain imaging and behavioural studies, which suggests that gustatory language is indeed grounded in sensorimotor experience, thus supporting a modal and embodied account of semantic representation (but see Speed and Majid [2019] for a critical evaluation of these findings). It must be stressed however that embodiment is better conceived as a theoretical framework that encompasses related positions, and that different positions interpret the relationship between the body and the mind in a slightly different manner (e.g., Bergen 2015: 12; Speed and Majid 2019; Winter 2019a: 59–65).

1.3 Ineffability

Our language and our conceptual systems are largely grounded through embodied cognition in concrete perceptions and elaborations of bodily states. The physiology and biology of humans have evolved to respond in the same manner to the same stimuli across the globe. The linguistic representations of our perceptual systems however vary across cultures and languages. This suggests that the relationship between our body perception and language is not one to one. The gap between them has also been referred to as *ineffability*, i.e., "the difficulty or impossibility of putting certain experiences into words" (Levinson and Majid 2014: 408). The authors differentiate between different levels of ineffability (*weak* vs. *strong*) and distinguish it from *codability*. A sensation "S" might be ineffable in any language, and therefore there might be no lexical item in any language to describe it. This is a case of *strong* ineffability. Conversely, if a sensation "S" is not expressible in a language L1, but it is in another, then we can talk about *weak* ineffability. For a perception being "expressible" means that it can be communicated, more precisely that it can be linguistically coded. Furthermore, it should be emphasised that linguistic *codability* is different from linguistic *conveyability* (Levinson and Majid 2014). A common strategy to linguistically convey a concept which is not directly coded in the lexicon is to rely on source-based language. This is readily found in English gustatory vocabulary, e.g., *smoky*, *spicy*, and *fishy*, where each word is metonymically based on the source of the taste sensation (see Paragraph 4.3).

Each sense may show different levels of (in)effability across languages. For instance, it is usually held that odours in English are largely ineffable, and that English lacks a specific olfaction vocabulary. Contrary to what was commonly held, this is far from being a universal characteristic of human languages. For instance, Maniq-speaking hunter-gatherers in Thailand have more smell terms in their language than English speakers (Wnuk and Majid 2014), while the Jahai in Peninsular Malaysia have words such as *ltpit* that describes a variety of perceptual qualities: from flowers, to ripe fruit, to the *binturong* (or bearcat): a mammal in the Viverridae family that "according to Wikipedia, smells *like popcorn*" (Majid and Burenhult 2014: 267).

Examples of ineffability may be found even in closer languages, for example between Italian and English. In the regional variety of Italian spoken in central Italy, the unpleasant flavour of raw eggs, badly washed dishes, and dirty water after floor-cleaning is called *ciarruttime*. In other regional varieties the same odour is referred to as *freschino*. English however does not present an equivalent word, thus instantiating a case of *weak ineffability*. Thus, the odour of *ciarruttime* is coded in Italian, but it is not coded in English. This does not mean however that English speakers cannot perceive it, nor that they cannot talk about it. The same perception may be conveyed by means of other linguistic strategies such as periphrasis, or source-based descriptions. The English word *tart* represents a good example related to taste, as it is not always coded in other languages. It describes a perception that is in-between sour and sweet. Italian lacks an exact correspondent to it, and to refer to such a sensation, Italian speakers would use a periphrasis, referring to both sweet and sour tastes. Thus, we may conclude that *tart* is *conveyable* in Italian, but it is not coded. In other words, Italian speakers can talk about it, but they do not have a lexical item to describe it. This is another case of weak ineffability.

1.4 Perception in cognitive linguistics

Only recently have researchers coalesced to develop a consistent branch of investigation on the senses, which Winter calls *Sensory linguistics* (2019a), even though the language of perception has received attention in Cognitive Linguistics (e.g., Sweetser 1990; Caballero 2007; Ibarretxe-Antuñano 2008; Caballero and Ibarretxe-Antuñano 2014; Caballero and Paradis 2015; Sandford 2016, 2018, 2021; among others). The need for a new area of investigation on the senses was already invoked by Howes:

> The embodiment paradigm is being *out-moded*, as more and more scholars [. . .] come to (and into) their senses and lay the foundations for a new science of *sensuous cognition* (in place of embodied cognition) and *Sensitive Linguistics* (in place of Cognitive Linguistics) which is attuned to the varieties of sensory expression and experience across cultures.
> (2013: 298)

Despite Howes' wish to radically change the theoretical approach to embodiment in linguistics, researchers have incorporated interest in and insights to the language of the senses within the embodiment and Cognitive Linguistic tradition, as testified by recent work.

Duly, Speed et al. (2019) edited a book specifically on *Perception Metaphor*. This relevant contribution offers a wide perspective on the state of the art on the study and account of perceptual metaphors in contemporary research, both from an empirical and theoretical point of view. The efforts with an empirical inspiration are represented by contributions that investigate the metaphorical elaboration of particular senses in specific languages. Cases in point are Steinbach-Eicke's contribution on taste metaphors in Hieroglyphic Egyptian, Proos's *Polysemy of the Estonian perception verb nägema, 'to see'*, Trojszczak's chapter on the metaphorical extensions of touch in Polish and English, and Julich's discussion of our understanding of music as moving. Among these, a couple of chapters investigate the diachronic development of perceptual metaphors (Anderson; Strik Lievers and De Felice), illustrating a promising approach to this field. I follow this type of analysis with specific reference to taste in English (see Paragraph 7.6). Whereas the theoretical contributions span from the debunking of the terminology of synaesthetic metaphors (Winter 2019b), to a discussion on the general characteristics of perceptual metaphors proposed by Ibarretxte-Antuñano (2019) and Kövecses (2019). Ibarretxe-Antuñano advances that both touch and taste are commonly used to structure experiential knowledge, and that this specific elaboration is based on intrinsic properties of the senses. The metaphorical mapping is seen as an instantiation of the general metaphor COGNITION IS PERCEPTION, which mainly involves general terms in the domain of TASTE (for a similar discussion on KNOWING IS TASTING, INTELLIGENCE IS FLAVOUR see Bagli 2017; and KNOWING IS SEEING, see Sandford 2012, 2019). Kövecses adds another two general metaphors to account for the general role of perception in metaphorical elaboration, namely THE GENERAL ATMOSPHERE OF SOMETHING IS PERCEPTION, and EMOTION IS PERCEPTION.

The field and scientific interest in the sensory domains is constantly expanding. Since the beginning of my research in 2013, I have witnessed growing attention in research on sensory perception in linguistics. As I revise my book going into publication, numerous contributions are appearing across scientific research. For instance, the UK Cognitive Linguistics Conference 2020 at the University of Birmingham hosted a pre-conference workshop on *Figurativity in English Perception language* (organised by other scholars and me); see also Salzinger (2020), Speed and Majid (2020), and Sandford (2021).

Feelings and emotions as well have been largely investigated in Cognitive Linguistics literature. These are conventionally seen as the result of metaphorical elaboration within Conceptual Metaphor Theory. Notably, emotions and perception are widely correlated (e.g., Chu and Downes 2000; Willander and Larsson 2007), to the point that Prinz (2006) suggests that emotions might be regarded as a form of perception. There are many points of resemblance between the two (for a discussion, see Kövecses 2019). Perhaps the most notable example of structuring an emotion domain via metaphorical mapping is the ANGER IS A HOT FLUID IN A CONTAINER (e.g., Kövecses 2010).

According to recent data, the conceptual metaphor EMOTION IS PERCEPTION may be grounded in the neural architecture of our cognitive systems, especially for taste and smell. The neural pathways that process information coming from the chemical senses involve areas (e.g., the amygdala) that are also involved in the processing of emotions (Winter 2019a). The conceptual metaphors identified and reviewed in Chapters 7, 8, and 9 largely structure emotional concepts, such as LOVE (for SWEET), or DISAPPOINTMENT (for BITTER). Crucially, sweetness provides access to the general domain of PLEASANT, while bitterness provides access to UNPLEASANT. The theoretical background against which my analyses are set recognises emotions as resulting from conceptualisation mechanisms, though direct ties between emotions and the senses have been posited.

1.5 Tastes we live by

The progression of my argument is divided in two sections. The first section is entitled *The words of taste*, in which I concentrate on the lexical items that encode this perceptual modality in English. It undertakes an onomasiological perspective to the study of the domain of TASTE: the aim of this section is to identify the lexical items that make up this semantic domain in English. In Chapter 2, I review the physiology of taste and of gustatory perception, highlighting its physical multisensoriality and its psychological reconstruction. I also review the evolutionary role of different taste types, which motivate the conceptual mechanisms that are activated in usage. Chapter 3 contains specific theoretical tenets. Particularly, I review the notion of basic categorial terms, and their relationship to salience and entrenchment. Furthermore, I discuss different methodologies to describe a semantic domain in a fully usage-based perspective, and advocate freelistings.

Chapter 4 addresses the question of the identification of the most salient words of taste that correspond to the Basic Taste Terms in English, through the application of the Cognitive Salience Index to a list of lexical items. The methodology of the Cognitive Salience Index is widely applied in anthropology, less so in linguistic studies, and to the best of my knowledge has never been applied to taste in English, as the lexicon of taste has always been defined mainly through lexicographic methodologies. In Chapter 5, I classify each lexical item listed in Chapter 4 according to their most strongly associated sensory modality as resulting from a comparison to sensory norms. This chapter aims at verifying the distinct modalities that we use to elaborate the sense of taste.

I propose two different studies involving categorisation techniques in Chapter 6, to unravel the semantic relationship and network that structures the internal organisation of the category of taste. The first study is aimed at eliciting conflation patterns among taste types, while the second focuses on the possibility of representing taste terms according to family resemblance structures involving different dimensions of flavour, such as taste types, chemesthesis (e.g., spiciness), texture, and mouthfeel.

The second part of the book is entitled *The taste of words*, and it focuses on the investigation of the conceptual elaboration of the lexicon of taste in English. It represents a semasiological investigation in the domain of TASTE, and it reports on the figurative meaning of the lexical items identified in the first section.

Thus, Chapter 7 proposes a review of central concepts in Conceptual Metaphor Theory that shape the discussions that follow. Moreover, I consider the well-established role of metaphors in the creation of polysemy, as well as the notion of *dead metaphor* employed as an interpretative tool for the metaphorical extensions that sometimes are so conventional that their metaphorical nature is no longer transparent. More specifically, Chapter 7 reviews linguistic data coming from Mapping Metaphor with the Historical Thesaurus Project (MMP) developed at the University of Glasgow, focusing on the category of taste. The MMP "exploits lexicographical evidence representing the English language over a period of more than a millennium" (Anderson 2019: 65). This chapter explores the conceptual mechanisms that drive semantic change in English through time. This research benefitted also from the insights of the people working on this ambitious project during a four-month stay while working on my Ph.D. Some of these data already appeared in Bagli (2017), but they are presented here in a new form, and more importantly are interpreted relying on different conceptual metaphors.

Chapter 8 extends the analysis of conceptual usage of the gustatory lexicon in English to contemporary English, relying on data elicited from the COCA (Corpus of Contemporary American English, Davies 2008) to elucidate on the meaning of taste words when they are used figuratively. The results reveal the variegated usages of the different taste types, which are consistently used to structure target domains according to an evaluative, rather than an exclusively descriptive scale. The conceptual elaboration of taste words is grounded in embodied responses, driven by the biological role of the corresponding taste types, according to the specific cultural context. The contexts and instances that taste words conceptualise are manifold and argue for a multifaceted account of figurative elaborations.

Chapter 9 focuses on so-called synaesthetic metaphors to analyse how we use TASTE to talk about other sensory modalities. Specifically, it offers an alternative account to a traditional analysis previously proposed by many scholars including myself (Bagli 2016). The present analysis takes into account recent contributions on this phenomenon and reviews the theoretical limitations of labelling them as "synaesthetic" and calls them "intrafield" (Mattisof

1978; Vanhove 2008; O'Meara et al. 2019; Winter 2019a, b). At a closer look, the intrafield metaphors retrieved through corpus analysis may be considered either as metonymical, because they describe integrated sensory modalities, or as motivated by other and more generalised conceptual mechanisms.

In Chapter 10, I provide some general conclusions, wrapping up the main results of my analyses, with the aim to delineate what linguistic elaboration of the domain of TASTE can tell us about the nature of our minds and conceptual systems. Moreover, it proposes new directions of research to better understand the conceptual elaboration of gustatory language. This includes linguistic anthropological research and also more biologically oriented research on intrafield expressions.

2 Taste

2.1 Taste in philosophy

The sense of taste has often been downplayed and classified as an inferior sense for centuries. Ever since the first attempts of philosophical inquiry into nature and humanity, the senses have been ranked according to their worthiness of being discussed and studied. In ancient Greece (especially in Plato and Aristotle) this is most evident in discussion about the highest achievements of the human mind, such as knowledge, morals, and art, with taste being the sense that would less contribute to these efforts. Sight and hearing[4] instead were considered more worthy of philosophical attention (Korsmeyer 2002: 11, Rudolph 2018: 1).

The functional importance of taste in nutrition is undeniable, and this is perhaps one of the main reasons for its disparagement: taste has an almost instinctual and animalistic nature, and it requires an intimacy with its objects of perception. For instance, in Plato's dialogue Gorgias, Socrates provides a classification of different types of art, by opposing it to *kolakeia,* a term which is often translated with *flattery*. He states that while medicine is considered "art", because it knows what food is best for the body, gastronomy is considered flattery because it *claims* to know what food is best for the body. It is defined as ugly (as the other different types of flattery) because its aim is to please the body with no other actual interest in human benefits (Gorgias 464e). Socrates argues that gastronomy is not rational because it is unable to explain its nature, its objects, and its tools: it is an irrational activity (Gorgias 465a). This judgement of cooking and gustatory experiences is to be found in Aristotle as well, who asserts that "taste and touch are the most 'slavish and bestial' of the senses, with which self-control and wantonness are concerned" (Rudolph 2018: 10). The hedonic value of gustatory perceptions played a key role in the disparagement of this modality from ancient Greece to the Modern era.

Besides moral judgements on eating and cooking, philosophers more concerned with theory of perception advanced physiological and psychological hypotheses on the nature of the senses, including taste. The first philosopher to describe gustatory perception was Alcmaeon of Croton (fl. 500–450 BCE), who already distinguished the tongue as the dedicated organ to perception of taste, and as such taste is more commonly considered a type of touch (Rudolph 2018: 8).

---

4 I adopt the following labels for the senses: touch, taste, smell, sight or vision, and hearing or sound, though clearly derivative adjectives are haptic, gustatory, olfactory, visual, and auditory. I use sight and vision, hearing and sound interchangeably.

Philosophers, doctors and scientists of the ancient world recognised a variable number of basic tastes (Beare 1906; Boulay 2018; Paulas 2018; Totelin 2018), but most of them already included the terms that contemporary physiology distinguishes as taste primaries. Medieval and Renaissance accounts of taste physiology are largely based on ancient sources. Thus, for instance, Fernel in the sixteenth century offers a list of tastes that reflect Pliny's list, while Haller in the eighteenth century also included flavours such as *urinous* and *spirituous* (Rudolph 2018: 4). Notwithstanding the scientific investigations and accounts, taste has been mainly associated with gluttony, and its aesthetic and cognitive value has been largely overlooked by philosophers and scientists.

One of the first attempts to re-evaluate taste sensations in Western culture comes from Jean-Anthelme Brillat-Savarin ([1825] 1949), who published a book with a rather self-explicatory title: *The Physiology of Taste, or, Meditations of Transcendent Gastronomy.* The book is a collection of aphorisms, rules, and essays on various topics including food, pleasure, sex, dinners, gastronomy, and taste. The book also contains famous quotations, such as the proverbial "Tell me what you eat, and I shall tell you what you are", which as Korsmeyer (2002: 71) notes, anticipates Feuerbach's materialistic assertion "You are what you eat". Brillat-Savarin is considered the father of modern gastronomy, and his role in the Western re-evaluation of the sense of taste should not be underestimated. Contemporary food-related literature is abundant: there are many contributions of gastronomy, cookbooks, history of food items, and food blogs. However, there are not as many books specifically related to taste.

A recent philosophical investigation in this neglected sensory modality is authored by Korsmeyer (2002), who on one hand, aims at explaining why the sense of taste has received minimal attention by philosophers and why it has been classified as one of the "lowest" senses. On the other hand, her objective is to propose a philosophical investigation on taste, by arguing that indeed it does have aesthetic significance and epistemological validity. She identifies the motivation for such neglect in the nature of the proximal senses (touch, taste, and smell) as opposed to the distal senses (sight and hearing). Proximal senses require that an object to be perceived must enter the body of the perceiver, and thus necessitate direct engagement of the body with the object perceived. On the other hand, philosophers considered sight and hearing as not requiring such intimacy and are therefore less habit-forming and distracting from the road to knowledge and wisdom. The author presents a brief philosophical history of taste from ancient Greece to the 18th century, where many philosophers, from Kant to Hegel were interested in taste as a metaphor for aesthetic preference. The main argument of Korsmeyer is that indeed taste, the *physical* sense of taste, is an aesthetic sense. Food and food practices convey meaning, and our neurophysiological knowledge of how taste functions allows us to grasp a better understanding of this sense. In her own words: "I mount a brief for a 'philosophy of food' that defends the aesthetic character of taste and eating and draws parallels between foods and arts in terms of their symbolic, cognitive functions" (Korsmeyer 2002: 10).

Two other important contributions to the description and conceptualisation of taste are authored by Cavalieri. *Gusto, l'intelligenza del palato* (2011) contains sections that describe taste from various perspectives: philosophy, physiology, and anthropology, including an overview of the lexis of wine tastings in Italian (for a similar overview in English, see Lehrer 2009). The aim of her book is to explore taste from a broad perspective, and thus it is very useful as a first reading into a critical evaluation of this undervalued sense. A more specific book by the same author is *E l'uomo inventò i sapori* (2014), which takes on an evolutionary perspective on the development of gustatory sensations. In this book, the author reconstructs the development of food preferences and taste perception, from non-human primates to molecular gastronomy. She reviews the claims advanced by *The Cooking Hypothesis* (Wrangham 2010), according to which the domestication of fire represents a turning point in human evolution. Particularly, it caused relevant changes in hominin diets, and subsequently to their cognitive evolution: cooked meat enhances the energy intake and decreases the time needed for digestion. Furthermore, the greater consumption of meat corresponds to a lower consumption of vegetables, which again results in more energy in less time. The extra energy might have been used by the brain, which got bigger; extra time allowed the hominins to organise their social lives, thus creating tools, cooperating, and (potentially) even developing gender roles. Allegedly, this also exposed hominins to appreciation of different food types and enabled the development of different tastes. For instance, the usage of fire allowed hominins to start consuming cereals and starchy foods, which would have been indigestible without being cooked. Conversely, it enabled us to exclude toxic, tannin-rich vegetables from our diets, which however are particularly appreciated by chimpanzees (Cavalieri 2014: 68). Another important leap in the evolutionary history of taste is the spreading of agriculture and the domestication of animals, with the subsequent revolution and spreading of culinary habits and cultures.

Lastly, Rudolph (2018) edited a book which collects various contributions on the role of taste in the ancient world, offering insights on literature, poetry, and philosophy. It also contains archaeological data on the dietary habits and practices of ancient populations. This contribution, although not specifically on the language of taste, gives an unprecedented perspective on the importance of this sensory modality and on the history of its development, thus contributing to the impetus towards a reassessment of taste (and the lower senses) in philosophical, anthropological and linguistic research.

2.2 How many senses?

Western folk theory of the senses and perception are largely indebted to ancient Greek philosophical tradition that recognised five senses, namely touch, taste, smell, sight, and hearing. Traditionally, the partition of human sensorium in five categories is attributed to Aristotle (Sorabji 1971). This distinction is in fact a cultural product: not all cultures share the same division of the perceptual continuum, and even in Western cultural tradition the number and quality of the senses has varied greatly from ancient Greek to contemporary Theories (Howes 1991; Classen 1993; MacPherson 2011; Matthen 2015). Some candidates to be added to the five traditional senses are *proprioception* (awareness of movement of the body), *kinaesthesia* (a sense of movement), thirst, and even a sense of number (Matthen 2015: 567). Crucially, one of the most recent and most credited additions to the human sensorium is *nociception*, or the sense of pain. Contrary to what was previously thought, perception of pain is separate from that of touch (Craig 2003; Hardcastle 2015), and it has its own neural pathways and mechanisms (Basbaum et al. 2009) that often interfere with those of touch. Nonetheless, in this book I deliberately use the domain of TOUCH in a broad fashion, and I consider adjectives that describe painful haptic stimuli as part of this semantic domain. I distinguish however between TOUCH and PAINFUL TOUCH in the discussion of intrafield metaphors in Chapter 9.

The frailty of the five senses model is suggested both by cultural, physiological, and neuropsychological data. The example of taste is paradigmatic: this sense is in fact a complex reconstruction of different and intricate sensory modalities, that intervene simultaneously to recreate a unique and uniform perceptual Gestalt that scientists call flavour (see discussion below). The experience of flavour is both multimodal and unified in a phenomenologically single event. Critically, multisensory experience is more than the sum of its parts. Smith reports that "we sometimes just see, and sometimes just hear, a plastic bottle being crushed, but when we both see and hear it, this gives more neural activation than the sum of activation involved in the seeing and the hearing. This superadditivity in the neural pattern of responding to combined information is one sign of multisensory integration" (Smith 2015: 319). Information transmitted by separate channels is then reassembled, reconstructed, and integrated. This is true also regarding sight and touch: we see a texture and process its "feel", shape, and size at the same time. Subsequently, it is pertinent to my methodology that I recognise the simultaneity of these phenomena, even though I consider them singularly.

The answer as to how many senses there are largely depends on the criteria used to identify them, and on the definition that we give to a *sense*. For instance, if one argues that the senses should collect information from the world *outside* of the human body, then proprioception is not a good candidate to be considered a sense. However, if one argues that a sense should have *its own* organ of perception, then proprioception would pass the test, as there are nervous terminations and dedicated receptors in the muscles, tendons, and ligaments (MacPherson 2011: 16–17). If one argues that different senses should process different types of energy, then we would not even have five senses anymore: taste and smell might be grouped as the chemical senses, touch and hearing as mechanic, while vision would be a light-processing sense generically speaking.

There is no easy way out from this philosophical and scientific debate, at least for now. In this book however I had to make a choice as far as how many senses I recognise. Considering that my main concern is the linguistic and therefore necessarily cultural description and construction of taste in English, I choose to adopt the five senses folk model. This is the model that most people in the West are accustomed to: it is the model that is being taught in schools, and children learn to partition the senses in five categories as they grow up. As it will become evident in the following chapters, I formulate my research questions with reference to taste, and its relationship to the other senses. Nonetheless, the data retrieved and analysed in the following chapters suggest that English really sponsors multisensoriality, perhaps more than we could imagine in an aprioristic position.

2.3 Physiology of taste

The physiological mechanisms that constitute gustatory perception are complicated and rely on an intricate network of receptors and nerves, most of which have been discovered only recently, while some others are still a matter of debate and discussion among scholars. I maintain that an understanding of the biological foundations and inner workings of taste is essential in order to map the experiential grounding of the conceptualisation process of TASTE.

One of the first things to pinpoint is the difference between taste and flavour. The biological understanding of taste (or gustation) is limited to the specific gustatory sensations mediated by a "specialized anatomically and physiologically defined chemosensory gustatory system" (Bachmanov and Beauchamp 2007: 389). The label flavour refers to the multisensory experience of food consumption, including information about its smell, texture, and temperature perceived by other sensory systems: namely olfactory and somatosensory (e.g., Bachmanov and Beauchamp 2007: 389; Smith 2015: 317–8). As Spence, Smith, and Auvray note, taste and flavour can and should be considered as overlapping labels in perceptual experience (2015: 247–274).

The gustatory system in vertebrates recognises at least five different taste qualities (Antinucci and Risso 2017: 2), and mammalian gustatory perception is mainly localised in the oral cavity. Humans taste with the edges and dorsal surface of the tongue, the soft palate (i.e., the back-part of the palate), and part of the throat. However, there are no receptors on the lips, on the inside of our cheeks, under the tongue, or on the hard palate (i.e., the foremost part of the palate, behind the upper incisors) (Breslin 2013). Recently, proteins that allow taste perception in more unusual places, such as the gastric and intestinal tract have been discovered (San Gabriel 2015). Together, these tissues consist in the gustatory epithelia. Taste Receptor Cells are organised in taste buds, a microscopic cluster of receptors, shaped like a rosette; each taste bud is located within gustatory papillae, which in turn are divided into three major types: fungiform, foliate, and circumvallate. Some areas of the tongue are more sensible to certain tastes than other areas. The division however is not as rigid as it was previously held in earlier accounts of physiology (Cavalieri 2011: 42).

Taste Receptor Cells are epithelial chemoreceptor cells, which at the outset contain thin fibres (microvilli), which is where chemical transduction of taste takes place. The chemical information retrieved by the receptors is transferred to the nerves that innervate the tongue: the facial nerve (VII nerve), the glossopharyngeal nerve (IX), and the vagus nerve (X), (Smith and Vogt 1997; Holley 2006). The VII nerve is divided in two main branches: the chorda tympani nerve, which innervates the anterior part of the tongue, and the greater petrosal nerve, which innervates the soft palate. The IX nerve sends fibres to the rest of the tongue, and possibly to the Taste Receptor Cells in the pharynx. The X nerve innervates the epiglottis, the larynx, and the upper part of the oesophagus (Bachmanov and Beauchamp 2007: 389). Together, these nerves transmit information to the brain stem, where reflexes of acceptance and rejection are controlled. Strong sweet tastes are accepted, while strong bitter tastes are rejected. This reflexive mechanism has been observed even in decerebrate animals (Grill and Norgren 1978) and in anencephalic humans (Steiner 1973). In its journey from the caudal to the rostral area of the brain, the information is split in two different flows. The first is a more dorsal path through the primary and secondary gustatory regions, where conscious taste sensations arise (Breslin and Spector 2008). The second is the ventral forebrain, where functions such as affective and emotional processing, memory, and learning are carried out. Finally, the information from the two pathways is integrated (Breslin 2013).

Although there is still debate about the number and nature of taste qualities, scholars agree that there are at least five: *sweet, sour, bitter, salty,* and *umami*. Other proposed transduction mechanisms include *oleogustus* (Running, Craig, and Mattes 2015) and *starchy* (Lapis, Penner, and Lim 2016). The first of the proposed mechanisms responds uniquely to Non-Esterified Fatty Acids, which elicit a rancid and unpleasant taste. The second mechanism corresponds to perception of carbohydrates, which were commonly held to be perceived through the perceptual mechanism of sweetness. This transduction process has only been observed indirectly by inhibiting sweet receptors in the mouth of a pool of participants. Both terms however are not of interest to the focus of this book, as both of them belong to specific medical jargon, and have resisted entrance in common parlance.

The five taste qualities may be further divided in two groups: sweet, bitter, and umami are mediated by G protein-coupled receptors, while sour and salty are mediated by ion channels (Antinucci and Risso 2017). Bitter taste is transduced by receptors in the T2Rs family; T1R2/T1R3 receptors transduce sweet sensations; T1R1/T1R3 transduce umami qualities; salty is transduced through the epithelial sodium channel; and sour through the acid sensing ion channels (Antinucci and Risso 2017; Breslin 2013). Each of these receptors responds to a distinct class of chemicals: sugars (e.g., glucose) and certain amino acids (e.g., glycine) taste sweet, tannins and alkaloids taste bitter, acidic substances (not specifically associated to any specific group of nutrients) taste sour, metal ions and salts (especially NaCl) are salty, and monosodium glutamate tastes umami (Bachmanov et al. 2014; Breslin and Spector 2008). Sweet substances evoke an innately pleasant response, while bitter and sour substances do not (Steiner et al. 2001); and a weak salty and umami taste are preferred by humans (Okiyama and Beauchamp 1998).

Crucially, the information coming from Taste Receptor Cells is integrated with information pertaining to other sensory modalities and transmitted through separate neural pathways, and yet deeply integrated in a unique Gestalt, which is commonly referred to as flavour (Bachmanov and Beauchamp 2007; Smith 2015: 317). Flavour perception is a multisensory phenomenon, and it involves gustatory, olfactory, and tactile information. Volatile substances during ingestion of food are perceived by the olfactory receptors, while tactile sensations in the mouth – most accurately referred to as *chemesthesis* (Smith 2015: 316) – are perceived through the trigeminal nerve. This nerve is responsible for transmitting information about chemical irritation, nociception (perception of pain), temperature, texture, and consistency of food (Delwiche 2004; Auvray and Spence 2008: 1024). Among these sensations, *spiciness* is not properly a taste, as it is not perceived through gustation. Rather, spiciness is a flavour as it is perceived through the trigeminal nerve, which innervates the face, the nose, and part of the palate, and which is responsible for perception of temperature, among other sensations. The trigeminal nerve is also responsible for perception of effervescence of drinks, texture of food (described by adjectives such as *creamy, rough, hard*) and mouthfeel. Chapter 6 explores how native speakers of English partition the lexicon of TASTE.

Olfaction plays a fundamental role in flavour perception. The component of olfaction that is particularly relevant for this purpose is labelled as retronasal olfaction (as opposed to orthonasal olfaction, see Smith 2015: 325–326; Rozin 1982). Whenever we ingest something, we may be thinking we are *tasting* it, while in fact we are mainly *smelling* it via our retronasal receptors, which capture volatile molecules in the nasal cavity and transmit them to the brain, which in turn reconstructs the whole Gestalt experience and places it in the mouth. This effect is similar to cases of phantom limb (Soler et al. 2010), in which individuals report feeling pain in a limb that had been severed and is no longer part of the body. According to Smith (2015: 324) this might happen because the sensation is immediately labelled as taste, and as such the smell component

> goes missing (or unnoticed) phenomenologically. That smell doesn't appear as a separable part of the complex experiences generated by the interaction of taste (and touch) and retronasal olfaction doesn't mean that we can't focus our attention on the dimension of flavour it contributes (e.g., fruitness) to our experience. (Smith 2015: 324)

The integration of olfaction, chemesthesis, and gustation is so common and automatic that has led to the formulation of the hypothesis that together they indeed form a separate sense from the others, thus questioning the Western partitioning of perception (Auvray and Spence 2008; Prescott 1999).

2.4 The evolutionary value of different tastes

According to embodied cognition, biological and evolutionary perspectives on the mind and conceptual organisation play paramount roles. Gustatory functions and the ability to discriminate different tastes are thus fundamental, and as Bachmanov and Beauchamp (2007: 390) remark, "probably, taste evolved to ensure animals choose food appropriate for body needs". Taste preferences and perceptions change from species to species, and there are traces of intraspecific variation of sensibility to specific taste types even in *Homo sapiens* (Bachmanov et al. 2014; Bachmanov and Beauchamp 2007). Vertebrates can perceive at least the five different taste qualities, even if some classes of animals have lost their ability to perceive some of them (Antinucci and Risso 2017). For instance, felines are reported to have lost their ability to taste sweetness reflecting their carnivore diet (Li et al. 2005, 2009), while aquatic mammals show almost no taste system, with few or no taste buds at all (Yoshimura and Kobayashi 1997), possibly as a consequence of their diets and feeding behaviour, i.e., no mastication of food and large quantities of sodium contained in marine water.

Human food choices are different from those of other animals, but the difference is not so dramatic if we compare our preferences with those of other apes. Our last common ancestor with great apes presumably roamed the earth around 7 to 8 million years ago (e.g., Wood 2010). If we assume that the diets of contemporary great apes mirror those of our last common ancestor, then this was an omnivore who fed on tropical fruit, leaves, and insects (Milton 1999). Despite the diets of early hominids expanded dramatically between 4.4 and 2.3 million years ago (Breslin 2013), *Homo sapiens* retained common food preferences with our closest living relative, namely chimpanzees. Particularly, a preference for fruits and acids, a source of sugars and vitamin C, which is necessary for life and which great apes cannot synthesise (Milton and Jenness 1987).

Perception of *sweetness* guides the ingestion of sugars and food with a high caloric content, both in humans and great apes. The appreciation of this taste has been observed even before birth, and new-born infants of human and non-human apes show positive facial reactions when exposed to this taste (Steiner et al. 2001). The evolution of sweet perception in primates is linked to the evolution of plants belonging to the Angiospermae group (one of the most numerous groups of land plants), which produces fruits with a high sugar content. The diversification of early mammals was roughly contemporary to the rise of angiosperms, and it occurred at the end of the Mesozoic era (Chen, Strömberg, and Wilson 2019). The sugar contained in the fruit of these plants was a valuable source of energy for primates, while the plants benefitted from fruit consumption for seed dispersal. Furthermore, fruit consumption triggered the evolution of the tripartite colour vision system of primates, a fundamental skill for the recognition of ripe fruit (Hladik and Pasquet 2004; Morris 1967). The gustatory perception of sweetness therefore is the result of evolutionary selective pressure that corresponds to the necessity of caloric intake. For instance, in modern primates a larger body mass corresponds to lower thresholds of sensitivity to sugars: this tendency allows species with a larger body (which need a higher energy intake) to include a wider range of fruit in their diets (Hladik and Pasquet 2004). Perception of sweetness is also tied to consumption of honey, one of the most valuable sources of energy in the savannah (Orians 2014). The positive embodied response to perception of sweetness hence I argue motivates the positive semantic elaboration of sweet in language.

Perception of *bitterness* signals the presence of toxic substances in the food, mainly alkaloids and tannins that are dangerous for the human body at high concentrations (Antinucci and Risso 2017: 2). Infants of both human and non-human primates show rejection to bitter substances (Rosenstein and Oster 1988; Steiner et al. 2001; Hladik and Pasquet 2004), revealing an automatic, embodied reaction to bitterness. The facial expressions that the babies produce in reaction to *bitter* are reminiscent of facial reactions to pain. Facial reactions represent an important means of non-linguistic communication in humans, especially in the communication of internal states and pain in infants-caregiver interactions (Prkachin 2009). This refusal may be culturally overridden through learning, as showed by cultural practices around the globe. Human diets contain bitter tasting foods, which are often valued and looked for. Notably, researchers observed that some of the great apes include minor quantities of bitter vegetables in their diets, possibly as a rudimental form of medicine and personal care, as in prevention of parasites (Hladik et al. 2010). Huffman and Seifu (1989) report on a case of a lethargic chimpanzee in Tanzania that was observed consuming *Vernonia amygdalina*, a local medicinal plant, which is normally avoided because of its bitter taste. The association between vegetable-based pharmacopeia and bitterness is related to metaphorical realisations found in the Epicurean philosophical tradition, and which may be related to metaphorical mappings retrieved in contemporary English (see Paragraph 8.4). Perception of bitter substances relates to the presence of a specific pool of genes, which determines different thresholds of sensitivity among individuals (Bachmanov et al. 2014). Recent investigations show that *Homo neanderthalensis* was already exposed to these genetic variations, thus suggesting that the inter-personal variation predates the divergence of evolutionary lineages leading to Neanderthals and *Homo sapiens* (Lalueza-Fox et al. 2009). The negative response to bitter tastants motivates the figurative elaboration of this domain to refer to negative experiences and feelings.

The reason behind the human ability to perceive and even appreciate *sour* substances is a matter of debate. Arguably, vitamin C is the only sour stimulus that has nutritional value. Since primates lost the ability to synthesise this vitamin, being able to detect it and ingest it from food sources is an important skill to possess. Thus, perception of sour tastants may be motivated by the necessity of ingesting vitamin C (Breslin 2013). Although it is not tied to an identifiable group of nutrients, this taste quality is consistently desirable in foods, and artificial additives are employed in industry to make the food sour. Sour perception may have evolved together with sweetness perception to signal ripeness of fruit. Furthermore, it is also an indicator of fermentation. Vinegar is another example of a desired taste in cooking and preserving foods. It also appears to have positive effects on the body's bacteria balance. Strong sourness however is typically undesirable and rejected in a protective instinct to avoid potentially corrosive substances that may damage the tissues in the oral cavity and the whole body (Breslin and Spector 2008: R149; Cavalieri 2014).

The evolution of *salt* perception seems to be more recent in human evolution. The prototypical compound that elicits a salty taste (NaCl) is considered a flavour enhancer: it enables the evaporation of water molecules in the food, thus enabling flavour perception through retronasal pathways (Cavalieri 2014: 111–2). The adaptive significance of such perception is related to the indispensable role that sodium has for life. No other ion may replace sodium, and animals are frequently depleted of such substance through excretory and secretory processes (e.g., urine and sweat) (Breslin and Spector 2008: R149). Consequently, a physiological mechanism to signal levels of this substance is necessary to balance the levels of this element in the body. While carnivores ingest salt through meat, herbivores show a salt appetite. It has become customary to set out "salt licks" for animals to help them reduce sodium depletion. Humans as omnivores have a sodium intake that is between that of carnivores and herbivores, thus the appetite for saline substances is a consequence of specific diets (Breslin 2013). The usage of salt in culinary traditions varies greatly, but it may date back to an early species in the genus *Homo*. Notably, Japanese macaques (*Macaca fuscata*) acquired the habit of dipping potatoes in sea water to make them taste better (Kawai 1956; Hladik 2004). In a more recent stage of human history, NaCl also acquired a further role as food preservative and therefore as a useful commodity. This cultural role is reflected in the English word *salary*, which ultimately derives from Latin *salarium*, and it refers to money allowed to Roman soldiers for the purchase of salt, hence, their pay (OED *salary*, n.).[5] Salt taxes were also applied around the world, as were salt tariffs to cross rivers or boundaries, and these were the cause of many revolts, uprisings, and revolutions in China, France, Spain, Russia, England, Italy, and the Roman Empire. Its importance is also evinced in toponyms, e.g., *Salzstraße*, (Salzbury), *Solnitsata* (The Saltworks), *Via Salaria* (the Salt Route), and *Salt Lake*; see also Cutting (2008).

The evolution of *umami* perception is related to the presence of amino acids and proteins in food. In human diets, it is mainly found in cooked or aged meats, cheeses, tomatoes, and seafood (see Beauchamp 2009; and discussion in Osawa 2011: 22 for counter evidence). The word *umami* was first introduced in the academic debate by Ikeda ([1909] 2002), who discovered that the sensations induced by exposure to glutamate salts are different from the previously well-

---

[5] Oxford English Dictionary (OED) online, oed.com. References from the OED report the *part of speech* and the number of the meaning discussed.

known and established four basic taste types (Bachmanov et al. 2014). As such, *umami* is a Japanese loan word, which means 'delicious' and 'savoury'. In English, umami sensations are typically coded by the adjective *savoury* (Osawa and Ellen 2014). Exposure to this tastant seems to stimulate sweet receptors (Hellekant and Ninomiya 1991; but see Breslin and Spector 2008: R148 for a non-confusion between sweet and umami). The presence of glutamate however is not as high in fresh, unprocessed meats as it is in processed meat, thus suggesting that humans developed receptors to umami as a response to the inclusion of easily digestible proteins in their diets (Breslin 2013). This may be presumed also by the fact that chimpanzees (*Pan troglodytes*) can taste umami compounds, but they do not have specific receptors for it. This implies that umami taste receptors did not appear in primates before the domestication of fire that could guarantee the cooking and/or storage of meat (Wrangham 2010). However, specific receptors for the taste of meat proteins might have existed in extinct carnivores, such as some dinosaurs. This hypothesis is supported by the conversion of the ancestral umami receptor to the sweet receptor in hummingbirds, which possibly genetically inherited their umami sensitivity from an earlier dinosaur ancestor and later reconverted it to taste pollen (Baldwin et al. 2014; Antinucci and Risso 2017: 6).

Finally, *spiciness* perception needs discussion, although it is not one of the taste types. Some plants evolved a defensive mechanism based on toxic substances to deter teeth-bearing animals from consuming them. Capsaicin is one of those chemicals aimed at the nociceptors of many animals, and responsible for our perception of spiciness (Caterina et al. 1997; Tewksbury and Nabhan 2001). Exposure to such stimuli leads to heat and irritation of the mucosae, and as such capsaicin has been observed to increase pain-sensitivity and avoidance in both humans (Klein et al. 2013) and rats (Gilchrist, Allard, and Simone 1996). Animals also display a rejection of spicy foods, even if such phenomenon may be reversed through repetitive exposure, and cultural appreciation in humans (Rozin, Gruss, and Berk 1979; Carstens et al. 2002). Rozin and Kennel (1983) investigated appreciation of spiciness in domesticated chimpanzees, showing that despite instinctual refusal, these primates came to prefer spicy crackers over non-spicy ones after a period of exposure.

The physiological mechanisms that connect our gustatory experiences to cognition evolved over millions of years, and sometimes the hedonic response that humans have when exposed to them is instinctual and automatic, without even reaching the central nervous system. According to my hypothesis, the complex architecture and multimodal composition of the gustatory system is mirrored in the linguistic and conceptual organisation of the lexical items that describe it. Furthermore, the evolutionary value and embodied response to each tastant inform and motivate their conceptual elaboration via figurative mechanisms.

2.5 The linguistic representation of taste: A brief literary review

There are a number of studies that have specifically dealt with this modality and its linguistic representation, even though Western philosophical tradition has downplayed the importance of taste among other perceptions. Most studies are aimed at describing the language of taste either as used amongst specialists and in specialised communicative contexts (i.e., the language of wine, Lehrer 1983), or in languages where taste is more widely represented than in Western languages (e.g., Lim 2015; Rhee and Koo 2017 on Korean); while more recent studies investigate the language of food. Although this line of research has produced crucial results to consider, the perspective I take here is slightly different. My main interest is to investigate the role of taste in common and familiar English parlance. I do not focus on technical and specialised vocabulary, and the people who took part in my study are laypeople, and not experts in taste-related disciplines. Therefore, to the best of my knowledge, this research can be considered to be a first attempt to describe the language and role of taste in everyday English.

The first investigations in the domain of the linguistic conceptualisation of taste appear in the early years of the 20th century, and despite evident methodological issues about the collection of the linguistic data, they represent a valuable contribution to the description of this sense in a cross-linguistic perspective, and one of the few attempts proposed to reach this aim. These linguists reveal a strong anthropological perspective to language description. They mainly focus on the vocabulary of perception of what they inopportunely call "primitive" people. The researchers did not belong to the cultures they were describing, and definitely were not native speakers of the language. This position gave them an ethnographic approach, which reflects the approach of this book.

Chamberlain (1903) presents a survey of taste terms in Algonquian languages of North America. His paper is a collection of words in these languages, divided in different categories corresponding to their English equivalent. Firstly, he lists all the words in different languages that have a general meaning of *taste*. Secondly, he enumerates all the words that express a hedonic value (good tasting, bad tasting). Thirdly, he lists the linguistic items that indicate lack of taste (i.e., insipid or tasteless). Lastly, Chamberlain reports on the different taste sensations: apart from the basic five taste qualities (*sweet, sour, salty, bitter, spicy*) he also refers to categories such as *acid, astringent, peppermint, pungent,* and *rancid.*

Myers (1904) is a relevant attempt at classifying the language of taste. He was a psychologist at King's College in London, and reports on his studies on the Torres Straits populations that he carried out with Seligmann. The two researchers ran a set of taste recognition tests, having informants taste different

solutions containing sugar, salt, acid, and quinine to retrieve information about the gustatory sensations of sweet, salt, sour, and bitter, respectively. He summarises the results as follows:
- The literal meaning of the phrase commonly used in the Torres Straits to denote sweetness is 'tasting good'.
- The same phrase is applicable to denote saltness.
- The usual word for saltness is derived from seawater.
- The taste-names for salt and sour tend to be confused.
- There is no specific name for the bitter taste (Myers 1904: 119).

He continues with an examination of the taste-names in Indo-European languages and claims that the same characteristics of taste vocabulary hold in those languages too. He also reports the results of experiments carried out with the help of several non-specialists (such as missionaries and officials). The instructions he gave however lacked precision and sound methodology, therefore it is difficult to consider his results as scientifically valid. Nonetheless, the research reported is of high value, especially for his attempt to trace a general state of the art of taste terms in various languages and cultures. Finally, Rivers (1905) contains a section on taste terms of the Todas, a population from southern India. Rivers used the same methodology proposed by Myers, thus eliciting the names of different tastants by the informants. He reports on some difficulties about carrying out the tests, but also found terms for the main four different qualities. Furthermore, the author also reports on some confusion between sour and salt tastes.

The next relevant contribution to the study of taste in language comes decades later with Lehrer. The American linguist investigates the vocabulary of wine in a series of publications (Lehrer 1975, 1983). Her main interest is the vocabulary of wine tasting, its internal organisation and the mechanisms of semantic extensions. As she reports in the first chapter:

> I was concerned with two questions. First, assuming that some of the wine words mean something, even if they are to be interpreted subjectively and evaluatively, what is the structure of this vocabulary? Second, how do speakers use these words and what do they understand when they hear them? (Lehrer 1983: 4)

Lehrer demonstrates the vastness of wine vocabulary in English, which is often expanded through various mechanisms of meaning extension and word formation. These mechanisms are not exclusively related to wine vocabulary, rather they might be found in other semantic domains – for instance metaphor; and morphological processes such as affixation with the suffix -*y*. Lehrer's contribution to the study of taste is of outstanding theoretical and practical value, and her morphological observations have been applied in the discussion of my data set (Chapters 4–6). The overall focus however is slightly different, as I concentrate on the lexicon of taste elicited by native speakers in a neutral and non-taste related context.

A recent example of the anthropological and cultural perspective to the study of taste related terms is represented by Kuipers (1984). The anthropologist published a report of his ethnographic fieldwork with the Weyéwa, a population in Sumba, Indonesia who speak the homonymous language belonging to the Austronesian family. The focus of his report is the role that this culture gives to taste and the tasting experience. Kuipers notices that the social visit is organised according to taste perception: "the quality, size, freshness, quantity, and variety of the ingredients are factors in the evaluation of their taste on the wealth and prestige of the giver, and also perhaps on the disposition of the host towards the guest" (Kuipers 1984: 541). On the basis of this observation, Kuipers proposes a set of basic taste words in Weyéwa: *sour, sweet, salty, bitter, tart, pungent, bland*, alongside a set of taste terms that refer to food texture. The most compelling part however is his survey of the "ritual uses of taste vocabulary". He reports that in Weyéwa ritual language the couple *bitter-bland* is extended metaphorically to refer to objects prohibited or permitted respectively. The notion of *bland* in Weyéwa however is less negative than in English (Kuipers 1984: 548–550). Kuipers' paper is relevant for my research for two main reasons: (i) he describes the language of taste in a given culture through participant observation, and (ii) he investigates the cultural and metaphorical meanings of taste words. He argues that there is a fundamental difference between culture and physiology. As much as physiological accounts can be of help in the definition of taste, when considering how laypeople use taste terms in specific linguistic and social contexts, it is crucial to avoid over-relying on physiological definitions (Kuipers 1984: 85). I fundamentally agree, but I also maintain that information coming from physiology needs to be integrated in our description of cognitive and perceptual phenomena, especially considering the framework of embodied cognition. Therefore, the present book adopts a hybrid perspective on physiological descriptions. On the one hand, these are fundamental to our understanding of linguistic phenomena (see e.g., Majid and Levinson 2008); on the other hand, language often partitions perception with little or no concern of the underlying physiological phenomena. This creates a substantial gap between these two analytic dimensions as in the case of the five senses folk-model.

Further pieces of evidence of the discrepancy between linguistic conceptualisation and physiology may be retrieved in Backhouse (1994). He explores the semantics of taste terms in Japanese, taking a lexical semantics approach developed from Lyons' (1977) approach. The results of Backhouse's investigations suggest that gustatory sensations in language cannot be restricted to just five qualities, thus confirming the multisensoriality of taste. Despite being far from an embodied cognitive perspective, Backhouse recognises the role of distinct modalities in the creation of what we would now refer to as flavour. As he puts it, the lexicon of taste in Japanese "ranges over the parameters of gustation, the tongue sensations of pungency, astringency and harshness, and olfaction" (Backhouse 1994: 160).

A relevant study regarding English taste words is authored by Ankerstein and Pereira (2013), who provide evidence for the notorious paucity of taste terms in English by carrying out an object description task. The authors asked native speaker informants to list different features of vegetables and fruit. As they noted, "whilst taste was rated as an important (the most important?) modality in knowledge of fruits and vegetables, the number of individual taste features given in the feature generation task was low and largely restricted to three of the four basic taste words: 'sweet', 'sour', and 'bitter'" (Ankerstein and Pereira 2013: 313). Furthermore, the two researchers verify collocations for a set of 28 taste terms (retrieved from the website descriptivewords.org) in the COCA. The aim of the corpus analysis was to verify the use of taste words in language. The results of the corpus analysis

> showed that many of our taste words, including the taste primary "salty", are derivative, based on noun stems. Many of the taste words listed were also shown to be ambiguous (polysemous) or vague, describing not only taste but food quality. Other words were also not specific, for example "sweet". It can describe the taste of an apple, pear, or banana and does not offer a clear description of a particular taste.
> (Ankerstein and Pereira 2013: 312)

Thus, they conclude that English reveals a poverty of taste words (Ankerstein and Pereira 2013: 305), but that this does not mirror a generalised lack of knowledge about taste or inability to perceive tastes. The perspective in which the authors discuss their results is that of the Sapir-Whorf hypothesis, therefore their primary interest was to investigate the relationship between language, cognition, and perception, and to what extent one influences the other (Ankerstein and Pereira 2013: 305).

The insights provided by Ankerstein and Pereira tackle the thorny issue of the richness of specialised vocabulary to talk about the senses, or lack thereof. It is undeniable that there are not many words that *uniquely* refer to gustation, but there are not many words that uniquely refer to *any* sensory modality outside of specialised terminology. The linguistic data presented in this book offer a different picture, namely that the transfer of lexical material from one modality to the other is so common in English that identifying a single, uni-sensory adjective may be considered exceptional. Human experience is a multifaceted, multisensory, and integrated phenomenon, and the linguistic system of English fully recognises this complexity. In this light, the question of whether a single lexeme uniquely describes one modality as opposed to another is undermined by recognising perception as a continuum, as opposed to a collection of discrete entities.

Lastly, there have been recent attempts to describe the figurative elaboration of gustatory sensations. For instance, Steinbach-Eicke (2019) proposes a diachronic analysis of taste metaphors in ancient Hieroglyphic Egyptian texts. Although there is only one lexicalised verb of gustatory perception in these texts, she reviews the metaphorically extended meanings and proposes the following conceptual metaphors: PHYSICAL FEELING/TOUCHING IS TASTING, EMOTIONAL FEELING IS TASTING, EXPERIENCING IS TASTING, KNOWING IS TASTING. These metaphorical realisations are consistent with the ones found in English and reported in this book, and the distance in phylogenesis, time, and cultural systems between Ancient Egyptian and Contemporary English suggests an ancient, embodied trend in the semantic extension of gustatory language emerging from human cognitive architecture.

3 The words of taste

3.1 Introduction

The first issue to be addressed is the identification of the words that constitute the semantic domain of TASTE in English, which would answer the question, what are the words that describe taste in English? The use of the word *domain* is to be intended as Evans defines them, i.e., "relatively complex knowledge structures which relate to coherent aspects of experience" (2007: 62). To reiterate, I investigate the domain of TASTE in a usage-based perspective, with a bottom-up approach (Barlow and Kemmer 2000), in keeping with the methodological tenets of Cognitive Linguistics. I am interested in describing this semantic domain as speakers perceive it, discarding specialised terminology, jargon, or genre specific language (i.e., food blogs, or recipes). In this chapter, I discuss the main methodological and theoretical tenets that structure my investigation to retrieve the words of taste.

The question about the underlying structure of the domain of TASTE needs to be handled carefully for a number of reasons. Firstly, English is a widely investigated language in Western academia, to the extent that some scholars have rightly advocated for a wider inclusion of less-represented languages and more cross-linguistic investigations (e.g., Majid and Levinson 2015). While on one hand the interest in Western languages has led to a plethora of contributions describing English, it has nonetheless meant that some aspects of the structure of English have often been left unexplored. English gustatory terms have been reported and investigated, but usage-based and bottom-up approaches are still lacking, which instead are paramount in Cognitive Linguistics.

Secondly, describing any semantic domain needs some methodological clarifications. What are the *boundaries* of a semantic domain? What qualifies a word as part of a domain and not another domain? A possible answer to these questions comes from our understanding of fundamental cognitive phenomena such as categorisation (see Paragraph 3.3; 3.4), salience, and entrenchment (see Paragraph 3.5). The internal structure of domains is better thought of as gradable, with some members that may be more representative than others along a continuum. This view of semantic structure advocates for a dynamic construal of what might be considered part of a domain. The methodology that I adopted for the elicitation of taste words is freelistings and the Cognitive Salience Index (Sutrop 2001), which allows to create a graded and continuous representation of the semantic domain (see Chapter 4).

Lastly, as I have ascertained that the physiological multisensoriality of taste is better accounted for as flavour, i.e., as a spectrum including gustation, olfaction, and chemesthesis, it follows that it is crucial to verify if this complexity is mirrored also on a linguistic level (see Spence, Smith, and Auvray 2015). To confirm this, in Chapter 5 I compare a list of lexemes retrieved with a bottom-up approach with precompiled lists of words normed along perceptual dimensions, in keeping with the approach of sensory linguistics. As an example, consider the following description of the taste of asparagus:

(3) But quite often, its taste is described as **distinct**, yet reminiscent of **broccoli**, **Chinese long beans** or **green beans** with an **undertone of an earthy grass flavor** with some **bitterness**. Compared to green asparagus, the white variety is slightly more **sweet-bitter** but has less of the **grassy** taste.[6]

Which of the words highlighted in (3) is considered a taste word in English? Furthermore, in the brief passage, the taste of asparagus seems better described with reference to a source of a similar quality, for instance *reminiscent of broccoli* or *grassy taste*. This linguistic strategy is commonly referred to as source-based language (Cacciari 2008; Winter 2019a: 23–25, see Paragraph 4.3), and it involves using the source of a sensation as an index for another type of food. As Winter (2019a: 24) notes however, this relationship is semantically opaque. When we describe the taste of asparagus as *grassy* are we describing the mild bitterness of the asparagus? Maybe we are using it to convey information about texture, crossmodal information about the *colour* of the flavour (compare *green beans*), or the olfactory qualities of the object.

Moreover, how entrenched is the adjective *grassy* in the linguistic representation of taste of English speakers? Do speakers normally use this word to refer to the taste of something, or is it just a peculiar usage for this specific reason? While the meaning of such an item is certainly grasped by speakers of English, this does not mean that its status in the domain of TASTE is entrenched enough to be considered a taste word, and to enable a speaker to produce it frequently.

3.2 Methodological tenets: Usage-based approach

The usage-based approach adopted in this book may be exemplified with reference to a basic distinction in cultural anthropology: emic vs. etic approaches. The dichotomy first originated in linguistics, in the writings of the missionary linguist Kenneth Pike (1967), and they were coined in reference to the distinction

---

[6] https://vegbyte.com/what-does-asparagus-taste-like/; last accessed 25 September 2020.

between phon*emic* and phon*etic*. An *emic* approach would favour the *structure* of language, while the *etic* approach could not yield such information. The terms were later borrowed from anthropology, where they still belong and are more frequently used. In anthropology however the terms changed their meaning, and Harris (1968: 571) provides the following definition: "Emic statements refer to logico-temporal systems whose phenomenal distinctions or 'things' are built up out of contrasts and discriminations significant, meaningful, real, accurate, or in some other fashion regarded as appropriate by the actors themselves" (1968: 571).

Thus, in cultural anthropology, an emic statement is a description of a phenomenon, or a category, from the point of view of the individuals that developed and regularly use such phenomenon. If we apply this approach to linguistics, an emic approach to a linguistic phenomenon would mean designing a methodology that involves native speakers as the primary source of information. In contrast to this, an etic statement depends upon "phenomenal distinctions judged appropriate by the community of scientific observers" (Harris 1968: 575), thus interpreting cultural phenomena according to the beliefs of the scientist analysing it. This approach lies its foundations on the assumption that cultural actors (i.e., speakers) are too involved in their culture to interpret it from the point of view of an outsider. Conversely, an ethnographer working in an etic perspective should be able to observe a cultural phenomenon and describe it objectively and comprehensively (Kottak 2007: 29).

The emic approach to the domain of TASTE is particularly evident in the establishment of basic taste terms and in the identification of conceptual mechanisms. Physiology identifies a limited set of basic transduction processes, and as such it limits the set of basic taste terms to only five: *sweet, sour, bitter, salty,* and *umami*. Folk-knowledge also includes terms such as *spicy*, and sometimes *savoury*. A linguistic description of the sense of taste must rely on a cultural construal of taste itself, retrieved in an emic perspective. Thus, the data retrieved from elicited conditions are validated and integrated with information from various sources. More technical data, such as psycholinguistic norming studies, corpora, free sorting tasks, are coupled with popular and accessible information, such as websites, blogs, and forums to reconstruct a multifaceted understanding of taste. The two models go hand in hand, and it is not possible to eschew one without the other. Similarly, in the identification of conceptual mechanisms, I adopt the labels of the five-senses folk model to spell out phenomena of semantic transfer from one modality to another despite their physiological basis (particularly evident in the case of nociception).

Research has debated the role of subjective introspection in Cognitive Linguistics and the cognitive sciences. The work of cognitive linguists is often criticised because it relies too heavily on personal intuitions and introspection (e.g., Gibbs 2007: 5), and these critiques have been voiced within Cognitive Linguistics as well. Dąbrowska (2016) reviews the *Seven deadly sins of Cognitive Linguistics*, and the role given to introspection is one of them. The problem with introspection is that (i) "many aspects of our mental life are not accessible through introspection", and (ii) "introspective judgements are influenced by our knowledge and beliefs, and often demonstrably false" (Dąbrowska 2016: 480).

Introspective analyses however are also a valuable source of information. As Gibbs points out, "the trained intuitions of cognitive linguists have provided detailed insights into possible language-mind-body interactions that serve as the source of experimental hypotheses on the workings of the cognitive unconscious" (2007: 3). Linguists' intuitions and reliance on introspection are necessary tools especially in the description and interpretation of meaning (Talmy 2018). Intuitions might be the source of hypotheses that need to be tested with more empirical methodologies, and introspection is just one of the methodologies adopted in Cognitive Linguistics (Talmy 2007).

3.3 Basic level terms

Categorisation is one of the most basic processes of the human mind. We categorise objects at any time, even without necessarily realising it. The mental process of categorisation often happens without surfacing to the level of consciousness. Whenever we utter phrases like "an asparagus is a vegetable", we are in fact using our ability to categorise objects in real life, by way of assigning an item X (the asparagus) to a superordinate category Y (vegetable) that encompasses objects similar to X. Research originated in ethnobiology in the second half of the 20th century has shown that the internal structure of categories is graded, and gradable. This view is in sharp contrast to earlier descriptions of category structure, according to which each member had an equal status: an item would be either part (or not) of a given category. The German philosopher Wittgenstein was one of the first to notice the fallacy of this conception of category creation in his *Philosophical Investigations* (1953). He considers various types of games and tries to identify common patterns to them all. To do so, he identifies defining features of one, and notices that some features are lost when passing to the next one, while some others are gained:

> Look for example at board-games, with their multifarious relationships. Now pass to card-games; here you find many correspondences with the first group, but many common features drop out, and others appear. When we pass next to ballgames, much that is common is retained, but much is lost. – Are they all 'amusing'? Compare chess with noughts and crosses. Or is there always winning and losing, or competition between players? Think of

patience. In ball games there is winning and losing; but when a child throws his ball at the wall and catches it again, this feature has disappeared. Look at the parts played by skill and luck, and at the difference between skill in chess and skill in tennis. Think now of games like ring-a-ring-a-roses; here is the element of amusement but how many other characteristic features have disappeared! And we can go through the many, many other groups of games in the same way; can see how similarities crop up and disappear. And the result of this examination is: we see a complicated network of similarities overlapping and criss-crossing: sometimes overall similarities, sometimes similarities of detail.

67. I can think of no better expression to characterise these similarities than "family resemblances"; for the various resemblances between members of a family: build, features, color of eyes, gait, temperament, etc. etc. overlap and criss-cross in the same way. – And I shall say: 'games' form a family. (Wittgenstein 1953: 31e–33e)

This description of categories suggests that members of a category do not necessarily share the same features, but some members may have features that others do not have, and have in turn features shared by members of other categories. Consequently, some items may be better representatives of a category than others, and the distinction between members and non-members may be distributed on a gradient of membership. In other words: membership in a category is not binary; boundaries of inclusion are not clear-cut, rather they are fuzzy; and members in a category do not share an equal status.

Wittgenstein's intuitions were explored and confirmed in later, empirical research. A case in point is the ethnobotanical line of inquiry led by Berlin, Breedlove, and Raven (1973, 1974; Berlin 1978). These scholars found that the level that encompassed the largest number of names, as well as the one that speakers would choose more often was the level that they called generic, with categories like *oak* or *willow*. Other (more general) levels of categorisation were unique beginners, i.e., *plant*; *life forms*, or *tree*; while more distinct levels were specific, i.e., *white beans*; and varietal, i.e., *red common bean*. Their claims were later psychologically confirmed by a series of experiments by Rosch et al. (1976), who extended ethnobiologists' claims out of the natural domain to common objects. Their results show a number of characteristics shared by what they call basic level categories: i.e., the most inclusive level of abstraction at which objects have common attributes, they have greater cognitive primacy than terms at other levels of categorisation, and terms found at this level tend to be acquired earlier by children.

In another famous study, Labov (1973) investigated the concepts of cups, bowls, and vases with a pool of English speakers by pairing visual manipulation and object recognition. In his research, he shows that there are no clear-cut boundaries between the category of cups and bowls, but that one object could slowly turn into the other in a gradient of attributes shared by different entities on a scale from more cup-like to more bowl-like, without necessarily establishing a precise point where one would turn into the other. Taylor (1995: 49) provides a practical example for the appreciation of basic level terms. If asked to draw or to visualise a "piece of furniture", one feels that some details are missing, and it seems legit to ask, "what kind of furniture?". Conversely, a request to draw a bed or a chair seems more feasible and does not require further information. This is because terms such as *bed* and *chair* are basic level terms and lie on a maximally inclusive level of abstraction.

Compelling evidence from these studies contributed to affirmation of a new theoretical approach to the description of categorisation and highlighted the inadequacy of the structuralist and functionalist view that was prominent. The new version of categorisation is one of the basic assumptions in the cognitive enterprise, and this theoretical model, based on empirical data, may be applied to various disciplines: psychology, anthropology, and linguistics. The two main characteristics of cognitive categories are prototypicality (e.g., Battig and Montague 1969; Heider 1971; Labov 1973; Rosch 1973, 1975a, 1978; Coleman and Kay 1981; Kempton 1981; Pulman 1983); and the existence of basic level terms (e.g., Rosch 1975b, 1976; Rosch and Mervis 1975; Downing 1977; Pulman 1983). The amount of literature produced in this line of research is overwhelming and a complete review exceeds the scope of this book (see Lakoff 1987: 46–54; Taylor 1995: 46–51; Croft and Cruse 2004: 74–106; Schmid 2007; Ramscar and Port 2015 for a comprehensive overview).

Drawing together various sources in the linguistic tradition, basic level terms show the following characteristics:
- they should be physiologically motivated;
- they tend to be short and morphologically simple (Berlin and Kay 1969; Sutrop 2001);
- their application is not restricted to a narrow class of objects (Berlin and Kay 1969);
- they tend to be acquired earlier in first-language acquisition (Brown 1958, 1965);
- they are salient and entrenched (Berlin and Kay 1969; Geeraerts 2000, 2010; Sutrop 2001; Schmid 2007).

One of the most popular and discussed examples of basic level terms is perhaps Basic Colour Terms (BCT). Linguistic literature on BCTs is vast and has produced considerable breakthroughs in our understanding of the interaction of bodily perception, language, and culture. Current research on colour perception and language considers eleven BCTs in English: Black and White, Red, Yellow, Green, Blue, Grey, Brown, Purple, Pink, and Orange (Biggam 1997, 2012; Casson

1997; Dedrick et al. 2005; Sandford 2012, 2021). Early research in the domain of colours represented one of the first empirical investigations that pushed for a reconsideration of the cognitive structure of categories. This line of research showed similar patterns of development of what they called basic colour terms, as well as the tendency to attribute strikingly similar hues to the same colour concepts, disregarding the language system of the participants. Their original results have been criticised, particularly because of their methodology and their universalist approach (McNeill 1972; Sampson 1980) before being empirically confirmed by a series of experiments led by psychologist Eleanor Heider (1971) (better known under her later name of Eleanor Rosch). Her empirical findings show that focal colours are stable across different languages, and that they are both perceptually and cognitively more salient than non-focal colours. Furthermore, she also demonstrated that categories representing focal colours are more easily remembered if an individual speaks a language with basic terms corresponding to those colours, but also that focal colours are learned more quickly than non-focal ones. For an updated version of the original basic colour term study by Berlin and Kay (1969), see *The World Colour Survey* (Kay et al. 2009).

Considering the criteria listed above, here are some examples from colour vocabulary to better understand them. Firstly, the eleven BCTs are morphologically simple: they do not comprise more than one morpheme each (an example of a non-morphologically simple colour term is *yellowish*, which is not a basic colour term). A possible violation of this criterion is represented by the word *orange*, which, despite being morphologically simple (i.e., it does not comprise recognisable and meaningful suffixes) it is derived metonymically from the homonymous fruit. It must be noted however, that most BCTs ultimately derive from real world entities (e.g., pink used to refer to carnation, see Sandford 2021), and may therefore be described as examples of source-based language.

Secondly, the application of BCTs is not restricted to a narrow class of objects: compare, for example, the pairing *blonde* and *yellow*. Both terms refer to similar hues, but the term *blonde* typically refers to the colour of one's hair, or it is contextually restricted to the colour of beers, especially lager. English does not allow, for instance, to describe someone's hair as *yellow*, nor to describe the hue of a lemon as *blonde*. Similar examples of pairings are *brunette-brown*; *auburn-red*. The contextual restrictions operating on the first term of the pairings suggests that they are not BCTs.

Thirdly, data from Age of Acquisition norms (Kuperman, Gonzales, and Brysbaert 2012) show that BCTs are acquired at an early age: *white* 4.06 years; *black* 3.56; *red* 3.68; *yellow* 3.20; *green* 3.79; *grey* 5.74; *brown* 5.20; *purple* 3.60; *pink* 3.80; *orange* 3.26 (for a comparison, the earliest acquired words are: *momma* 1.58;

mama 1.89; *mum* 2.00; *daddy* 2.56; *my* 2.72; *see* 3.06; *I* 2.79; *finger* 3.43; while the latest acquired are e.g. *pederasty* 20.00; *sagacity* 19.00; *megalomania* 18.92; *incertitude* 18.33). The relatively early age of acquisition suggests that these are BCTs.

Finally, BCTs need to be salient: Geeraerts (2000, 2010) describes basic level terms as onomasiologically salient, i.e., they are salient across a range of possible names for the same concept. For instance, if asked to name the colour of a poppy, speakers have a range of possibilities, including *scarlet*, *magenta*, *red*, *red-orange*, etc. The onomasiological salience of a term is calculated as a ratio between the frequency of potential referents to an object in a corpus (i.e., in this case all the possible lexical items that describe the colour red) and the frequency of occurrence of each single item. According to Schmid (2007), more entrenched lexical and cognitive units rest at the level of basic terms. Furthermore, Sutrop (2001), in keeping with Berlin and Kay (1969) defines basic level terms as psychologically salient, i.e., they have a tendency to be named in the first positions in elicited lists; they are stable in reference across informants and occasions of use; and they are present in the idiolects of all informants.

3.4 Basic taste terms

The notion of Basic Taste Terms (BTTs) requires a careful and thorough discussion, as it may refer to different, albeit related ideas. BTTs in English are commonly held to correspond to the basic tastes described by physiologists, i.e., *sweet*, *bitter*, *sour*, *salty*, and *umami*. Even within physiology however there are different accounts of the meaning of basic tastes. As noted by Ishii and O'Mahony (1987b), the issue of basic tastes is particularly confusing because we still lack a definition of *primacy*, as it may refer to "the number of taste receptors, the number of transduction mechanisms, the number of neural codes, channels or fibre types or the number of gustatory processes, areas or cell types" (1987b: 46). This terminological confusion adds up to the confusion derived by different possible accounts of gustatory perception. There is still no consensus on whether taste is limited to a set of taste primaries, is a continuum, or is multisensory.

The perceptual models at stake are two: on one hand, the visual synthetic model; on the other, the auditory analytic model. The visual model describes perception as synthetic, because different hues may result as a synthesis of basic, primary hues. For instance, the hue *violet* results from the mixture of red and blue, but the two components are blended in the result, and no longer distinguishable: they are synthesised. Conversely, the auditory model describes perception as analytic: in a succession of tones, each single element composing the symphony (i.e., the mixture) is still perceived as a single-distinguished tone. Scholars have been arguing about the two possible models, and provide evidence supporting both positions. For instance, McBurney (1974) is in defence of the notion of basic tastes, while Erickson and Covey (1980), Erickson (1982, 2008) suggest that the quadripartite (or pentapartite, and more) view of taste lacks substantial evidence, and that is rather influenced by cultural, linguistic, and social behaviour.

In a more psychological and linguistic perspective, Majid and Levinson (2008) strongly disagree with Erickson's position (2008) and provide cross-cultural, linguistic evidence supporting the idea of basic tastes (see also Cutting 2008). They suggest that recurrent lexicalisation patterns across different languages of salient taste prototypes make plausible the existence of psychological foci for basic tastes. These lexicalisation patterns converge despite a wide array of linguistic, cultural, and culinary practices which include a considerable variety of ecological possibilities and staples. The evidence they review suggests that *sweet* and *bitter* are the most psychologically distant concepts, whereas *sour* and *bitter*, and *sweet* and *salty* are the most similar to one another when compared to others.

How does the idea of basic tastes compare to colour primaries? Are we to consider the two notions of basicness as similar to one another? Korsmeyer (2002) analyses this parallelism and advocates for non-identity between the theoretical concept of basic colours and basic tastes, in that the former represent "categories of taste, not substances to be mixed" (Korsmeyer 2002: 77). She exemplifies her statement in reference to lemonade: an introspective taster would still be able to identify the components that went into the drink, despite the overall lemonade taste produced by the mixture. Although different categories of taste do not correspond to colour primaries, and they cannot be blended together in the same way as colours can, they may serve as "reference points" (Korsmeyer 2002: 77). This terminology is reminiscent of psychological and linguistic prototypes: i.e., focal points of reference for the description of the multitude of gustatory perceptions.

In sum, basic tastes may refer to two ideas, which, albeit strongly connected, are different. Basic tastes in physiology loosely refer to the transduction types that operate on the papillae, and they are: *sweet, bitter, sour, salty* and *umami* (unanimously accepted), and *oleogustus* and *starchy* (proposed and debated, see Chapter 2). In Cognitive Linguistics, BTTs refer to a psychologically salient level of categorisation. Although linguistic BTTs are based and largely correspond to the physiological basic tastes, there is not a one-to-one correspondence between the two sets of terms.

3.5 Salience and entrenchment

What does it mean for a BTT to be "psychologically salient"? Salience is a fundamental cognitive phenomenon, and as such its status is discussed in psychology, linguistics, and anthropology. Its common meaning is rather simple and intuitive: salience is the property of objects who attract our attention more than others; it is the property of items that stand out from the rest of their peers. Salience is a crucial concept in the grounding of language in our mental and cognitive abilities, and it has been defined and operationalised in various circumstances. In recent linguistic contributions, salience is also strongly connected to context and expectations. Schmid and Günther (2016) propose a *Unified Socio-Cognitive Framework for Salience in Language*, which aims at unifying the various ways in which salience is used in linguistics.

Salience is intimately connected also with the notion of entrenchment, which was first proposed by Langacker (1987: 59–60) who defines it as the property by which a certain linguistic unit becomes entrenched through repetitive usage in a given linguistic community, thus losing its incidental status. More recently, Schmid defines it as "the continual reorganization of linguistic knowledge in the minds of speakers, which is driven by repeated usage activities in usage events and subject to the exigencies of the conventionalization processes taking place in speech communities" (Schmid 2020: 2). Entrenched linguistic units therefore are stored in long-term memory and are activated with less effort than required by less entrenched units, as a consequence of their salience and frequency of activation. Schmid proposes that the terms with the highest level of entrenchment are found at the basic level (Geeraerts 2010: 201; Divjak and Caldwell-Harris 2015).

Schmid and Günther identify two main parameters to classify salience, namely context and expectations. Context may be linguistic, situational, social or it may refer to the general cognitive context of each speaker. The other variable is expectations, and it refers to the "state of the cognitive system immediately prior to processing a given linguistic cue" (Schmid and Günther 2016: 2). Expectations may be violated or confirmed. The combination of these four variables gives rise to comparative aspects as cross listed in Table 1 (derived from Schmid and Günther 2016), which accounts for the different types of salience in language.

A linguistic unit may be salient if it violates expectations in the current context of usage (case 1a in Table 1). The expectations are dictated by the current linguistic, situational, and/or social context. A linguistic unit in a collocation may become salient if it is not usually associated in that context. For instance, in the unacceptable *cool as an asparagus* (as opposed to *cool as a cucumber*),

Table 1: Various types of salience in Language, derived from Schmid and Günther (2016).

	current context	long-term memory
violation of expectation	1a. salience by novelty	1b. salience by novelty
confirmation of expectation	2a. salience by contextual entrenchment	2b. salience by context-free entrenchment

the word *asparagus* becomes salient because it violates the expectations created on the basis of the linguistic and collocational context of occurrence.

The second usage of the notion of salience describes linguistic units that are completely novel to the hearer, to the extent that the word in question is new and its meaning unknown (case 1b in Table 1). For instance, the word *oleogustus* for the description of a rancid, fatty taste that is found in oily foods may become salient for speakers who do not know its meaning. This aspect of salience is particularly evident during the stages of language acquisition but may be found at all levels of competence when facing new, unusual words.

The selection of a linguistic unit might be salient because it confirms the expectation of usage in the current context (case 2a in Table 1): for instance, when looking at a round, hand-size fruit with a stem found in the fruit section of a supermarket, it is most likely that we would call it an *apple*, as opposed to *plant*, *pear*, *grape*, *Fuji*, or *Granny Smith*. In this case, the word *apple* is salient because it was the first that came to mind in that context. This usage of the concept of salience is the onomasiological salience described by Geeraerts (2000, 2010), and it refers to basic level terms in a category.

The fourth case of usage of the concept *salience* in Cognitive Linguistics is the property of linguistic units that emerge from the general cognitive context of the speaker, without activation through contextual cues (case 2b in Table 1). For instance, when asked "what are common edible fruits?", we would expect that the word *apple* be one of the first words that comes to mind; despite being good candidates, *cherry* or *banana* might come to mind later.

The property of objects to be promptly activated during speech processing is defined by Schmid (2007) as cognitive salience. Cognitively salient concepts may acquire this status as a consequence of their physical and/or cultural characteristics in real-life situations. For example, the word *asparagus* may become more salient in certain periods of the year (e.g., during spring), when they are more commonly harvested and therefore present in the vegetable section of supermarkets. Schmid (2007) calls this characteristic *ontological* salience: some entities in the world are more likely to attract our attention than others. Ontologically salient items attract our attention more easily and immediately than other entities, thus resulting in cognitively salient concepts, which in turn are also more frequently activated than others because they are the first concepts that come to mind.

The activation of a concept in working memory during speech production however may result in the activation of similar or associated concepts through conscious mental elaborations or through *spreading activation* (Anderson 1983: 85–125; Schmid 2007). For instance, the activation of the concept *asparagus* may involve recruitment of associated concepts, such as *risotto*, *bitterness*, *Spring*. This mechanism is particularly effective in the description of linguistic frames or domains using a bottom-up approach, and it is exploited in the present research to produce salient lexical items in the domain of TASTE.

Cognitively salient concepts are more frequently activated than others, and therefore enter the focus of attention more frequently. As a result, these cognitive units have a better chance to become entrenched. When speakers of a language utter speech events, their lexical, grammatical, phonological, and syntactic choices are selected among linguistic units and constructions that are stored in long-term memory. In online speech events however, competent speakers of a language do not browse over the thousands, even hundred-thousands of words that they know and are stored in their brains. Rather, they produce speech in a seemingly automatic and rapid fashion, by relying on a pool of "pre-packaged concepts readily encodable by words" (Schmid 2007: 118). The units of language at their disposal are said to be entrenched.

To sum up: ontologically salient items enter the focus of attention and become cognitively salient. Cognitively salient items are more likely to be activated, and thus stand better chances to become entrenched. Entrenched items tend to be retrieved more easily from memory, are mentioned more frequently, and are found more commonly at the basic level of a category. Thus, we may conclude that Basic Level Terms are both entrenched and salient, and therefore candidates to become BTTs need also to be entrenched and salient.

3.6 Freelistings and salience

A standard methodology to investigate salience and entrenchment of items in long-term memory is the freelisting technique. The underlying idea is that more salient and entrenched units in language tend to be retrieved earlier in a lexical retrieval task, an assumption better formulated by Schmid and Günther (2016: 2), who state that "the general long-term memory-based context includes the full range of entrenched linguistic knowledge and routines, i.e., the individual's current linguistic competence". Therefore, investigation of salience in long-term memory provides insights on salient and entrenched units in a given linguistic category.

Anthropologists have long known and used the methodology of freelisting. It is a qualitative procedure that can be easily quantified through simple operations and the application of an algorithm. It is as simple as having a group of people listing "as many X as you can think of", where X are items in a domain, or a category. For example, applications of this method include medicinal plants used by members in a given society (e.g., Nolan 2001, 2004; Mathez-Stiefel et al. 2012), barriers to self-care in a group of American patients (Bayliss et al. 2003), decision-making for ADHD (Fiks et al. 2011), among others (for more examples, see Bernard 2011; Quinlan 2017). Notably, a number of researchers investigated the domain of COLOUR with this procedure (Smith 1995; Uusküla and Sutrop 2007 on Hungarian; Uusküla 2007 on Finnish; Uusküla 2008 on Czech; Sandford 2016 on American English vs. Italian), while Osawa (2011) and Osawa and Ellen (2014) investigated taste terms in Japanese.

There are numerous advantages to this procedure:
- it provides a large amount of data in a small amount of time (in literate societies it can be performed with more than one speaker at a time, for example in a classroom);
- it offers insight on the items in a category (or in a cultural domain);
- when operationalised, it informs the researcher on which items are most important and salient; but most importantly
- the data retrieved are elicited through native speakers, with little to no involvement or bias from the researcher.

This usage-based approach elicits an emic description of categories under scrutiny. The freelisting procedure rests on three underlying assumptions, exemplified by Quinlan (2017):
1. Informants perform a freelisting task with an ego-centred perspective: thus, earliest examples are also the most familiar for them. For instance, Romney and D'Andrade (1964) interviewed American middle-schoolers on kinship terms. Their results showed that terms such as *mother* were more frequent among the overall group of participants, as opposed to *son* or *daughter*. They relate these results with the fact that participants presumably did not have any sons or daughters but were sons or daughters. Furthermore, the order of frequency of such terms corresponds to an order of familiarity: *mother* was generally listed before *aunt*, and *aunt* before *great-aunt*.
2. The length of the lists produced by informants corresponds to their knowledge about the subject. For instance, Brewer (1995) found that participants who listed more Countries were also better at recognizing them on a map.

3. Order of retrieval from memory corresponds to the order of elaboration of the category. For instance, Gatewood (1983) asked 40 adults from Pennsylvania to list as many names of trees as they could think of. Participants were consistent in mentioning *oak*, *cherry*, and *pine* earlier than *orange* or *banana*. The order and frequency of mention is assumed to correspond to geographically prominent items in the domain of participants, as a result of everyday exposure.

The last assumption resonates with the nature of the cognitive system and its situatedness in a sociocultural environment. The construction of linguistic categories and cultural domains is connected to the environment in which an individual dwells. We have seen how frequency of exposure to given stimuli corresponds to more frequently activated concepts, which in turn will result in more entrenched entities in the lexicon of the speaker.

3.7 Comparison to other methodologies

I adopt the freelisting methodology to describe the domain of TASTE, as it elicits lexical items in a full emic and usage-based perspective. To illustrate my methodological choice, I review here other possibly viable methodologies that have been applied with a similar objective. I do not use these procedures to elicit the terms that describe the domain of TASTE. I do use the results of norm-based lists however in comparison to the terms emerging from the freelisting to discuss the multisensoriality of taste in Chapter 5.

3.7.1 Before Cognitive Linguistics

The most comprehensive example of linguistic research dedicated to the description of taste is Backhouse's monograph *The Lexical Field of Taste, A Semantic Study of Japanese Taste Terms* (1994). In this seminal study, Backhouse applies constructionist theories of language and semantics to describe the lexical field of gustatory sensations in Japanese. Before the investigation, the author was self-reportedly "familiar, to a greater or lesser degree, with a range of Japanese lexical items whose meaning seemed to relate in some way to 'taste' in the widest sense" (Backhouse 1994: 32). Backhouse is not a native speaker of Japanese, and in order to investigate the "lexical field" of taste he recognised his need of validation from native speakers. As a matter of fact, his findings are "based chiefly on the speech of one informant, the wife of the investigator who was raised and educated in Tokyo" (Backhouse 1994: 34).

One can easily see how relying on just a single informant may lead to biases in the collection and interpretation of data. To avoid this, Backhouse assumes that "the structure of the core terms will be stable across speakers of the variety" (1994: 34), and that one would expect variation in the application of these terms, but not in their intralingual relationship. Recent research however in the Cognitive Linguistics tradition has ascertained that individuals differ consistently from each other in both their linguistic and conceptual systems (Dąbrowska 2012, 2015). Therefore, while the methodology adopted by Backhouse reflects the intention of this book of having an emic approach to language description through the interpretation of native speakers, it does not fit the intention of achieving an accurate description of the semantic domain of TASTE. Backhouse's data do not consider individual differences in linguistic competence and production.

3.7.2 Corpora-based lists

Another method of eliciting items for a linguistic analysis is through the usage of corpora. For instance, Ronga (2016) selected texts and collected a corpus of one million tokens. The focus of her research is synaesthetic pairings between gustatory descriptors and other modalities in Italian. The sources of the texts varied: from wine magazines to cookery books and websites; the types of food being described included wine, tea, and cheese. This methodology for mining linguistic data is in line with a usage-based approach to linguistic description: the researcher uses methods of corpus analysis to retrieve linguistic data, with little reliance on personal introspection, as the items retrieved are already validated by their usage.

There are however some counterpoints to this approach which do not fit well with the emic perspective to the description of the semantic domain of TASTE. Firstly, the corpus created by the researcher is highly specialised, and therefore it reflects the usage of gustatory words in a specific genre, and not in common parlance and conceptualisation. To address this problem, Ronga decided to exclude technical terms from the analysis, by selecting only those texts that were addressed to non-professionals, leaving texts addressed to possible purchasers. While this is an ingenious way of avoiding specialised terminology, it does not rule out the possibility that some of those words could be understood by speakers, but never actually produced.

Secondly, the researcher intervenes in establishing *what* is a gustatory word or not. She classified different adjectives with different labels and asked a pool of native speakers to verify her intuition. While the process of aggregating different introspection values is vital in the description of language, the high multisensoriality of the lexicon of taste in English could represent further impediments to reaching this objective. Asking a speaker whether a word such as *crisp* is more a gustatory or an auditory word requires making an exclusive decision between two sensory modalities. Furthermore, the task elicits a binary choice that does not fit with most recent findings in sensory linguistics, which instead regards perception and its lexicon as multisensory and continuous (Winter 2019a). As a consequence, this method may yield only partial and biased results. While Ronga's paradigm is in line with Cognitive Linguistics and the usage-based approach to linguistic description, it endorses an etic approach to the study of the semantic domain of TASTE in English, which is at odds with the intention of unravelling taste words through an emic approach.

3.7.3 Lexicographic analysis

Perhaps the most common method to retrieve sensory specific lexicon is through lexicographic analysis. Typically, a researcher identifies a set of lexemes to start their investigation in a given semantic domain and identifies the items in such a domain through dictionaries and thesauri (e.g., Ronga et al. 2012; Bagli 2018). In both contributions, the authors validated their original insights with a pool of native speakers, by asking them to rate each lexical item in a sensory modality. For instance, Bagli (2018) asked if the lexemes could be used as a descriptor of taste; while Ronga et al. (2012) asked participants to categorise each word in eight different domains (audition, touch, pain, temperature, taste, olfaction, colour and non-colour related vision).

While both approaches address the issue of introspection by validation of native speakers, both methodologies do not rule out the possibility of inaccuracy, specifically because the original lists may not be complete and therefore may not mirror a comprehensive list of adjectives that speakers would use and recognise as salient in the selected domain. The original list of words to be rated is chosen by the researcher and verified by native speakers only in a second moment. The list may contain recognisable though unusual items in the vocabulary of a native speaker; while leaving out potentially salient items that are not listed because they escape lexicographic relations (for instance: they are neither synonyms nor antonyms to the original terms). Thus, although validation of a pool of native speakers allows one to reach a better representation of a specific domain, the methodology adopted may not yield a comprehensive list.

3.7.4 Norm-based lists

Validation by native speakers is the key component to avoid relying too heavily on personal introspection on the side of the researcher. A possible method to do this is through rating. The methodology of rating is highly endorsed in sensory linguistics investigations (see Winter 2019a: 132–135). Moreover, Winter uses this tool to advocate for a continuum in the English sensory lexicon. I follow his lead in explaining what norms are, before highlighting some flaws of this approach.

Rating studies offer a way out of the problem of too much arbitrariness in linguistic investigations, since they offer a list of words that has been reviewed and evaluated by a pool of speakers along a dimension of interest. Thus, researchers have recently contributed with norms for iconicity (e.g., Perry et al. 2015), emotional valence (Warriner et al. 2013), haptic sensation (Stadtlander and Murdoch 2000 for rough or smooth surfaces), concreteness (Brysbaert, Warriner, and Kuperman 2014), among others.

Perceptual modality norms (e.g., McRae et al. 2005; Vinson and Vigliocco 2008) tend to measure the degree in which a single property is exclusively associated to a single modality. Yet, Lynott and Connell instead enable researchers to evaluate the extent to which each property can be considered unimodal, bimodal, or multimodal, while also considering the association strength of each property through the measure "Modality Exclusivity" (2009: 560). They asked a group of fifty-five English native speakers to rate a list of 423 sensory adjectives along different modalities. The goal of the research is to produce norms that measure two distinct, yet related parameters. Firstly, the degree to which each adjective is associated to the different modalities (be it auditory, gustatory, haptic, olfactory, or visual). Secondly, the degree of exclusivity of the association of each adjective to a dominant modality. Furthermore, they asked participants to rate their familiarity with the word they were asked to rate. The scores of each property are measured on a five-value vector "reflecting that item's experiential strength on each modality" (Lynott and Connell 2009: 560). Modality Exclusivity was calculated as the range of values for each modality, divided by the sum. Values in this dimension range from 0 to 1, where a perceptual quality scoring the same value in each modality will have an Exclusivity Rate (ER) equal to 0, and a completely unimodal property, scoring 0 on every modality except one will have an Exclusivity Rate of 1. For instance, the word *oily* was rated by speakers more strongly as visual, then haptic, gustatory, olfactory, and lastly auditory. As a result, the exclusivity modality is not very high (0.28), thus suggesting a high multisensoriality of this term.

The description of the semantic domain of TASTE in English could be achieved by collecting the lexical items that were more strongly associated with the gustatory dimension in Lynott and Connell's norms. This methodology would limit introspection and provide the researcher with a set of rated words. However, there are at least two main points against starting by norms.

Firstly, the authors collected these words "from a range of sources (dictionaries, thesauri, etc.), where each word described an object property that could pertain to one or more sensory modalities (e.g., crackling, glowing, thin, acidic, yellow)" (Lynott and Connell 2009: 559). The original list of adjectives under scrutiny was manually created by the researchers. In other words, it fundamentally relies on the initial introspection of researchers who decided which word was to be considered a "sensory" word, thus imposing an initial arbitrary boundary.

Secondly, considering the high multisensoriality of the lexicon of taste, it would not be sufficient to consider only the words that have been most associated with the gustatory modality via norms. By doing this, the results would have been limited just to the gustatory modality, and the researcher would have no further indication on which other items are used as describing other flavour dimensions, i.e., those more strongly associated with other modalities, but still relevant to the description of TASTE. Thus, exclusively relying on norms does not completely fit my objective.

In conclusion, I employ the freelisting methodology, as it fully enables me to ascertain the lexical items in taste in a usage-based and emic perspective. Nonetheless, I want to stress the importance of multiple approaches to unravel the same issue. The complexity of our linguistic and conceptual systems is not to be glimpsed through a single paradigm or a single methodology, and therefore a varied approach to the study of these phenomena should be endorsed. The current investigation aims at providing an example of how plural methodologies may interact and provide access to different facets of the same issue, thus furthering our understanding.

4 The semantic domain of TASTE in English

4.1 The Cognitive Salience Index

The most common way to operationalise data coming from freelistings is the calculation of the Cognitive Salience Index (CSI). The CSI is an algorithm that combines the frequency and the order of mention of words in a list of lexical items elicited from a population of native speakers through freelisting. There have been different proposals on how to calculate this score. The two main variables taken into consideration are order of mention of an item and its overall frequency in the aggregated lists. For instance, Weller and Romney (1988) and Borgatti (1990) assume that frequency of use equals salience, thus discarding the order of mention as an indicator of this measure. Romney and D'Andrade (1964) instead employed only order of mention as an indicator of salience. A consistent development is represented by Smith (1993), who combines the two elements to create the Salience Index, an easily calculated algorithm, which was refined later by Smith et al. (1995). Although it combines the different variables, it was shown that Smith's Salience Index was influenced by the length of individual lists. Eventually, Sutrop (2001) presents the Cognitive Salience Index: a refined version of the algorithm that does not depend on the length of individual lists and combines the two parameters. As such, the CSI might be considered the most comprehensive version of the index.

The CSI is defined as the ratio between frequency (F) of mention of an item and the number (N) of participants in the test multiplied by the mean position (mP) of the term in the lists. That is:

$$CSI = F/(N \cdot mP)$$

The results of the algorithm are normed to oscillate between 0 and 1, with higher results corresponding to higher levels of salience. Extreme results are practically impossible to obtain: for an item to score a CSI of 1, it should be listed by all participants always in first position. The CSI is also reliable with smaller samples of informants (Sutrop 2001: 267). The parameter of frequency refers to the occurrence of any single item in the entire corpus of elicited items, that is: the number of times an item appears. Frequency alone is not sufficient to define the boundaries of a cognitive (or cultural) domain of knowledge. In the treatment of data, items with extremely low frequency must be eliminated. Terms that are named only by a small number of informants could be accidental or occasional terms. A rule of thumb reported by Sutrop suggests deleting some of the terms from the general list, according to the following criterion. If the number of informants is small, then it is advisable to delete items that have a frequency of 1. If however the number of participants is large, the researcher may delete the terms mentioned by three or fewer subjects. Unfortunately, the author does not specify what are to be considered "small" or "large" numbers in a clear-cut way. He only gives examples: twenty participants would be a "small" sample; "fifty-eighty" instead allow for deletion of items mentioned by three or fewer people (Sutrop 2001: 265). It is safe to assume that the items that are listed with a lower frequency than this are either in passive use or are used only in some idiolects.

The other important parameter for the calculation of the CSI is the mean position of items in the list. This parameter represents the average position that a term has in the aggregated lists in which it appears. It is calculated as the sum of the rankings of each single term (Rj), divided by the specific frequency (F) of that term:

$$mP = \left(\sum Rj/F\right).$$

It is generally held that there is a direct correlation between the mean position and the frequency of the term: more frequent items are listed sooner, while less frequent items are listed later. For this reason, the researcher who intends to define the boundaries of a domain may ignore data about the mean position of items (Sutrop 2001: 265). Conversely, mean position on its own is not sufficient to accurately describe salient terms in a domain, as items may be positioned in a high rank as a result of the conscious activation of a concept in working memory during speech or lexical retrieval tasks. Thus, the two parameters of frequency and mean position need to be combined to have a more nuanced description of the basic status of terms within a domain. More specifically, the two variables operationalise two distinct characteristics of basic terms, namely: frequency corresponds to their presence in all idiolects of all informants (i.e., entrenchment), while mean position corresponds to the tendency to occur in first position of elicited lists (i.e., their ontological salience). Drawing on these observations, we may evince that the CSI is a valuable method to establish cognitively salient and entrenched items in a domain under scrutiny.

4.1.1 Specific methodology

The methodology adopted for this study follows the standard methodology described in the literature for freelisting. I conducted a series of written interviews with the participation of students at the Umbra Institute, an American Study

Abroad program in Perugia (Italy) and a group of students at the University of Glasgow. The choice of interviewing students in a classroom gave me the opportunity to collect a large quantity of data in a short period of time. I conducted a total of fifty-two interviews, but I was able to use only forty of them, due to the presence in the two classes of non-native speakers of English. The mean age of participants was 22 years old.

The questionnaire consisted of three different sections. The front page was the report sheet, on which informants were asked to list the items. The second page included demographic questions (gender, native language, provenance, age) and the instructions of the test. The third and last page reported the Consent from, signed both by participants and I. Informants were allowed three minutes to complete the task, to avoid overthinking and conscious elaboration of the question, which could potentially result in inclusion of unnecessary and non-salient items (Sandford 2016). The instructions were reported on the second page of the questionnaire, and I read them aloud to the informants before starting the test:

> **INSTRUCTIONS**
> You are asked to list as many words as possible in the report sheet. A lexical hint will be provided in due time. You are given three minutes to complete the task. The test is anonymous. There are no incorrect answers.

I gave the last part of the instructions orally shortly before starting the test. It was not included in the printed version to avoid bias. The oral instruction was: "I would like you to write down all the different words that describe different tastes". After the last part of the instructions, I would start the timer and tell informants they could start writing and when they should stop.

4.1.2 Results

The pool of informants produced a total of 248 different types for 829 tokens. The length of the lists varied dramatically: the longest list included 42 items, while the shortest contained only 7 items. Informants produced an average of 20 items per person. Gender did not affect the production task: female participants (27 total) elicited 20.8 items per person on average (562 total), while male participants (13 total) listed 20.6 items per person on average (268 total). Before calculating the CSI, I eliminated items which had a frequency lower than 3, in keeping with Sutrop's indications (Sutrop 2001: 265). This yielded a list of 52 items. The items are distributed on a continuum of salience, from the most salient to the least, and it is not possible to unequivocally establish a clear-cut break in the continuum with standardised measures. However, as suggested by Quinlan (2017), there are visible breaks in the list that may help identify boundaries.

Table 2 shows the most salient items in the domain of taste in English. Column 1 contains a numerical progression that reflects the rank of salience (R) of the items listed in Column 2. I use this value throughout the chapter to refer to the position in the CSI of the items in question, e.g., R1 *sweet*. The others are: Column 3 frequency of mention (F) (a total of 40 possible), Column 4 mP, and Column 5 CSI. Results are ordered by salience; spelling errors are normalised. I did not round up the figures of the CSI, to enable a more nuanced distinction of salience. While the ranking leaves no space for interpretation, the difference in the CSI values is often small, almost insignificant. Yet, the CSI produces a spectrum of salience, and the items are organised along this gradient.

Table 2: Lexical items in the CSI.

CSI Rank (R)	Item	F	mP	CSI
1	sweet	40	3.90	0.256410
2	sour	35	4.20	0.208333
3	salty	32	5.20	0.153846
4	bitter	31	6.16	0.125812
5	spicy	23	8.87	0.064825
6	savoury	21	10.00	0.052500
7	hot	19	9.58	0.049582
8	delicious	18	11.44	0.039336
9	umami	6	5.00	0.030000
10	cold	9	7.89	0.028517
11	yummy	7	6.57	0.026636
12	creamy	10	9.70	0.025773
13	fruity	14	14.79	0.023665
14	tangy	9	10.11	0.022255
15	soft	9	10.20	0.022059
16	disgusting	14	15.93	0.021971
17	smooth	10	11.40	0.021930
18	bland	14	16.29	0.021486

Table 2 (continued)

CSI Rank (R)	Item	F	mP	CSI
19	strong	11	13.10	0.020992
20	sharp	8	10.13	0.019743
21	flavourful	9	12.67	0.017758
22	cheesy	8	11.50	0.017391
23	dry	9	13.30	0.016917
24	meaty	10	14.90	0.016779
25	fresh	9	13.67	0.016459
26	good	8	12.25	0.016327
27	sugary	9	15.70	0.014331
28	tart	4	7.00	0.014286
29	bad	7	12.29	0.014239
30	tasty	4	7.25	0.013793
31	smoky	5	10.60	0.011792
32	gross	7	16.14	0.010843
33	rough	6	14.50	0.010345
34	pungent	4	9.75	0.010256
35	weak	7	17.40	0.010057
36	fishy	7	17.80	0.009831
37	sickly	5	12.80	0.009766
38	juicy	4	10.50	0.009524
39	flavour	5	13.60	0.009191
40	acidic	5	13.80	0.009058
41	burnt	4	11.50	0.008696
42	hard	4	11.50	0.008696
43	chewy	5	15.20	0.008224
44	rich	5	15.40	0.008117
45	oily	4	13.00	0.007692
46	full	4	13.50	0.007407

Table 2 (continued)

CSI Rank (R)	Item	F	mP	CSI
47	light	5	17.20	0.007267
48	stale	4	14.25	0.007018
49	plain	5	18.40	0.006793
50	raw	5	18.60	0.006720
51	crunchy	4	15.00	0.006667
52	boring	4	22.50	0.004444

Although I did not explicitly request participants to produce adjectives, all the items listed through the CSI belong to this word class with the exception of R39 *flavour*, which belongs to the category of nouns. The participants' consistency in listing adjectives may be a result of the specific instructions provided, namely "words that describe different tastes", thus suggesting a descriptive function of the words listed. The elicitation of adjectives proved to be helpful especially in the investigation of their metaphorisation.

The list of salient taste terms in English starts with the four basic transduction processes described by physiology, and that are commonly held to be BTTs: R1 *sweet*, R2 *sour*, R3 *salty*, and R4 *bitter*. They seem to form a first cluster: they share similar frequencies (higher than 30) and close range of CSI [0.256410–0.125812] across the four items. The word R1 *sweet* is the only one in the entire list that has been mentioned by 100% of informants, as evidenced by its frequency, which equals 40. The other items present a descending frequency of mention: R2 *sour*, F= 35; R3 *salty*, F= 32; R4 *bitter*, F= 31.

The difference in CSI values between R4 *bitter* and the following item R5 *spicy* suggests that the first break is after R4: [0.125812–0.064825]. This boundary is followed by a second group of less salient items. This second group starts with the item R5 *spicy*, followed by R6 *savoury*, R7 *hot*, and R8 *delicious*. The items in the second cluster of salience share a similar range of CSI values [0.064825–0.039336] and similar Frequencies [23–19].

After these two groups, the CSI trend flattens, and the differences in salience between the terms are limited. The following item in line is R9 *umami*. Despite the low frequency, this term is surprisingly high in the ranking, as a result of its high score in mean position (mP= 5.00). This means that although only 6 informants mentioned the word *umami*, they always did so in fifth position, and presumably after the four classical basic terms. This may be a result of *spreading activation*, i.e., the activation of a concept in working memory triggered by activation of close-related concepts. Its position after the four basic tastes reflects the recent Western inclusion of this lexical item in the list of basic taste terms. Furthermore, its low score on the frequency parameter suggests a low level of entrenchment in the idiolects of participants, as confirmed by its low frequency in the COCA (F= 154).

The high difference in frequency between R8 *delicious* (F= 18) and R9 *umami* (F= 6) suggests that this last term marks the beginning of a descending trend in salience with no more visible or meaningful breaks. For the first eight items, the trend of frequency follows that of the CSI, which is: the most salient items are also the most frequent. After R9 *umami*, there is no direct correspondence: for instance, R13 *fruity* has double the frequency of R11 *yummy*, yet their CSI is inverted because of their mPs, thus suggesting that R13 *fruity* is more entrenched but less salient than R11 *yummy*. The differences among the items at the bottom of the list are extremely limited, but there is a correspondence in their parameters: for instance, R49 *plain* has a CSI of 0.006793 and F= 5; R50 *raw* has a CSI of 0.006720 and F= 5; R51 *crunchy* has a CSI of 0.006667 and F= 4; lastly R52 *boring* has a CSI of 0.004444 and F= 4. This suggests that effects of salience are most evident and informative at the beginning of the list and about items that are more frequently mentioned. Nonetheless, in keeping with theoretical literature on the subject, items with low frequency and low CSI are still included in the description of the domain of TASTE. The 52 items retrieved through the CSI aggregate the answers of forty native speakers of English, and therefore should be regarded as pertaining to TASTE, although at different levels and through different linguistic and conceptual strategies. The list of words presented in Table 2 is organised with a descending order, from most to least salient items.

4.2 Basic taste terms reassessed

The CSI measures the salience and entrenchment of items elicited within a free-listing technique. Table 2 reports the items (R1 *sweet*, R2 *sour*, R3 *salty*, and R4 *bitter*) which confirms their status of BTT. The following items in the list (R5 *spicy*, R6 *savoury*, R7 *hot*, and R8 *delicious*) do not describe a physiological taste yet show characteristics that may advocate for their inclusion among BTTs. The term R5 *spicy* does not technically refer to gustation, but as Majid and Levinson (2008) suggested, it may be considered a basic taste term in English. The adjective *savoury* does not correspond to any particular taste, and yet cross-linguistic evidence suggests that usage of this term (or equivalent) often conflates and covers sensations which physiology codes as *umami* (Osawa and Ellen 2014). The adjective R7 *hot* is almost a synonym to R5 *spicy*, and it has inspired influential research on the theoretical status of figurative language in reference to embodied cognition and the neurological underpinnings of gustatory sensation (see Chapter 9; Rakova 2003; Winter 2019a). Lastly, the term R8 *delicious* has a broad reference and does not really describe a specific type of gustatory sensation, rather it expresses an evaluation of the hedonic appreciation of a gustatory sensation. In a categorisation perspective, it may be regarded as a hypernym, as it typically conveys an evaluation of food, and therefore may refer to any of the taste types. Yet, its values in the CSI and other parameters (for instance age of acquisition) do not remove all doubt about its potential nature of BTT.

The criteria for identification of BTTs as outlined in the previous chapter are reported here for ease of exposure:
– they should be physiologically motivated.
– they tend to be short and morphologically simple (Berlin and Kay 1969; Sutrop 2001);
– their application is not restricted to a narrow class of objects (Berlin and Kay 1969);
– they tend to be acquired earlier in first-language acquisition (Brown 1958, 1965);
– they are salient and entrenched (Berlin and Kay 1969; Geeraerts 2000, 2010; Schmid 2007; Sutrop 2001).

The eight terms in the first ranks of the CSI list present mixed characteristics that sometimes violate, yet more often confirm these criteria of BTTs.

4.2.1 Application of the criteria

From a morphological point of view, most of the types are morphologically simple, as most of them are monomorphemic: R1 *sweet*, R2 *sour*, R4 *bitter*, R7 *hot*. The other items follow the common structure SOURCE+Y: R3 *salty*, R5 *spicy*, R6 *savoury*. This structure is the result of derivational processes of affixation with the suffix *-y*, a common phenomenon of lexical expansion, especially in the domains of TASTE and SMELL. The word R8 *delicious* is morphologically more complex than the others. It presents a bound root derived from Latin and the addition of the suffix *-ous*. The bound root is also complex, and consists of two separate morphemes, namely *de* and **lect*, which are also found in words such as *delicate*, and *delectable*.

The second criterion predicts that basic level terms are not restricted in their use. Indeed, the application of the eight most salient items does not seem to be restricted to a narrow class of objects, and they all seem to be involved in figurative mechanisms of meaning expansion (see Chapters 7–9). The terms R1 *sweet,* R2 *sour,* R3 *salty,* R4 *bitter,* and R5 *spicy* code identifiable gustatory perceptions which apply to a wide range of items, whereas R6 *savoury* may refer to *umami*. The remaining two terms seem to show quite a reverse pattern: they refer to a wide class of objects that may include items that are not even in the category of taste. From a lexicographic point of view, the item *hot* mainly refers to haptic perception, more precisely to the sensation of temperature. Its gustatory dimension is reported by dictionaries and verified through norms, and however has other meanings. The item R8 *delicious,* as mentioned above, does not refer to an identifiable type of gustatory perception, rather it refers to *any* type of gustatory perception that elicits a pleasant hedonic response.

The third criterion concerns the age of acquisition of basic level terms. In psycholinguistic literature, the age of acquisition variable is largely investigated, and it predicts an array of linguistic phenomena. It is intimately connected to the speed at which a word is recognised, processed, and produced by a speaker, possibly because its meaning is more accessible as it has been stored longer in the memory of a speaker (Ghyselink, Custers, and Brysbaert 2004). Furthermore, lexical items found at the basic level tend to be learned at an early stage of language acquisition, possibly as a consequence of their entrenchment, salience, and morphological structure. One possible way to verify the age of acquisition of the eight terms is through the norms proposed by Kuperman, Gonzales, and Brysbaert (2012). Table 3 reports the data for age of acquisition (expressed in years) of the eight most salient items in the CSI list.

Table 3: Age of acquisition for the eight most salient items in the CSI list.

CSI Rank	Word	Age
1	sweet	4.53
2	sour	4.89
3	salty	5.33
4	bitter	8.81
5	spicy	5.06
6	savory	13.78
7	hot	3.37
8	delicious	6.50

The earliest learned word is *hot* (3.37 years). The dataset does not specify whether the meaning refers to temperature or to taste. My best guess is that the gustatory facet is learned later than the temperature facet: as I review in Paragraph 5.2.2, *hot* is predominantly a haptic word, and its meaning in the gustatory domain heavily relies on temperature description, which suggests that the haptic facet is more salient and learned earlier.

The BTTs seem to be learned at an age that ranges between 4 and 7 years. For a comparison, basic colour terms are learned between 3 and 6 years old (see Paragraph 3.3), thus slightly earlier than taste terms. The word R11 *yummy*, although not as salient as the other terms, is the first lexeme among those in the CSI to be learned at 3.42 years old. A remarkable outlier in this group is the age of acquisition of the BTT R4 *bitter* (8.81 years), and of the adjective R6 *savoury* (13.78 years).

Ventura and Worobey (2013) discuss how the late acquisition of *bitter* may be tied to the generally negative hedonic value of this taste and argue that infants show a preference for solutions with higher concentrations of other tastants such as sweet, salt, and even sour as opposed to bitter, for which children show higher sensitivity. Specific preferences for this taste appear later on in life as a learned behaviour, as a consequence of social and cultural adaptation, as well as caregiver's pressures. These taste specific reactions are believed to represent an adaptive, evolutionary based response to ecological uncertainty and varied food environments (Reed and Knaapila 2010). This may translate into learning the word for bitter at a significantly later stage than other BTTs. If compared to age of acquisition of other words elicited by the CSI, related items such as R4 *bitter*, R28 *tart*, R14 *tangy* appear to be learned (roughly) at the age of 8, and R40 *acidic* slightly later (age 11.21), thus suggesting that the conceptualisation and verbalization of this perceptual quality may occur later in life.

4.2.2 Discussion

To summarise, the five criteria identified and described previously provide a useful guide for the identification of basic level terms but should not be regarded as a strict rule for their recognition. Each of the eight terms respect and violate different criteria. All of them are salient (although at different degrees) and are the most salient items in the CSI. The first four have long been considered BTTs on the basis of their physiological uniqueness, and the CSI confirms their status, although R2 *salty* is not morphologically simple, and R4 *bitter* seems to be learned later than other terms. In other words, R1 *sweet* and R2 *sour* fit five criteria; while R3 *salty* and R4 *bitter* fit four criteria. The physiological criterion does not hold for the term R5 *spicy*, which is not morphologically simple, but it is acquired earlier than R4 *bitter*. In an emic construal of taste, R5 *spicy* is supported by usage and folk-knowledge: a quick search on Google reveals users in different blogs asking "is spicy a taste",[7] or even "why is spicy not a basic taste",[8] thus suggesting that some people regard it as a taste term. The term R6 *savoury* not only violates the criterion of morphological simplicity, but also that of age of acquisition; moreover, it covers a range of perceptions that are associated to the linguistically less frequent word *umami*, one of the basic transduction processes (Ventura and Worobey 2013). R5 *spicy* and R6 *savoury* fit 3 criteria. Nonetheless, if we consider *savoury* to correspond to *umami* it fulfils 4 criteria, but the investigation regards lexemes and not their meaning. The items that seem suspicious are R7 *hot* and R8 *delicious*. Their position in the CSI advocates for inclusion, which is the only verified criterion. R7 *hot* is more strongly associated to another sensory domain, and the R8 *delicious* has a general, superordinate meaning that may encompass those of other BTTs.

Cognitive semantics sponsors dynamic models of language descriptions with a usage-based approach, and it is in those lines that I would like to propose a gradient of basicness, combining together the different pieces of evidence reviewed in this chapter. Notably, this gradient follows the gradient of salience. Hence, R1 *sweet* and R2 *sour* are the terms that respect most criteria, and therefore seem "more basic" than others: they are physiologically motivated, morphologically simple, not restricted to a narrow class of objects, acquired early, and most salient. From a purely theoretical linguistic point of view, R1 *sweet* and R2 *sour* are the prototypical salient terms. The other terms do not fulfil some of the criteria. The adjective R3 *salty* fails at the morphological criterion, and it is acquired slightly later. R4 *bitter* fails the acquisition criterion; while R5 *spicy* is not supported by physiology, but acquired early, even earlier than R3 *salty*. Lastly, R6 *savoury* seems the least basic of the BTTs: it is acquired much later than the others, it is morphologically derived from a noun, and it is only partially supported by physiology. Nonetheless, their status is much more basic than, for instance R28 *tart*, which shows characteristics such as morphological simplicity, but lacks width of reference (it is mainly associated to fruit), age of acquisition, and, most notably, salience. Reflecting the pattern followed in BCT application I identify these terms as Primary BTTs: *sweet, sour, salty, bitter*; while Secondary BTTs are *spicy, savoury*; I consider *hot*, and *delicious* as not basic.

---

7 https://www.quora.com/Is-spicy-a-taste-or-a-feeling, last accessed 30 September 2020.
8 https://www.quora.com/Why-isnt-spicy-considered-one-of-the-five-basic-tastes, last accessed 30 September 2020.

4.3 Source-based language

The morphological analysis of the items elicited with the CSI reveals that 33% of adjectives produced by native speakers of English to describe taste follow the construction SOURCE+Y (e.g., R24 *meaty*, R27 *sugary*, R31 *smoky*). This pattern results from a derivational process, which was already noted by Lehrer (2009: 19–20) in the lexicon of wine descriptors. In her dataset, the suffix *-y* is the commonest mechanism of lexical expansion. It is added to concrete nouns, the source of the taste, and it produces adjectives with the meaning of "having" or "resembling", and as Lehrer notes "sometimes the word can mean either" (Lehrer 2009: 19). It is not always feasible to disentangle the two facets, which may be construed at the same time (see Chapter 6).

Source-based language is a common strategy in describing perceptual properties of objects via referring to the source of the specific perception (e.g., Croijmans and Majid 2016; Majid et al. 2018; Winter 2019a). It involves using a concrete object as a proxy to the description of a perceptual quality of another object. For instance, consider the taste of two wild herbs with similar taste (and looks), but of completely different species: common hop (*Humulus lupulus*) and wild asparagus (*Asparagus acutifolius*). Sprouts of both species are commonly found in Mediterranean regions and consumed as a delicacy in rural areas of Italy. Crucially, the two herbs have a similar taste, which may be described as *herbaceous*, *bitter*, and *metallic* (or *asparagusy*). If asked to taste, say hop sprouts, a naïve taster could easily utter a sentence of the type *"it tastes like asparagus"*. This sentence links the perceptual qualities of a product (hop, in this case) to a prototypical source that elicits similar sensations (asparagus). A speaker who eats hops may perceive a taste similar to that of asparagus (indeed, wild hop sprouts do taste *like* wild asparagus), compare it to a mental representation of a previous experience (the memory of the taste of asparagus) and judge that the two perceptions are close enough to be linked to one another. In this respect, source-based language involves evaluation of a current perception, comparison to other possible similar perceptions stored in long-term memory, and finally attribution of the current sensation to the category elaborated from a prototypical, central example (asparagus, in this case). The elaboration of a gustatory attribute from a central, prototypical source, and its attribution to other objects that possess similar perceptual qualities may be described as a metonymy PRODUCER FOR PRODUCT, or SOURCE OF SENSATION FOR THE SENSATION (see also Cacciari 2008: 426; Winter 2019a: 24). The linguistic reference to a prototypical source of the sensation, be it morphologically encoded in the lexicon (i.e., *asparagusy*) or created in discourse (i.e., *it tastes like asparagus*), stands for its taste.

Another possible account for source-based language is the one more extensively sponsored by Winter (2019a: 23–25), and it involves the semiotic relationship of indexicality. According to the American philosopher Pierce (1903), signs come in three different types: *icons*, *indices*, and *symbols*, and they all involve a different relationship with the object they signify. Icons show a perceptual resemblance with the signified object (e.g., the full moon on the calendar looks like a full moon, and it signals the day in which this phenomenon will be manifest), while symbols are arbitrarily associated with their referent (e.g., the word *moon* with the Earth's satellite: there is nothing in the structure of the word that resembles, or points at its meaning). Indices are different: they show a connection of contiguity with the object, which might be causal (smoke indices fire), or it might show some physical proximity between them. This is the case of *pointing*, one of the most prototypical examples of an index in human communication (Clark 2003), (and among chimpanzees: Leavens et al. 2005). When we indicate the full moon in a starry night, we are using our finger as an index to refer to *that* object – the full moon in this case. In source-based language, we use the adjectives or phrases we utter as an index pointing in a certain direction, which is the source of the perceptual quality we want to convey in language. Thus, when a speaker utters *it tastes like asparagus* while eating wild hops, they are linguistically pointing at asparagus as the source of the taste they are experiencing.

In experts' speech and conversations, source-based language is particularly common (e.g., Lehrer 2009; Crojimans and Majiid 2016) because it allows for higher accuracy (Plümacher 2007), provided that the source of the perception is shared among the participants of the conversation. Obviously, reference to a source which is obscure to one of the participants does not mean much to the other: if I describe the taste of common hops as *like asparagus*, my listener needs to know what asparagus taste like for communication to be successful. At the same time, the meaning conveyed by source-based language may hide some levels of vagueness especially among non-experts. When I describe the taste of common hops as asparagus, do I mean that it is *bitter*, *herbaceous*, or *metallic*? It becomes evident that the meaning of source-based language needs to be conventionalised for it to be effective and to avoid any form of vagueness.

The reliance on morphological derivation (i.e., suffix -*y*) and the use of comparison (e.g., *It tastes like . . .*) represent an interface between metonymy and indexicality. Both communicative strategies require a degree of relatedness between the concepts involved; as noted by Radden, "it makes perfect sense viewing metonymic relations as indexical" (2018: 171).

4.3.1 Which sources?

Table 4 reports the adjectives in the elicited list that present the suffix -y. Some of them are derived from a concrete entity, and therefore may be regarded as prototypical cases of source-based language. It must be noted however that not all of them have as a root a concrete noun, e.g., *chewy, yummy,* or *tasty*. Yet, I argue that the usage of the -y suffix is motivated by similar processes that grant a conflation of the two phenomena.

Table 4: Source-based lexicon in the CSI list.

CSI Rank	Adjective	Root	Root type
3	salty	salt	food
5	spicy	spice	food
6	savoury	savour	property
11	yummy	yum	exclamation
12	creamy	cream	food
13	fruity	fruit	food
14	tangy	tang	property
22	cheesy	cheese	food
24	meaty	meat	food
27	sugary	sugar	food
30	tasty	taste	property
31	smoky	smoke	process
36	fishy	fish	food
38	juicy	juice	food
43	chewy	chew	process
45	oily	oil	food
51	crunchy	crunch	process

The most common grammatical root for the adjectives in Table 4 is a type of food or substance (e.g., *salt, fruit, sugar*), but it may also be an action or process (i.e., *to chew, to crunch, to smoke*), a general property of the object (i.e., *savour, tang, taste*), or even an interjection resulting from the experience of food (*yum!*).

Food items represent 59% of grammatical roots, and they are either general items used as a condiment (i.e., *salt, spice, sugar, oil*); or basic level terms in the category of food (i.e., *cream, fruit, cheese, meat, fish, juice*). The adjectives derived from processes make up for 17% of the list, and they show the width of application of the derivational suffix *-y*, which not only is denominal and may also be deverbal.

According to the OED, the general meaning of the suffix *-y* is "having the qualities of" or "full of" (OED *-y* suffix1, 1). The adjectives with a root that corresponds to a concrete source instantiate an indexical relationship with their source, and in this regard, they represent a case of prototypical source-based language. For instance, when a speaker describes a cocktail as *fruity*, they make indexical reference to the prototypical source of that specific gustatory experience, namely *fruit*, which is also the morphological root of the adjective. From a cognitive point of view, there is no difference between describing the cocktail as *fruity* or with the paraphrase *it tastes like fruit*. There is no way to ascertain whether the meaning imparted by the suffix is either the first or the second listed in the OED.

The meaning of adjectives based on processes (*chewy, crunchy*, and *smoky*) are also motivated by metonymic mechanisms, but their morphological root does not correspond to the source of the quality, rather to the action that metonymically stands for the source. When speakers describe a steak as being *chewy*, they are referring to the particular texture of the steak, which requires a lot of time *to be chewed*, and as a result, it is *chew-y*. In this account, the adjectives whose roots correspond to processes may be considered a case of source-based language, in which the source of the sensation is not a specific food, but a process metonymically associated with a type of food, more specifically with a physical property of a given food (e.g., texture in the case of *chewy*). The same holds true for the roots of the adjectives *crunchy* (derived from *to crunch*), and for *smoky* (the action of smoking food to preserve it stands metonymically for the resulting taste).

Adjectives whose root is a general property instead are motivated only by the second meaning of the *-y* suffix, namely "full of", since their meaning is so general that saying something "*tastes like taste/tang/savour" does not make sense. Nonetheless, the morphological roots of these adjectives function as a vehicle to access the entire sensorial experience of perceiving something that is "full of taste". For instance, a "*tasty snack*" may be paraphrased as "It is full of taste". Thus, I argue that these adjectives may also be considered as cases of source-based language, since their morphological root metonymically stands for the source of the property.

Lastly, the adjective *yummy* derives from the word *yum!*, an interjection that is prototypically uttered when someone tastes a delicious food. Following

Goffman (1978), this interjection may be classified as a response cry: that is as "exclamatory interjections that are not full-fledged words" (Goffman 1978: 800). It is similar in usage and function to other expressions such as *ouch!* for pain, or *ew!* for refusal or unappreciation of food. The relationship that holds between the grammatical root of the adjective and the object being described is metonymical. When a speaker describes a cake as *yummy*, they are using the interjection caused by the cake (*yum!*) to stand for the whole gustatory experience of the food.

I argue that adjectives following the morphological construction SOURCE+Y are to be considered source-based language, at least in the case of gustatory adjectives. This construction is highly productive and may be applied to countless sources, including non-perceptual items (e.g., *dreamy* may be paraphrased as "it has the quality of a *dream*"). Duly, adjectives following this construction may be analysed as metonymies and as source-based language. Furthermore, the array of sources used by source-based adjectives in the list mirrors the level of salience of the vocabulary retrieved. In most cases, these sources represent food items that show basic level term characteristics, and this mirrors their salient and entrenched status. Adjectives that sport this structure but are not as salient are, for instance, *oniony, chocolatey, citrusy, lemony* etc., which were normed by Lynott and Connell's study, though were not retrieved through my freelisting.

4.4 What are the most salient words of taste that correspond to the basic taste terms in English?

The freelisting task has elicited a considerable number of lexemes, which have been operationalised with the CSI to calculate salience. The most salient items in the list correspond to primary BTTs in English: *sweet, sour, salty, bitter*; while secondary BTTs are *spicy*, and *savoury*. The distinction between primary and secondary BTTs has been borrowed from colour studies terminology. Primary BTTs are the terms on which both experts and naïve speakers agree. They are taught through schooling, physiologically motivated, and quickly retrieved when explicitly asked "what are the words that describe taste". Secondary BTTs do not technically correspond to gustation, but they share some characteristics with primary BTTs: they are salient and learnt at a young age. Furthermore, *spicy* is also considered to be a BTT by many speakers, thus reinforcing its inclusion as one of the BTTs in an emic description of taste.

Besides the most salient items, the majority of adjectives in the list may be considered as examples of source-based language, lexicalised following the derivational construction SOURCE+Y. The physical sources of these adjectives vary, and they are not always concrete objects. The semantic analysis reveals that metonymy is a key mechanism in the conceptual motivation of source-based language.

Finally, the results of the freelisting, and the resulting CSI scores, show that these methodologies are valid tools to retrieve lexical items and to describe specific semantic domains, providing a considerable amount of data in an emic, usage-based approach.

5 The multisensory lexicon of taste

5.1 Introduction

The most striking characteristics of the words elicited by the CSI is their multisensory nature, which suggests the intervention of different modalities in the linguistic elaboration of taste. For instance, adjectives such as R7 *hot*, R10 *cold*, R15 *soft*, R33 *rough*, R42 *hard* may be ascribed to the domain of haptic sensations; R51 *crunchy* may be considered an auditory word, and R31 *smoky* and R41 *burnt* may be regarded either as olfactory or as visual, but not specifically gustatory. At the same time, they were listed by a group of native speakers of English answering the simple question of writing all the words that could describe taste. This urges for a classification of these lexical items across modalities.

Perception is a highly multisensory phenomenon, and it integrates different stimuli coming from different neural pathways into a single Gestalt. This claim has received neuropsychological validation, for example by observing the areas of activation in the brain during processing of stimuli transmitted by separate channels (e.g., Smith 2015, see Chapter 2). Spence, Smith, and Auvray (2015) pinpoint the differences between taste and flavour, by demonstrating that flavour integrates olfactory and somatosensory information to gustation. This difference could explain the multisensory nature of the lexicon retrieved through freelisting: the adjectives in the list may reflect the elaboration of flavour as opposed to being restricted to the elaboration of gustation.

Although the partitioning of the sensorium into mutually exclusive categories reflects a highly entrenched and controversial folk-model, it represents a useful analytical tool to gain insights into the lexicon of perception and into its multisensory nature. One could verify the strongest association of a lexical item to a given modality: rather than asking "is *sharp* a haptic or gustatory word", one should formulate the question as "is *sharp* **more** a haptic or a gustatory word?". Lynott and Connell's norms offer an opportunity to answer this question and disentangle the multisensoriality of the lexicon of taste.

Norms represent a valuable tool for sensory linguists. Winter (2019a: 132–135) presents a long list of advantages to the usage of norms, and why this paradigm should be included in cognitive and sensory linguistics more often. First of all, they represent a limitation to arbitrariness and personal introspection, by aggregating introspections of a large number of people. Secondly, they quantify the association strength in a usage-based perspective, thus limiting the reliance on dictionaries and lexicographical resources to disentangle the belonging of a word to a given modality. Lastly, the norms offer a glimpse on the relationship between perceptual experience and its conceptual representation, highlighting "the continuity between conceptual and perceptual knowledge" (Lynott and Connell 2009: 558), and helping researchers grounding human conceptual processes in embodied perception and cognition.

This leads to the formulation of two hypotheses. Either (i) the elaboration of the semantic domain of TASTE, as evidenced by the freelisting, reflects the multisensoriality of flavour, or (ii) it includes more modalities than those integrated in flavour. In order to verify (ii), the lexicon of TASTE should include adjectives that have been rated by informants in Lynott and Connell as visual and auditory, which are two perceptual modalities that do not concur with the realisation of flavour. Crucially, neuropsychological data suggest participation of these modalities in the reconstruction of the Gestalt of taste perception (e.g., Van Doorn, Wuillemin, and Spence 2014).

5.2 Norming taste

From a comparison between the list of adjectives from the CSI and Lynott and Connell's norms, it becomes evident that some of the words retrieved through freelisting are not present in the norms. The adjectives that were normed however received a familiarity score of 1 out of 1, thus adding another piece of evidence to their entrenched status. The exceptions were R28 *tart* and R34 *pungent*, whose familiarity rate is 0.9. Furthermore, the items R21 *flavourful* and R52 *crunchy* are not present in Lynott and Connell's norms, but there are the adjective *flavoursome* and the deverbal adjective *crunching*. I considered the norm values for these forms as potentially referring to the items in the CSI as well, given the close semantic and morphological relationship of the words. Applying all the norms, the words that were normed as gustatory represent 51.3% of the list; haptic words represent 20.5% of the list; olfactory 12.8%; visual 12.8%; and auditory 2.5%. The presence of adjectives belonging to visual and auditory modalities suggests that the semantic elaboration of taste consists of more modalities than those integrated in flavour, thus reflecting a more inclusive Gestalt informed by the five different sensory modalities, albeit in different proportions.

I review and discuss the items in each of the modalities, report on their modality associations, and their Modality Exclusivity Rates (ER). Furthermore, in order to allow for a more nuanced understanding of the extent to which a given lexical item belongs to a modality other than gustatory, I introduce the ΔP value. It is calculated as the mathematical difference in perceptual association between the Dominant Modality for each lexical item and its value in the modality under scrutiny (i.e., the gustatory modality in this case). Lower figures in the

ΔP value correspond to items closer to the gustatory dimension. This value is obviously not available for items in the gustatory modality thus their ER is discussed instead. For instance, the word R33 *rough* from the CSI ranking (Table 5), normed as predominantly haptic, presents the following parameters:

Table 5: Modality Norms (Lynott and Connell 2009) for R 33 rough.

CSI Rank	Word	ER	2	3	4	5	ΔP
33	rough	0.39	visual	auditory	gustatory	olfactory	3.29

The first column reports the CSI Rank of the word listed in the second column. The third column reports its Exclusivity Rate, the following columns each report the modalities in which the property was coded: in the case of R33 *rough*, it was secondly normed as visual, then as auditory, then as gustatory, and lastly as olfactory. The last column reports the ΔP value to show the extent to which each property is associated to taste. Theoretically, ΔP may vary between a maximum value of 5 (if the dominant modality is 5 and gustatory is 0) and a minimum of 0.01. A result of 0 would mean that an item was coded with the same value in two modalities, including the gustatory, in which case it would be listed under gustatory. I report only the numerical values of the ER and ΔP to avoid confusion in the exposure with unnecessary numbers. Where reported, figures have been rounded to the second decimal to allow for an easier visualisation and discussion.

5.2.1 Gustatory terms

Listed in Table 6 are the 20 CSI items coded as gustatory. All together, they represent 51.3% of the elicited terms.

Table 6: Adjectives normed as gustatory.

CSI Rank	Item	ER	2	3	4	5
4	bitter	0.54	olfactory	visual	auditory	haptic
2	sour	0.53	olfactory	visual	auditory	haptic
3	salty	0.52	visual	olfactory	haptic	auditory
14	tangy	0.50	olfactory	visual	haptic	olfactory

Table 6 (continued)

CSI Rank	Item	ER	2	3	4	5
28	tart	0.43	visual	olfactory	haptic	auditory
6	savoury	0.41	olfactory	visual	haptic	auditory
21	flavourful	0.40	olfactory	visual	haptic	auditory
5	spicy	0.40	olfactory	visual	haptic	auditory
30	tasty	0.39	olfactory	visual	haptic	auditory
18	bland	0.37	olfactory	visual	auditory	haptic
43	chewy	0.35	visual	haptic	auditory	olfactory
24	meaty	0.35	visual	olfactory	haptic	auditory
40	acidic	0.34	olfactory	visual	haptic	auditory
1	sweet	0.34	olfactory	visual	auditory	haptic
13	fruity	0.33	olfactory	visual	haptic	auditory
22	cheesy	0.32	olfactory	visual	auditory	haptic
12	creamy	0.31	visual	haptic	olfactory	auditory
48	stale	0.25	olfactory	visual	haptic	auditory
38	juicy	0.23	visual	olfactory	haptic	auditory
8	delicious	0.23	olfactory	visual	haptic	olfactory

The word R4 *bitter* has the highest ER (0.54), shortly followed by R2 *sour* (0.53), and R3 *salty* (0.52). Crucially, these items correspond to the majority of BTTs. The word R1 *sweet* received a lower ER= 0.34, thus highlighting its multisensorial nature. The second most dominant modality was olfactory for all of them but R3 *salty*, which was coded mainly as visual, and only thirdly as olfactory. The other BTTs present the visual modality in third position. The difference between the ratings of visual and olfactory for R3 *salty* is very low, i.e., 0.14, suggesting that the two modalities scored almost equal strength for this item. The remaining BTTs, R5 *spicy* and R6 *savoury* present a similar score for ER, i.e., 0.4 and 0.41 respectively. Strikingly, these two terms scored 5 points out of 5 for their belonging to the gustatory modality. This means that 100% of participants rated these items in these modalities with the maximum strength. The other term that reached a unanimous rating was R30 *tasty*, which however was also coded as olfactory, and visual, with an ER= 0.39.

The other terms are organised on a regular, descending gradient. Still, I recognise three clusters on the basis of the numerical difference between two contiguous values of the ER in the list. The difference between the ER of R14 *tangy* and R28 *tart* equals 0.07, while the difference in ER between R12 *creamy* and R48 *stale* equals 0.06. The application of the norms to my list suggests the existence of two breaks in the ER gradient, which create three clusters.

The first cluster is represented by words that scored an ER of approximately 0.5. These are the three BTTs reported above (R4 *bitter*, R2 *sour*, R3 *salty*) and R14 *tangy*. These words were more strongly coded as uniquely gustatory if compared to others. The second group of words normed as gustatory has an ER that ranges from 0.43 (R28 *tart*) to ER 0.31 (R12 *creamy*). These are R28 *tart*, R6 *savoury*, R21 *flavourful*, R5 *spicy*, R30 *tasty*, R18 *bland*, R43 *chewy*, R24 *meaty*, R40 *acidic*, R1 *sweet*, R13 *fruity*, R22 *cheesy*, and R12 *creamy*. The last cluster encompasses three items: R48 *stale* (ER= 0.25), R38 *juicy* (ER= 0.23), and R8 *delicious* (ER= 0.23).

The ER value is revealing of the specificity of association to a given modality. The majority of BTTs identified in the previous section present a relatively high ER score; with the exception of R1 *sweet*, which was also strongly coded as olfactory. The adjective R8 *delicious* received an even lower ER, thus reinforcing the hypothesis that its meaning lies at a higher level of categorisation. The term R7 *hot*, which was also in doubt of being a BTT, is not present in the list of gustatory terms, but it has been coded as haptic. Four items present considerably higher scores than the others in the haptic dimension. These are R12 *creamy*, R48 *stale*, R38 *juicy*, and R43 *chewy*: each of them refers to the consistency of a food item, as evidenced by the source of their source-based structure (with the exception of R48 *stale*, which is not source-based).

5.2.2 Haptic terms

The largest group of adjectives not normed as gustatory is represented by the adjectives normed as belonging to the haptic dimension. Table 7 reports these items ordered according to their ΔP (from lower to higher). Lower figures in the ΔP value correspond to closer items to the gustatory dimension.

The closest adjective to the gustatory dimension in the haptic group is R7 *hot* (ΔP= 0.43). Furthermore, it is also the adjective with the highest gustatory rating in the group, which equals 4.43. The following items are R23 *dry* (ΔP= 1.76), R10 *cold* (ΔP= 2.29), R17 *smooth* (ΔP= 3.1), R33 *rough* (ΔP= 3.29), R20 *sharp* (ΔP= 3.38), R15 *soft* (ΔP= 3.61), and R42 *hard* (ΔP= 3.71).

Table 7: Adjectives normed as haptic.

CSI Rank	Item	ER	2	3	4	5	ΔP
7	hot	0.25	gustatory	visual	olfactory	auditory	0.43
23	dry	0.35	visual	gustatory	olfactory	auditory	1.76
10	cold	0.34	visual	gustatory	olfactory	auditory	2.29
17	smooth	0.36	visual	gustatory	auditory	olfactory	3.10
33	rough	0.31	visual	auditory	gustatory	olfactory	3.29
20	sharp	0.37	visual	gustatory	auditory	olfactory	3.38
15	soft	0.34	visual	auditory	gustatory	olfactory	3.62
42	hard	0.42	visual	auditory	gustatory	olfactory	3.71

The presence of haptic terms in the linguistic elaboration of taste mirrors underlying physiological mechanisms that are salient in the lexicon. Items in the haptic modality refer to two different dimensions of haptic perception: *temperature* and *texture*. Both dimensions are perceived through the trigeminal nerve, and they are considered part of flavour instead of taste. Temperature terms are just *hot* and *cold*. *Hot* has a special status in the domain as it came to convey not just information about temperature, but also about spiciness. This semantic relationship is strongly embodied and discussed in detail in Paragraph 9.3.3.

5.2.3 Olfactory terms

The adjectives that were normed as mainly olfactory are five in total. Table 8 reports the items in the olfactory dimension ordered according to their ΔP score.

Table 8: Adjectives normed as olfactory.

Rank	Item	ER	2	3	4	5	ΔP
36	fishy	0.31	gustatory	visual	haptic	auditory	0.10
25	fresh	0.22	gustatory	visual	haptic	auditory	0.43
41	burnt	0.26	visual	gustatory	haptic	auditory	0.52
31	smoky	0.30	visual	gustatory	auditory	haptic	1.24
34	pungent	0.51	gustatory	visual	haptic	auditory	2.63

The adjective with the lowest ΔP is R36 *fishy* (ΔP= 0.10), a considerably small difference in preference. The preferred association to the olfactory modality may be related to frequent metaphorical expressions in English, e.g., *it smells fishy*, where the adjective is found in collocation with smell related words. Nonetheless, its gustatory dimension is still salient (ΔP= 0.10). The second item in line is R25 *fresh* (ΔP= 0.43), followed by R41 *burnt* (ΔP= 0.52), R31 *smoky* (ΔP= 1.23), and lastly R34 *pungent* (ΔP= 2.63). The adjective R25 *fresh* has also been coded in the visual modality, possibly as a way of assessing the state of conservation of food through its appearance. The dominant association of the adjectives R41 *burnt* and R31 *smoky* to the olfactory modality are hardly surprising: they are both related to the production of smoke, which propagates through air as result of combustion, and it is therefore mainly perceived through the nose. Some distinctions however should be made. The meaning of R31 *smoky* in the domain of TASTE refers to a peculiar gustatory quality of food items preserved through the culturally specific process of smoking, e.g., *smoked salmon*, that may elicit a *smoky* taste. The adjective R41 *burnt* instead refers to the gustatory characteristics of prolonged (often accidental) cooking. Finally, the adjective R34 *pungent* was strongly categorised in the smell dimension. It may be glossed as *stinging*, *biting*, and *sharp*, and it is a cognate with other Indo-European words to express nociception, some of which are found in the domain of taste in other languages (for instance, It. *piccante*, Eng. 'spicy', but which literally translates to 'stinging'). The connection of nociception, heat and spiciness is reviewed in detail in Chapter 9.

5.2.4 Visual terms

The five adjectives predominantly coded in the visual modality are reported in Table 9.

Table 9: Adjectives normed as visual.

CSI Rank	Item	ER	2	3	4	5	ΔP
45	oily	0.28	haptic	gustatory	olfactory	auditory	0.57
19	strong	0.13	haptic	gustatory	olfactory	auditory	0.62
49	plain	0.36	gustatory	haptic	olfactory	auditory	1.05
35	weak	0.18	haptic	gustatory	auditory	olfactory	1.52
47	light	0.31	haptic	gustatory	olfactory	auditory	2.57

The adjective with the lowest ΔP is R45 *oily* (ΔP= 0.57), followed by R19 *strong* (ΔP= 0.62), R49 *plain* (ΔP=1.05), R35 *weak* (ΔP= 1.52), and R47 *light* (ΔP= 2.57). The adjective R45 *oily* is a source-based adjective that points to oil as its prototypical source. Its predominant association to the visual modality is somewhat surprising, considering its source. From a quick survey on the COCA, it appears however that it collocates with *skin* and *hair* in contexts of makeup or aesthetics, thus partially motivating the strong association. It is also strongly associated with the gustatory dimension. The adjectives R19 *strong* and R49 *plain* are the two adjectives with the lowest ER score in the whole CSI list, thus suggesting that their meaning is very general, and may be used in reference to different modalities. The specific meaning of the visual adjectives in the gustatory modality may be the result of metaphorical shifts that conceptualise TASTE as PHYSICAL STRENGTH (*strong* and *weak*); as a COMPLEX EVENT (*plain*), and as INTENSITY (*light*). Furthermore, the dominant association of *light* to the visual modality mirrors its most salient meaning in reference to luminance perception.

5.2.5 Auditory terms

The auditory dimension collects only one item, R52 *crunchy* (Table 10). It must be noted that the modality norms for this adjective refer to the word *crunching*, but I considered them for the adjective *crunchy*. The ΔP equals 0.67, thus suggesting that the gustatory dimension is also relevant in its meaning construction.

Table 10: Adjectives normed as auditory.

Rank	Item	ER	2	3	4	5	ΔP
51	crunchy	0.29	gustatory	visual	haptic	olfactory	0.67

This adjective describes the texture component of food, in relation to the auditory sensations it elicits, particularly to refer to low-pitched sounds. Another adjective in the discourse of food that describes an auditory sensation is *crispy*, which, however, is not part of the CSI. The two adjectives describe the auditory qualities of the fracture of food products (Vincent 1998), and they mainly differ on the pitch of the sound they refer to: *crispy* tends to describe a higher pitch than R52 *crunchy*. Thus, for example, tortilla chips are *crispy*, but peanuts and almonds are *crunchy* (Vickers 1984). The different acoustic characteristics are also encoded in the phonetic structure of the adjectives, with *crispy* having a higher pitch than *crunchy* (Dacremont 1995; Dijksterkuis et al. 2007). The relationship between the sound of these words and their meaning is an example of *iconicity* or *sound-symbolism*. The phenomenon of sound-symbolism in the lexicon of the senses is mainly related to auditory adjectives (Dingemanse 2012), but there are traces of iconicity even in the gustatory and olfactory domain (for instance *chewy* is rated as one of the most iconic words in the gustatory modality, Winter et al. 2017).

5.3 The dark side of norms

Norms suffer from some bias in the original collection of adjectives. In Lynott and Connell, the original list of 423 adjectives was collected through a lexicographic analysis of dictionaries and thesauri (2009: 559). The most evident risk is ignoring relevant lexical items, while including irrelevant ones. As a matter of fact, some items retrieved through freelisting do not appear in the original list proposed by Lynott and Connell. These are: R9 *umami*, R11 *yummy*, R16 *disgusting*, R26 *good*, R27 *sugary*, R29 *bad*, R32 *gross*, R37 *sickly*, R39 *flavour*, R44 *rich*, R46 *full*, R50 *raw*, and R52 *boring*. In fact, some of these items are not markedly related to perception: it would be difficult to rate *rich* or *boring* against any of the sensory modalities. The other words which were not rated seem closer to the lexicon of perception. R9 *umami* might not have been as familiar and frequent in speakers' vocabularies in 2009 as it is now; and R37 *sickly* and R39 *flavour* are not prenominal adjectives, and therefore aprioristically excluded from the list. Nonetheless, I would rate R11 *yummy*, R16 *disgusting*, R27 *sugary*, R32 *gross* and R50 *raw* as related to gustatory, or more generically sensory experience. The exclusion of these words inadvertently reveals the methodological faults of a lexicographic analysis. However rigorous the analysis be, it may still be open to bias in the original selection of lexical items. In this regard, freelistings (operationalised through a CSI) allow the researcher to start with a list of salient adjectives.

Finally, the list compiled by Lynott and Connell (2009) contains words rated as gustatory that were not retrieved through the CSI (e.g., *oniony, chocolatey*), thus suggesting that although speakers recognise certain words, these words are not necessarily salient in the minds of the speakers. This is the downside and strength of the CSI: results elicited from this procedure may be partial, and some lexical items could potentially not be elicited. Yet, if an item is not listed, it most likely is not salient, and possibly dormant in a speaker's vocabulary. In other words, if confronted with a word, a speaker may recognise it, but may not use it, as noted also by Quinlan (2017).

5.4 Which modalities do we use to elaborate the sense of taste?

Generally speaking, the comparison between the adjectives retrieved through freelisting and Lynott and Connell (2009) reveal a composite and complex picture of interrelated meanings that are not easily classifiable. There are many lexical items that may have multiple meanings depending on the perceptual frame in which they are used: for example, *light* (visual, gustatory, haptic), or *sharp* (haptic, olfactory, gustatory), among others. The differences between the numbers and the indices reviewed in this chapter are often very small, thus suggesting an intricate interwoven network of meaning and senses. Some lexical items may be specific to a certain modality: for instance, R5 *spicy* was normed with 5 out of 5 in the gustatory dimension; but it was also normed as strongly olfactory and visual.

This comparison shows that the linguistic elaboration of the sense of taste is multisensory and includes stimuli coming from more modalities than those described by the label flavour. This is in keeping with a dynamic and continuous construal of perception. The adjectives in the CSI list mainly belong to the gustatory dimension, followed by haptic, olfactory and visual, and auditory. The adjectives primarily associated to the gustatory dimension were secondly most associated to the olfactory and visual dimensions. A consistent group of adjectives were also normed in the haptic dimension, thus reflecting the texture dimension of taste. Only one adjective was coded in the auditory dimension, and this suggests that the two senses are the most distant (Winter 2019a: 166). Nonetheless, adjectives pertaining to the three integrated dimensions of flavour account for the vast majority of adjectives in the list, thus suggesting a linguistic elaboration path that starting from taste expands to flavour, and finally integrates visual and auditory information.

Taken all together, the evidence reviewed in this chapter suggests that the senses interrelate and participate one in the construction of the other, and that clear-cut and mutually exclusive categories in the domain of the senses are useful analytic tools. Our perception and cognition, our bodies and our minds interrelate and interface through a constant flow of exchange of information, sensations, and lexicon.

6 Categorisation patterns

6.1 Naming tastes

Describing the exact sensorial and gustatory properties of food might prove difficult for laypeople and food-enthusiasts alike. Courses on appreciation and description of the taste of different food products abound: from wine to honey, from coffee to cheese. The lexicon of Western languages is scarce of specific olfactory and gustatory lexicon, and the level of agreement on specific taste qualities among different experts is an area of research with still some open questions (e.g., Croijmans and Majid 2016).

In the food industry, descriptive analysis of flavour is a crucial step to evaluate the sensory properties of a product. It typically involves identification and definition of the characteristics of a certain food item by a group of trained judges. These experiments typically consist of a first stage of concept alignment between participants, which is a necessary procedure to avoid little agreement among judges (O'Mahony 1991: 223). There are several standardising techniques available for a researcher (Cairncross and Sjöström 1950; Caul 1957; for more recent contributions see Stone and Sidel 2004; and Meilgaard et al. 2007, Lawless and Heymann 2010; Moskowitz et al. 2012). They all agree on training judges about the names given to the substances under scrutiny; therefore "an ad hoc language is created for communication about the sensory characteristics of the particular food product" (O'Mahony 1991: 223). Establishing a common language is not enough however: a further agreement to be reached is the extent to which a given stimulus can be included in an established label.

Furthermore, the boundaries of a "sensory concept" do not appear to be clearly defined. They present fuzzy edges similar to linguistic categories. Thus, in order to reach an acceptable level of agreement, researchers need to establish a prototype, or a "center of the concept" among the judges (O'Mahony 1990: 133). When confronted with real substances, judges may differ in their judgement of the taste properties. For instance, not all judges may agree on the definition of *bitter* or *sour* when associated with a specific tastant. Judges are usually trained by researchers with the presentation of a physical standard, so to define its characteristics and abstract a generalised concept for it. Typically, sucrose corresponds to *sweet*, NaCl (sodium chloride) corresponds to *salty*, QSO_4 (quinine sulfate) defines *bitterness*, and $C_6H_8O_7$ (citric acid) is used to define *sourness* (O'Mahony et al. 1979; O'Mahony and Alba 1980; O'Mahony 1990). Judges whose native language is English, show a pattern of confusion between two taste types, *sour* and *bitter*. Crucially, other languages present other confusions among taste types, as reported by Chamberlain (1903) and Myers (1904), and as discussed in the following section.

6.2 Conflation patterns: A cross-cultural perspective

The notion of basic taste types is largely debated, and there is no clear evidence of their numbers. This largely depends on the notion of basicness. Some languages only have two distinctive evaluative terms, which broadly correspond to *good* and *bad* (Myers 1904). Languages that also present descriptive terms may show various patterns of term conflation: for instance, *sweet* and *salty*, *salty* and *umami*, *sour* and *bitter* may be coded by the same linguistic label or may be strongly associated in various linguistic systems.

Myers (1904) was the first to report on what he then called "confusion" of different basic tastes, thus reinforcing Western classification models on "primitive" people. What used to be called "confusion", Osawa and Ellen (2014) advance should be called *conflation* of taste terms. The two phenomena should be distinguished: the term *conflation* refers to lexical conflation of two terms (e.g., Yora uses *wata* to refer both to *salty* and *sweet*), while I adopt the term *confusion* to talk about the misattribution of linguistic labels to two perceptual stimuli in presence of distinct lexical items (e.g., English *sour* and *bitter*).

The conflation of saltiness and sweetness is found in many linguistic families across the globe, in languages spoken by individuals who live in different environments and share different cultural systems. For instance, Shepard (2004) reports on two geographically close but genetically unrelated Amazonian languages: Matsigenka and Yora. Both languages present a single term to convey *salty* and *sweet* (Matsigenka: *pocha*, Yora: *wata*). Similar data have been reported for Tzeltal, a Mayan language (*chi'*, Brett 1994; Casagrande 2000; Brown 2011); Kenyah Leppo' ke (Borneo) conflates the two sensations in the lexical item *me* (Golin 2001); the word *hikok* in Iwamu (Papua New Guinea) is used to refer to tasty, salty, and sweet (Yoshida 1998, quoted in Osawa and Ellen 2014). There are various hypotheses regarding the development of this pattern. Shepard (2004) reports on earlier psychophysical data (Scott and Plata-Salaman 1991) that show how sodium deprived neurons shift from salt responsiveness to sweet, and therefore advances that such linguistic patterns may derive from this peculiar physiology. Myers (1904) offers another hypothesis. According to him, the conflation of the two sensations is due to their hedonic value. Both saltiness and sweetness are in fact pleasing substances, and elicit positive, embodied reactions (Wong 2000). A third possibility is advanced by Brett (1994) and reported by Osawa and Ellen (2014): the conflation of saltiness and sweetness is linked to specific food cultures and ecologies that bestow great value and salience on salt and sugar, often considered important and precious commodities. In Senegal, the Serer Ndut language (Dupire 1987) conflates saltiness, bitterness, and spiciness in one single term: *hay*, keeping it distinct from the terms for sweetness (*sen*) and from sour (*kɔb*). Similar patterns are reported by Osawa and Ellen (2014) for Aymara (Andean language in Peru, Bolivia, Chile and Argentina) and Maragoli (Tanzania).

A different case of conflation is that of umami-savory-salty. In a series of studies, O'Mahony and associates analysed these conflation patterns in speakers of English and other languages. Their results show how both Chinese and Japanese participants referred to monosodium glutamate as "glutamic", while English speakers would name it as "salty" (O'Mahony and Tsang 1980; O'Mahony and Ishii 1986; Ishii and O'Mahony 1987a; Ishii and O'Mahony 1990). Similar results are reported by Osawa (2011) for which *salty* was highly used by British speakers to describe monosodium glutamate, but not by Japanese participants, who in turn preferred *umami*-type descriptors. Moreover, monosodium glutamate sensations in Italian are often described as *saporito*, a general term that corresponds to English *savoury*. Unfortunately, I do not have scientific literature to back my claim: it is a personal observation as a native speaker of the language. Although Osawa and Ellen (2014) discuss some controversies and bias towards the results of physiological investigations, data reported in this chapter and personal observations on Italian support the hypothesis of conflation of these terms.

6.3 Taste association and confusion in English words

Contemporary English does not have any case of distinct concept conflated in the same lexical item. There are however relevant cases of association between different perceptual qualities that emerged from the data which call for a clarification. The first is the association of *hot* and *spicy*. The two terms can be used interchangeably, due to the fact that spiciness and heat occur simultaneously (see Paragraphs 5.2.3 and 9.3.3).

The sour-bitter confusion boasts a relatively robust documentation across different laboratories in the English-speaking world. Meiselman and Dzendolet (1967) tested a total of 120 American college students on two taste recognition tasks representing the four basic taste types. Their results show that only 16% of the males succeeded in identifying the solutions correctly; while the rates of success in the female group was considerably higher: 34%. In their second experiment, the authors attempted to apply a correction procedure to train their participants in the correct identification of the stimuli with no success. They conclude that "the fact that the sour-bitter quality confusion cannot be corrected by an informative procedure, suggests that this confusion is probably primarily physiological in origin. It may be that this confusion is a gustatory analogue of abnormal color vision" (Meiselman and Dzendolet 1967: 498).

Robinson (1970), almost in response to Meiselman and Dzendolet, designed a test which specifically concentrated on the sour/bitter confusion (although other substances were also tested). His results, elicited from 48 subjects at the University of Cardiff, confirm the pattern measured by Meiselman and Dzendolet. Crucially, Robinson observes that participants "often fail in identification even though they can discriminate and give the tastes different names" (Robinson 1970: 376). He therefore interprets his results as a difficulty in naming, rather than a difficulty in sensing the differences: "subjects seem to use the words 'sour' and 'bitter' badly" (Robinson 1970: 378), thus discrediting the comparison with a visual impairment. Crisinel, Jones, and Spence (2012) found similar results: their participants were able to distinguish between sour and bitter.

Gregson and Baker (1973) return to the issue with results elicited from (mostly) undergraduate students at the University of Canterbury (Christchurch, New Zealand). They developed a parameter to indicate the confusion between the two qualities. The authors conclude that "there is no justification in treating the acid-bitter confusion as either purely physiological or purely psychological" (Gregson and Baker 1973: 75), and that the estimation of taste intensity, disregarding evaluation of the taste quality, may precede evaluation of specific tastes. Overall, their experiments did not focus on the identification of taste qualities, as much as on discrimination of the concentration thresholds and intensity scaling of different substances.

McAuliffe and Meiselman (1974) designed an experiment setting to test the possibility of training participants in identifying different tastants, and their ability of retaining the information over time. The percentages of misnaming were lower than previous studies, but the authors claim that this was an effect of sampling differences. Notably, their findings show that exposure to stimuli, rather than instructions or feedback, produces "a significant and lasting effect on taste quality categorization" (McAuliffe and Meiselman 1974: 244).

O'Mahony and colleagues return to the topic with a set of 11 experiments (O'Mahony et al. 1979), with different foci. Their results show that expert participants (students in Food Science Technology at UC Davis) outperformed their untrained counterparts (students in the Psychology Department at the University of Bristol), in keeping with the observations by McAuliffe and Meiselman (1974) about exposure being more relevant than training. The authors summarise the analysis of their results in six points:

1. errors of applications of taste adjectives can be corrected through definitions and by giving the appropriate standard (this includes sour and bitter);
2. not all subjects remained consistent in time;
3. error frequency correlates with concentration of the stimuli: fewer errors occurred with higher concentrations;
4. if stimuli were too diluted, they could not always be distinguished from each other;
5. calling the sour stimulus (citric acid) *bitter* (13.3%) was more common than calling the bitter stimulus (quinine) *sour* (7.7%);
6. the authors noted tendencies to confuse *sour* and *salty*, and to identify citric acid as *sweet* (but not the reverse). While confusing sour and salty is reported also in other languages, the tendency to call sour stimuli *sweet* might be connected to low concentrations of citric acid reminiscent of citrus fruit.

Finally, the authors conclude that results on the confusion might be connected to culture and food consumption in Western societies and the relative paucity of prototypical bitter stimuli. Crucially, they note that the confusion might be rooted in language, more specifically in "the common habit in English of describing lemons as bitter" (O'Mahony et al. 1979: 316) and the application of the word bitter to generally negative stimuli. Following up on this confusion, O'Mahony and Alba (1980) tested taste recognition in American English and Mexican Spanish in a population of native speakers of both languages and bilinguals. Reportedly, the case of Spanish is of particular linguistic interest because there are three words available to describe the sour/bitter continuum: *ácido* (sour), *amargo* (bitter), and *agrio*. Allegedly, English-Spanish dictionaries translate *bitter* as *amargo*, and sometimes as *agrio*, while "in the reverse direction all give *amargo* as *bitter*" (O'Mahony and Alba 1980: 48). Furthermore, *sour* is listed as *agrio*, *ácido*, while *agrio* is unanimously listed as *sour* (O'Mahony and Alba 1980: 47–8). The authors included *acid* as an option in the experiments to create an equal number of conceptual categories between the two languages, despite the presence of the medial term *tart* in English.

Results for taste recognition in the two languages confirmed that the English sour-bitter confusion is reflected in Spanish by the *ácido-amargo* confusion. The medial term *agrio* was rarely elicited in the free response condition, and it did not seem to cause extra confusion in participants, unless "*agrio* was arbitrarily defined as meaning *ácido*" (O'Mahony and Alba 1980: 60). Its presence did not cause greater problems in the confusion, as it simply appeared to be an extra-term available for the descriptions, similarly to the term *acid* in English.

To date, most contributions on taste categorisation have been conducted in a laboratory in presence of actual physical stimuli, i.e., participants were asked to taste a solution with a specific taste quality. To the best of my knowledge, there has been no critical assessment of the linguistic relation that holds between the terms *sour* and *bitter*. Moreover, studies on taste naming suggest that the relationship between linguistic labels and perceptual stimuli is not straightforward, while cross-cultural assessment of conflation patterns show that languages around the globe partition sensory experience following different patterns.

In order to verify the categorisation patterns that hold between different gustatory concepts in the domain of taste of English, I designed two sorting tasks: a free sorting task and a closed sorting task. The free task aims at assessing the semantic association between the most salient gustatory adjectives in English, while the closed task unravels the network of conceptual family resemblances that structure the domain of TASTE. Both tasks have been carried out with the participation of native speakers of English, in keeping with the emic perspective in the study of taste sensations.

6.4 Free sorting task

6.4.1 Methodology

In the free sorting task, participants are asked to create categories by associating words together. The free sorting task is a procedure that enables the researcher to collect "similarity data in which each assessor groups together stimuli based on their perceived similarities" (Chollet, Valentin, and Abdi 2014). I conducted this study online through the platform OptimalSort, which enables the researchers to design various exploratory studies (Card sorting, Tree testing, Online surveys, etc.). The software enables the researcher to unravel categorisation patterns by looking at the frequency with which any card was categorised in any category, and to look at the members of each category. Results are calculated by the platform, and results are visualised in graphs (Dendrograms and Similarity matrices). Bagli (2018) is an earlier version of this procedure; Ramsay (2017, 2020) illustrate the use of OptimalSort in linguistic investigations.

6.4.2 Items

I selected the most salient words resulting from the CSI: *sweet, sour, salty, bitter, spicy, savoury, hot,* and *delicious,* for a number of reasons. First, the CSI index drops considerably between the eighth and the ninth word, thus suggesting a difference in salience. Second, the ninth word (*umami*), in spite of being one of the scientifically recognised taste terms, it is not as frequent (F= 6) as the others (e.g., delicious, F= 18). Thirdly, in this abridged group of items I recognised a potential pattern of associations, namely: *sour-bitter*; *spicy-hot*; *salty-savoury*; *sweet-delicious*.

6.4.3 Participants and instructions

I retrieved the participants with a snowball effect through friends, social media, and Facebook groups of expats living in Italy. A total number of 52 informants participated in the study (29 Female, 20 Male, 2 Transgender Male; 3.9% age 12–17; 62.7% age 18–30; 23.5% age 31–50; 7.8% age 51–65; 2% age more than 65; all native speakers). The large majority of informants (41.2%) received education at undergraduate level; 6% had some schooling, no diploma; 19.6% indicated High school graduate or equivalent; 25.5% had a Master or Postgraduate degree; and 7.8% of them had a Doctorate.

Instructions were shown on the screen as a welcome message. Participants were aware of the nature of the test: they knew that it was about taste words in English. They were further instructed on the nature of the task, which was "to organise a list of words into groups according to their meaning. The goal is to end up with groups of associated words".

6.4.4 Results

Figure 1 reports the dendrogram for the results of the survey. This view illustrates the proportion of informants who agreed about card groupings. The cards are listed on the left, and the horizontal axis measures the level of agreement; the left axis of the dendrogram represents 100% of agreement, while the right side corresponds to 0%.

The diagram shows the following strong association patterns: *hot – spicy* (80%); *sour – bitter* (78%); *savoury – salty* (58%). The two latter clusters form another one, although with a weaker association (20%). The pairing of *sweet – delicious* shows a low level of agreement (33%).

The visualisation method in Figure 2 is more detailed and informative of subtler associations. It is a Similarity matrix, and it shows the percentage of informants who grouped 2 cards in the same category. For each of the pairs, "the intersecting cell shows the percentage of participants who grouped these cards together" (OptimalSort instructions). The darker colour corresponds to a stronger association.

6.4 Free sorting task — 85

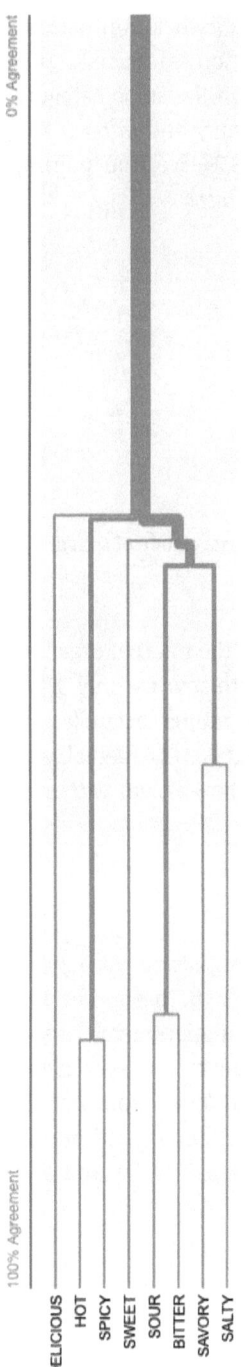

Figure 1: Dendrogram for the association of salient tastes.

This visualisation offers a finer grained picture of the association patterns between the most salient taste terms. Besides the association evidenced by the dendrogram, 43% of participants grouped *salty* and *sour* in the same category; similar ratings were produced for *sweet* and *sour* (41%), *salty* and *bitter* (41%), *spicy* and *salty* (39%), *savoury* and *delicious* (39%). At 33% we find pairings such as *savoury* and *sweet*, *delicious* and *sweet*, *sweet* and *bitter*.

Figure 2: Similarity matrix for the association of salient tastes.

The reverse pattern is also significant, and it is revealing of the internal organisation of the category. The term *delicious* was associated with *sour* by only 3% of participants, and even less (1%) with *bitter*. Similar low ratings occur for the word *hot* in association with *sweet* (3%), *sour* (9%), *bitter* (11%). The medial associations (those with percentages from 10% to 30%) do not show a clear pattern.

6.4.5 Discussion

The most notable clusters that emerge from the free sorting task are *spicy-hot*, *sour-bitter*, and *salty-savoury*, thus confirming my initial hypothesis. The first cluster is hardly surprising: the two lexical items stand in a relationship of synonymy[9] grounded in physical perception of capsaicin, which is so entrenched to be reported by dictionaries. The association of *sour* and *bitter* replicates the well-known phenomenon of the sour-bitter confusion. Although the present study does not verify the ability to recognise and distinguish bitter and sour

---

[9] In Cognitive Linguistics, the concept of synonymy is debated (e.g., Croft and Cruse 2004: 8; Littlemore 2015: 75). Arguably, each lexical item construes a different semantic facet. Nonetheless, I use synonymy to refer to the interchangeability of the two adjectives *spicy/ hot* in language use, based on lexicographic data.

stimuli, earlier research demonstrates that participants successfully discriminate between the two stimuli, and that the confusion arose in naming them. Previous research (O'Mahony and Ishii 1986; Osawa 2011) regarding recognition of the *umami* taste shows how participants tend to code this taste sensation as *salty* or *savoury*, thus indirectly demonstrating the association of the two in presence of physical stimuli. Salt operates as a flavour enhancer, so the addition of this substance to food results in a more vivid and richer flavour, which arguably may be described as *savoury*.

Contrary to the hypothesis, the items *sweet* and *delicious* are not strongly and unequivocally associated. Rather, the term *delicious* was associated both with *savoury* and with *sweet*, thus revealing its evaluative and more general meaning. As a consequence of this, its meaning is more viable of different construals that arise from personal experience and preference. Duly, some speakers may prefer savoury over sweet things. If the meaning of *delicious* might oscillate between *savoury* and *sweet*, it clearly cannot refer to *sour* or *bitter*. Once again, this exclusion pattern reflects physical perception of taste sensations: both *sour* and *bitter* are considered as hedonically not pleasing, unless when such properties are looked for in particular foods, e.g., beer or sour cream. In these contexts, negative hedonic response is culturally overridden, but these situations were clearly not accessed by the participants in this test.

Doty and colleagues (2017) report on the confusion between *salty* and *sour*, but with a lower frequency of the sour-bitter confusion. From a quick analysis of category construction, the association of *salty* and *sour* reported in this study may stem from the creation of general categories that include BTTs, or that include all terms other than *sweet* by virtue of the positive-negative hedonic value of the terms. The pairing *salty* and *bitter* has been noted in previous literature regarding cultures other than Western (Myers 1904), and also among English speakers (Doty et al. 2017). For some individuals, high concentrations of NaCl may indeed taste bitter: e.g., sea water. From an analysis of internal category construction however, it seems that the two lexical items were mainly located in the same category with other items to designate BTTs (similar to the association of *salty* and *sour*). The couple *sweet* and *sour* (41%) might reflect the name of a popular cocktail mix that typically consists of lemon juice and syrup; the pairing *spicy* and *salty* (39%) might emerge from an experiential bases of actual associations in food consumption, as testified also by the closed sorting task (see Paragraph 6.5.4).

The relevance of these findings lies in the absence of physical stimuli at the moment of the task. This suggests that the confusion between sour and bitter, replicated at a linguistic level, depends on the structure of the lexicon of English. Other semantic associations reflect patterns observed also in the presence of physical stimuli. The semantic association between *salty* and *savoury* might be motivated by a common reference to the umami transduction process, while the semantic association between *spicy* and *hot* is motivated by physiological reactions. The results of the free sorting task showcase the dynamic interplay between language and perception: on one hand, linguistic labelling in the linguistic system overrides perception, thus creating phenomena of naming confusion of physical stimuli in English. On the other hand, other associative patterns between the most salient adjectives are largely influenced by embodied experiences, thus providing support to modal views of semantic representation.

6.5 Closed sorting task

6.5.1 Methodology

In the closed sorting task, participants are asked to categorise a set of stimuli in fixed, ready-made categories on the basis of their meaning. The aim of this task is to unravel categorisation patterns in the linguistic category of taste descriptors in English. I employed the software OptimalSort. I ran a series of pilot tests to verify the best model of categorisation: I devised three tests before launching the definitive version. The tests varied in the number of categories available for participants. The 210 participants in the tests were all native speakers of English, and they were retrieved through Amazon Mechanical Turk and received $1 reimbursement.[10] Amazon Mechanical Turk has been used in various studies in linguistics (e.g., Winter, Pérez-Sobrino, and Brown 2019), and its validity for performing linguistic experiments has been verified by Sprouse (2011). The results were displayed by the software in terms of popularity matrices.

6.5.2 Items and categories

The items selected for the categorisation task are the 52 most salient terms emerged from the freelisting. I did not remove items whose meaning did not refer to specific taste types (e.g., *rich, good, boring, tasty*), because I did not want to alter the original dataset with an arbitrary choice. The categories under which the items could be categorised varied among the different pilot tests, as

---

[10] Funding for this research generously came from University of Genoa 2020 FRA (Fondi per la Ricerca d'Ateneo).

shown in Table 11. Some categories were fixed among different versions. These were: Sweet, Sour, Salty, Bitter, Spicy, Umami, and Not Sure.[11] These categories represent the Primary and Secondary BTTs established through the CSI, and the category Not Sure was included to allow participants to not categorise an item if they were doubtful of the most fitting category. I included *umami* and not *savoury* to verify the knowledge of this label by native speakers of English. In the second test, I included the category General Descriptors to limit the items that were otherwise categorised in the Not Sure category. In the third test, I excluded General Descriptors, but included the categories Texture and Mouthfeel to verify if these two could account for the items that were categorised in General Descriptor in Test 2. The results of Test 3 showed that not all of the items which were in the General Descriptors could be categorised as Texture and Mouthfeel, rather they migrated from General Descriptors to Not Sure. Hence, Test 4 presents all of the categories and corresponds to the final version of the test. I included all of the 10 categories proposed to have a more nuanced and distributed account of the categorisation patterns within the semantic domain of TASTE in English. I chose to distinguish between the two different albeit closely related categories of Texture and Mouthfeel for two main reasons. Firstly, because Mouthfeel may encompass adjectives related to temperature and other dimensions that were present in the list (i.e., *dry*); secondly, because I wanted to verify the perceived difference between the two Categories by native speakers of English.

Table 11: Pilot tests.

Test	Sweet	Sour	Salty	Bitter	Spicy	Umami	Texture	Mouthfeel	General Descriptors	Not Sure
1	Y	Y	Y	Y	Y	Y	N	N	N	Y
2	Y	Y	Y	Y	Y	Y	N	N	Y	Y
3	Y	Y	Y	Y	Y	Y	Y	Y	N	Y
4	Y	Y	Y	Y	Y	Y	Y	Y	Y	Y

Table 11 reports the different categories implemented for each pilot test. As evidenced from the Table, the variation in the different pilot tests was the category General Descriptors, which was inserted in Test 2 and 4. In Test 3 I also added the categories Texture and Mouthfeel. This process emerged as necessary to leave the conceptual space for the participants to categorise all of the items.

---

[11] In this Chapter, I use capital letters to distinguish Categories from *lexical items*.

6.5.3 Results

A 100 participants concluded the four pilot tests, and there were then 110 participants in the Final Test who completed the tasks (40 Female, 68 Male, 1 Gender Variant; 1 preferred not to answer to Gender; 53.6% age 18–30, 34.5% age 31–50; 10.9% age 51–65; 0.9% age more than 65), all native speakers of English. Table 12 reports the results of the definitive test: I included the lexical items grouped in each category with a frequency greater than 10%. Items are in **bold** when they are listed in the category with the strongest association: for instance, the item *sugary* in Sweet is in bold, because that association was the strongest for the item *sugary*. The numbers in (brackets) after each lexical item refer to the percentage of participants who agreed in the categorisation. Items marked by an *asterisk are listed with an equal association strength under different headings.

The category Sweet encompasses 3 items with high ratings: *sweet, sugary,* and *fruity,* and 8 items with lower scores. Sour contains 5 items, each of them with a strong association: *sour, tangy, tart, acidic,* and *sharp.* Salty and Bitter contain 1 strongly associated item (*salty* and *bitter*), plus 3 and 9 items respectively. Spicy and Umami include 2 items with strong association each: *spicy* and *hot,* and *umami* and *savoury,* and other 4 and 1 item respectively.

Texture consists of 8 strongly associated items: *rough, hard, smooth, crunchy, soft, chewy, creamy,* and *oily,* and 8 with lower scores. Mouthfeel has only 2 strong associations: *juicy* and *dry,* but 26 items with lower ratings. General Descriptors in turn present 27 items with strong association: *good, boring, bad, delicious, tasty, plain, disgusting, bland, flavour, fresh, gross, flavourful, weak, strong,*

Table 12: Taste categories.

Sweet – 11 items	Sour – 5 items	Salty – 4 items	Bitter – 10 items	Spicy – 6 items
sweet (85%)	*sour (80%)*	*salty (80%)*	*bitter (75%)*	*spicy (81%)*
sugary (78%)	*tangy (39%)*	savoury (15%)	burnt (22%)	*hot (45%)*
fruity (60%)	*tart (37%)*	fishy (12%)	acidic (20%)	smoky (16%)
sickly (20%)	*acidic (37%)*	smoky (10%)	tart (17%)	pungent (12%)
juicy (19%)	*sharp (22%)*		tangy (13%)	tangy (10%)
yummy (16%)			sharp (12%)	savoury (10%)
creamy (15%)			pungent (12%)	
delicious (14%)			raw (11%)	
rich (14%)			disgusting (11%)	
tasty (13%)			bad (10%)	
tart (11%)				

Table 12 (continued)

Umami – 7 items	Texture – 16 items	Mouthfeel – 27 items	GD – 38 items	NS – 18 items
umami (82%)	rough (55%)	juicy (37%)	good (26%)	sickly (25%)
savoury (25%)	hard (54%)	cold (35%)	boring (59%)	weak (22%)
*meaty (21%)	smooth (54%)	chewy (31%)	bad (59%)	full (22%)
cheesy (16%)	crunchy (53%)	dry (31%)	delicious (56%)	pungent (18%)
smoky (15%)	soft (50%)	oily (27%)	tasty (55%)	boring (17%)
fishy (14%)	chewy (41%)	smooth (23%)	plain (54%)	stale (17%)
rich (10%)	creamy (35%)	creamy (22%)	disgusting (54%)	bad (15%)
	oily (30%)	hot (22%)	bland (53%)	plain (15%)
	dry (28%)	light (21%)	flavour (53%)	disgusting (15%)
	*meaty (21%)	flavourful (18%)	fresh (52%)	cheesy (15%)
	light (21%)	rich (17%)	gross (50%)	fishy (14%)
	raw (21%)	fresh (17%)	flavourful (49%)	light (11%)
	burnt (20%)	crunchy (16%)	weak (49%)	flavour (10%)
	stale (19%)	cheesy (16%)	strong (48%)	gross (10%)
	juicy (13%)	rough (15%)	yummy (47%)	burnt (10%)
	rich (10%)	soft (15%)	full (42%)	sharp (10%)
		hard (14%)	cold (39%)	tart (10%)
		tasty (14%)	stale (35%)	
		sharp (13%)	raw (35%)	
		full (13%)	light (33%)	
		bland (13%)	rich (33%)	
		yummy (13%)	pungent (33%)	
		meaty (12%)	burnt (28%)	
		acidic (11%)	fishy (26%)	
		weak (11%)	smoky (25%)	
		stale (10%)	*sickly (25%)	
		smoky (10%)	cheesy (23%)	
			savoury (19%)	
			oily (18%)	
			sharp (18%)	
			hot (16%)	
			meaty (16%)	
			juicy (15%)	
			dry (15%)	
			soft (13%)	
			creamy (12%)	
			fruity (12%)	
			rough (11%)	

*yummy, full, cold, stale, raw, light, rich, pungent, burnt, fishy, smoky, *sickly,* and *cheesy,* and 11 items with lower scores. The Not Sure category is composed of 1 item with a strong connection: **sickly,* and 17 other items. The item *sickly* was associated with the same strength both in GD and in Not Sure.

Although in the detailed results virtually every item has been placed in every category, only few items display an exclusive and strong association in just one category. These are: *sugary* in Sweet, and *strong* and *good* in General Descriptors (besides the pairing of items in their "own" category, e.g., item *bitter* in category Bitter). It is illustrative also to consider the range of categories to which each item has been more commonly associated. Table 13 reports the list of adjectives ranked according to the CSI, with the first three categories to which they were assigned.

Table 13: Categorisation patterns.

CSI Rank (R)	Item	1	2	3
1	sweet	Sweet	/	/
2	sour	Sour	/	/
3	salty	Salty	/	/
4	bitter	Bitter	/	/
5	spicy	Spicy	/	/
6	savoury	Umami	Salty	Spicy
7	hot	Spicy	Mouthfeel	General Descriptors
8	delicious	General Descriptors	Sweet	/
9	umami	Umami	/	/
10	cold	General Descriptors	Mouthfeel	/
11	yummy	General Descriptors	Sweet	Mouthfeel
12	creamy	Texture	Mouthfeel	Sweet
13	fruity	Sweet	General Descriptors	/
14	tangy	Sour	Bitter	Spicy
15	soft	Texture	Mouthfeel	General Descriptors
16	disgusting	General Descriptors	Bitter	Not Sure
17	smooth	Texture	Mouthfeel	/
18	bland	General Descriptors	Mouthfeel	/
19	strong	General Descriptors	/	/
20	sharp	Sour	Bitter	Mouthfeel
21	flavourful	General Descriptors	Mouthfeel	/
22	cheesy	General Descriptors	Umami	Mouthfeel
23	dry	Mouthfeel	Texture	General Descriptors
24	meaty	Umami/ Texture	Mouthfeel	General Descriptors
25	fresh	General Descriptors	Mouthfeel	/
26	good	General Descriptors	/	/
27	sugary	Sweet	/	/

Table 13 (continued)

CSI Rank (R)	Item	1	2	3
28	tart	Sour	Bitter	Sweet
29	bad	General Descriptors	Bitter	Not Sure
30	tasty	General Descriptors	Mouthfeel	Sweet
31	smoky	General Descriptors	Spicy	Umami
32	gross	General Descriptors	Not Sure	/
33	rough	Texture	Mouthfeel	General Descriptors
34	pungent	General Descriptors	Bitter	Spicy
35	weak	General Descriptors	Not Sure	Mouthfeel
36	fishy	General Descriptors	Umami	Not Sure
37	sickly	General Descriptors / Not Sure	Sweet	/
38	juicy	Mouthfeel	Sweet	Texture
39	flavour	General Descriptors	Not Sure	/
40	acidic	Sour	Bitter	Mouthfeel
41	burnt	General Descriptors	Bitter	Texture
42	hard	Texture	Mouthfeel	/
43	chewy	Texture	Mouthfeel	/
44	rich	General Descriptors	Mouthfeel	Sweet
45	oily	Texture	Mouthfeel	General Descriptors
46	full	General Descriptors	Not Sure	Mouthfeel
47	light	General Descriptors	Texture/ Mouthfeel	Not Sure
48	stale	General Descriptors	Texture	Not Sure
49	plain	General Descriptors	Not Sure	Not Sure
50	raw	General Descriptors	Texture	Bitter
51	crunchy	Texture	Mouthfeel	/
52	boring	General Descriptors	Not Sure	/

The distributional patterns in different categories of each lexical item illustrates the family resemblances that structure the semantic domain of TASTE. The semantic relationships that exist between the different lexical items mirror their embodied value and reflect associations observed in taste recognition tasks.

6.5.4 Discussion

The results of the categorisation test show the elaboration of the semantic domain of TASTE in English in terms of family resemblances. Lexical items are closely intertwined with each other, creating a close-knit network of meaning across categories. Many items are present in more than one category and create patterns of family resemblance between different categories in the domain of taste.

The categories Sour and Bitter appear closely connected, and share a number of lexical items: *tangy, acidic, tart,* and *sharp*. The lexical overlap (i.e., the inclusion of the same lexical item in different categories) between the two categories denote the semantic sour-bitter continuum discussed in the previous section. Notably, *tart* is also in Sweet, and *tangy* is in Spicy. The association of *tart* to Sweet is motivated on experiential bases: the prototypical source of this taste is fruit (e.g., rhubarb, gooseberries), and a user in a thread in the online forum Quora describes it as "an acidic taste" but "lighter and a little sweet" than sour, like lemonade or an apple pie.[12]

The lexical item *tangy* is defined as "having a sharp, distinct or spicy taste" (OED *tangy*, adj., a). The lexicographic meaning is mirrored in the categorisation pattern, even if the *sharp* facet was perhaps more salient, since it was more strongly categorised in Sour. Nonetheless, participants were also able to access the *spicy* facet, as this item was categorised also in Spicy.

The item *sharp* was categorised in five different categories with similar ratings. The adjective *sharp* is highly multisensory, and it may refer to different dimensions across different modalities: according to the OED, the term originates in the domain of TOUCH, and it expanded to refer to other sensory domains, namely taste, olfaction, hearing, and sight. According to Lynott and Connell's norms, its strength of association is with the haptic, visual, gustatory, auditory, and olfactory dimensions respectively. Similarly, its meaning in the domain of taste is also associated with different categories.

Another observable cluster is Spicy-Salty-Umami. The adjectives *savoury* and *smoky* are present in the three different categories with different percentages, thus representing a bridge between the categories. Moreover, the adjective *fishy* is present in both Salty and Umami. The inclusion of Spicy in the continuum may be motivated by experience and confirms earlier observations in the free sorting task. In a recent study, Li and colleagues (2017) found that enjoyment of spicy food was correlated to less salt intake in individual dietary habits. Furthermore, they confirmed that administration of capsaicin in mice affected the saltiness receptors in the OFC (orbitofrontal cortex), the area of the brain typically associated with processing gustatory information. Researchers proved that preference for spicy food lowered the thresholds of saltiness tolerance. In a previous study on humans, Narukawa et al. (2011) showed that exposure to capsaicin could enhance salt perception: if salty food is also spicy, it is perceived as saltier. Data in the present study show a lexical overlap among the

---

[12] https://www.quora.com/Taste-sense-Is-there-a-technical-difference-between-tart-and-sour-If-so-what-is-it

three categories, thus partially confirming and expanding crosslinguistic data reviewed above (see Paragraph 6.2). Taken altogether, this evidence suggests the existence of a cluster of related linguistic meanings among the three different categories of Salty, Spicy, and Umami in keeping with findings coming from a more physiological angle.

The category Umami shares the items *meaty* and *rich* with the category Texture and Mouthfeel. The adjective *meaty*, like other source-based adjectives has at least two possible meaning facets: the taste facet (i.e., something *tastes* like meat) or the flavour/haptic facet (i.e., something *feels* like meat). The meaning purport of this item is clearly exemplified by the association of this adjective between the categories of Umami (i.e., taste facet), and Texture and Mouthfeel (i.e., flavour facet). The adjective *rich* instead was more strongly associated with the General Descriptors category, reflecting its metaphorical and supramodal nature. Its domain-specific meaning is also well-represented in the categorisation patterns evinced from these results. Lastly, the adjective *cheesy* is found in the category of Umami by virtue of its taste facet, and in Texture in reference to its flavour facet.

The categories of Texture and Mouthfeel share the great majority of their vocabulary. Arguably, the two categories are not very different, and questions in online forums abound on the difference between them. Although there is a technical difference, this may not be extremely clear to untrained speakers. Texture is the category that received the higher number of strongly associated items, and this may be a result of its most entrenched meaning. Nonetheless, the two categories share all of their items. Some of them have been categorised with (almost) equal percentages: *chewy* (41%-31%), *creamy* (35%-22%), *oily* (30%-27%), *dry* (28%-31%). Notably, *creamy* was also categorised in Sweet (15%), and it may be motivated by a phenomenon similar to *meaty*. In this case, the taste facet has been accessed by a relatively minor number of participants.

The category of General Descriptors consists of the highest number of items, most of which are truly highly general and do not refer to any taste type. Some of these adjectives however have been categorised also in more specific categories, although with lower ratings. For instance, *delicious, tasty, yummy, rich,* and *sickly* were categorised in Sweet. The most relevant case in this set is represented by the adjective *sickly*: it is a negative evaluative word, and it was associated to the category of Sweet, disregarding its generally positive meaning, possibly because of the collocation *sickly sweet*, which is used to describe the taste of something that is too sweet and therefore corresponds to a negative evaluation.

Other notable albeit isolated cases of lexical overlap are between Bitter and Texture, with the adjectives *raw* and *burnt*. The item *pungent* was categorised in General Descriptors, thus suggesting that it may be associated with different sensations. Secondly, it was associated to Bitter, and then to Spicy, two sensations that are conceptualised in reference to painful stimuli, in keeping with the etymology of the adjective *pungent*. It entered English from Latin via French, and is defined as "of pain, as if caused by a sharp point, piercing, stabbing" (OED *pungent*, adj., 1). The OED lists the meaning related to taste and smell only as fourth, as reflected in the results. Similar cases that relate nociception to gustatory qualities are the adjectives *sharp* and *tangy*. From a diachronic perspective, the BTT *bitter* originated from terms of nociception in several Indo-European languages (see Paragraph 9.5.2). The categorisation of *pungent*, *sharp*, and *tangy* in both Bitter and Spiciness illustrate the family resemblances between these adjectives. These are motivated by an underlying conceptualisation pattern grounded in nociception and negative hedonic responses. Furthermore, this pattern is observed in the conflation of *bitter* and *spicy* in other languages (see Paragraph 6.2), thus lending further support to the grounding of perceptual language in embodied experiences.

The items whose meaning was not clear, and about which speakers did not agree, are contained in the category Not Sure. There are no items that were exclusively listed under this heading, with the only (partial) exception of *sickly*, which was categorised with equal strength also under General Descriptors.

Moreover, the inclusion of items such as *savoury*, *meaty*, and *cheesy* in Umami suggests that participants in the study have an idea of its meaning; nonetheless the low percentages suggest that not many people do. The results of this categorisation test cannot be taken as definitive in verifying this claim. Lastly, *savoury* was most strongly categorised in Umami, then in Salty, and lastly in Spicy, thus providing a conceptual connection between different sensations that may arise together in human experience.

6.5.5 A brief comparison with the pilot tests

The categorisation of some items has remained stable across the pilot Tests, while others have changed. These changes between different models, although not reviewed quantitatively, may be informative on the level of agreement not only between participants, but also between models. It must also be noted that the results of the Tests cannot be safely compared, because the numbers of participants vary. There are however some tendencies that advocate further discussion. For instance, terms such as *tangy*, *acidic* and *tart* have been categorised in Sour across different models. The same holds true for *sugary* in Sweet, *hot* in Spicy. Other items have "changed" category. Notably, *cheesy, meaty, fishy, smoky* were Salty before the category of General Descriptors was introduced, thus suggesting again the availability of different meaning facets. On the other hand, the stability of items in the same category strongly suggests that their meaning is clear and well represented in the semantic domain for native English speakers.

6.6 What are the semantic relationships and network that structure the internal organisation of the category of taste?

The results of both sorting tasks show conceptualisation patterns and semantic associations within the domain of TASTE, and they offer insights into the relationship between perception and its linguistic representation. Cross-cultural data on the language of perception shows some cases of lexical conflation between physiologically distinct transduction mechanisms. Although English speakers correctly discriminate between sour and bitter substances when tasting them, they consistently fail to label them accurately. This phenomenon has been described as the sour-bitter confusion, and results of the free sorting task confirm that it is based on a strong semantic and conceptual association between the two terms. Other associative patterns emerging from the free sorting task involve the items *spicy* and *hot*, and *salty* and *savoury*, which instead label the same gustatory sensation. This is clearly motivated by physiological and embodied phenomena.

The categorisation patterns of gustatory adjectives reinforce the observations on the multisensoriality of taste and on the continuous nature of perception. The results of the closed sorting task illustrate an intricate network of semantic relations. Some of these items create conceptual clusters, populated by lexical items related through family resemblance, which in turn form a continuum among the six BTTs. The main clusters are Sour-Bitter, Spicy-Savoury-Salty, while Sweet is the most distinct category (see also Bagli 2018). Some of the lexical items with lower percentages of association strength are shared by many different categories, thus instantiating the family resemblance relationships.

Lastly, participants in the test identified the categories of Texture and Mouthfeel. The distinction between the two is not clear-cut, and this is evidenced by the lexical overlap between the categories, which reached its peak with adjectives such as *oily* and *dry*. From a morphological point of view, a vast majority of adjectives in this domain are source-based and are examples of the SOURCE-Y construction (see Paragraph 4.3). The diffusion of these adjectives across different categories is motivated by different meaning facets accessed by participants during categorisation. Sensory adjectives conceptualise and partition experience in language. The association between distinct lexical items and the categories shows the interconnectedness and dynamicity of semantic representation in the domain of TASTE, which is motivated by experience and physiology. The categorisation patterns evinced through the sorting tasks testify to the continuity and simultaneous nature of perception. Thus, unravelling their semantic relationship provides insights on the interplay between language and perception.

6.7 What are the words of taste?

In the first section of the book, I elicited the words of taste in an emic perspective, retrieved through a freelisting task and operationalised through the CSI. English displays a set of six BTTs: *sweet, sour, salty, bitter, spicy,* and *savoury*. Many of the lexical items that emerged in the task are morphologically derived through the application of the suffix *-y* to specific food and processes, thus creating examples of source-based language. Furthermore, different sensory modalities intervene in structuring the linguistic representation of the domain of TASTE, supporting the claim that language is grounded in and emerges from our embodied and perceptual mechanisms. Moreover, the family resemblance associations verified in this section illustrate a fine-grained picture of integrated sensations that participate in the linguistic elaboration of a unique Gestalt, reinforcing the claim that there is no single way to partition the senses.

In the next section of the book, I consider the six BTTs of English and their semantic expansion, both diachronically and synchronically. The conceptual mechanisms that spring from the usage of taste words offer compelling insights onto the nature of the mind and its relationship with culture, language and perception.

7 The taste of words

7.1 Introduction

The second section of the book is called *The taste of words*, and it focuses on the metaphorical and metonymic elaborations that expand the meaning potential of taste words in English. It builds on the first part in many respects. Firstly, it employs the results of previous research to further our understanding of the role that the sense of taste has in motivating cognition and language. Secondly, it complements the onomasiological approach by adopting a semasiological perspective, thus concentrating on the different meanings that the lexical items in the domain of TASTE may develop via conceptual operations.

After having discussed and retrieved items in the semantic domain of taste, this section discusses their elaboration, with the aim of analysing the conceptual mechanisms that drive the figurative usage of taste words in context. To answer this question, there are at least two possible paths. Both of them require a detailed analysis of data, and an interpretation of the conceptual elaborations of each lexical unit. In keeping with the usage-based approach, the data should represent real life utterances and situations of use, especially to avoid criticism of relying too heavily on introspection and intuition moved towards early contributions to the study of metaphor (e.g., Cameron 2003; Stefanowitsch 2006; Semino 2008).

The two ways of investigation are better exemplified with a recent contribution by Kövecses et al. (2019). The authors distinguish between the lexical approach and the corpus approach. The first approach reviews the semantic expansion of words as elicited through dictionaries and aims at recognizing regularities in the meanings of individual lexical items, while the second mines metaphorical realisations through corpora. The present book undertakes both lines of investigation; this chapter reports lexicographic data in a diachronic perspective, while Chapters 8–9 review corpus data coming from the COCA in a synchronic perspective.

There is an important caveat that needs to be stated. No matter how usage-based it may be, the interpretation of the various processes of meaning creation needs to be based on introspection. As I stated earlier, introspection is inevitable to some extent, especially in analyses of the meaning of utterances (Talmy 2007, 2018; Gries and Divjak 2010: 337; Dąbrowska 2015: 481). Surely, introspection must be correlated with information coming from other sources. In this book, the interpretation of the semantic elaborations of taste is based on data coming from different lines of evidence, such as lexicographic analysis, experimental and neuropsychological data, and biological responses to perceptual stimuli in an evolutionary perspective. While some of the conceptual metaphors discussed in this section have already been assessed through experimental protocols (e.g., LOVE IS SWEET, see Chan et al. 2013, Donging et al. 2015, Schaefer et al. 2020), others await confirmation and therefore should be regarded as hypothetical (such as CONFLICT IS BITTER).

To exemplify the concern of this section, consider the following expressions:

(4) (a) bitter weather;
 (b) bitter cold;
 (c) bitter divorce.

Expressions in (4) all share some characteristics, while retaining their difference. The usage of the same perceptual adjective *bitter* unifies them and suggests that they have something in common. At the same time, the referents of the adjective are different and this advocates for the differences between them. At closer inspection, we may even want to separate the expressions in (4a) and (4b) from that in (4c), as the first two utterances seem to share some meaning that (4c) does not. The meaning of *bitter* in (4a) and (4b) relates to temperature perception, and as such it may be considered as "synonymous" to *cold* (OED *bitter*, adj., 8). The meaning of the same lexical item in (4c) instead is not *cold*, but it still maintains a negative connotation, motivated by the conceptual metaphor CONFLICT IS BITTER. Finally, it must be noted that the three expressions convey a negative meaning, disregarding their referent. I argue that the conceptual mechanisms that unifies the different meanings of *bitter* in these examples is the metonymy BITTER FOR UNPLEASANT.

The second section of this book thus aims at identifying and classifying the metaphorical and metonymic realisations that employ the Primary and Secondary BTTs as a source domain in English, as evidenced through both lexicographic and corpus analysis. The array of figurative realisations that involve the lexicon of taste demonstrates that gustatory perception intervenes in conceptualisation processes, and that sensations arising from this modality play a long-underestimated role that deserves recognition.

7.2 Conceptual metaphors and polysemy

Metaphors are found at different levels in human capacity of meaning making. They may lie in *large* structures: an entire piece of art might be metaphorical. For instance, the directors of the 1999 sci-fi *The Matrix* recently confirmed that the entire film could be interpreted as a metaphor for gender transitioning. Both fans and critics speculated on this interpretation and found hints (i.e., metaphorical realisations) at different levels in the structure of the film. For example, the iconic scene in which the main character Neo is given the opportunity of choosing between the red or the blue pill has been interpreted as a metaphor for the beginning of gender transitioning (Keegan 2018: 33–4). Metaphors however do not only occur in large structures. Sometimes, a metaphor may be instantiated by a *single word*, thus altering the interpretation of an entire text (e.g., Thibodeau and Boroditsky 2011). In cognitive semantics, metaphors and metonymies are identified as cognitive mechanisms leading semantic change and motivating polysemy of lexical items. The way of dealing with metaphor may be across levels of complexity, both in macro and micro structures.

Here, I recall the structure of metaphors as they are understood in contemporary Cognitive Linguistics theory for the sake of exposure. In a nutshell, a conceptual metaphor connects two domains, i.e., a source and a target, and in its cognitively classic view is considered as projecting conceptual material from one domain to another. Typically, conceptual metaphors connect two unrelated domains by virtue of analogy, and the source is intended as more concrete than the target. For instance, in the case of *The Matrix*, the concrete source domain of CHOOSING A PILL is used to conceptualise the less concrete domain of CHOOSING A GENDER. The systematic correspondences that arise from the conceptual metaphor are defined as *mappings*. Crucially, conceptual metaphors are better accounted for as cognitive and conceptual mechanisms. They underlie and motivate *metaphorical realisations*, which may be found in language, but also in gestures (e.g., Núñez and Sweetser 2006), in visual representations (e.g., Forceville 2006; Pérez-Sobrino 2017), mathematics (Lakoff and Núñez 2001), and even in buildings (Stec and Sweetser 2012), to mention but a few. The present analysis specifically concentrates on verbal realisations.

Polysemy is the "association of two or more related senses with a single word form" (Taylor 1995: 99). The fortune of the study of polysemy in linguistics has changed with the passing of dominant theoretical frameworks, but it has puzzled philosophers and linguists since ancient Greece. The term *polysemy* derives from a combination of the Greek prefix *poly* ('multiple') and *sema* (sign, sense), and it reflects precisely what it is. It should be distinguished from *homonymy*, which describes the linguistic phenomenon of two separated meanings associated with the same word form.

For instance, the word *hop* in English displays both signs of polysemy and homonymy. According to the OED, *hop* (n.1) may refer to: the ripened sprouts of the female hop-plant (e.g., 1a: *This beer contains five different varieties of hop*); it may refer to the plant itself (e.g., 2: *Hop is cultivated throughout Europe*); in

Australian and New Zealand English it may also refer to beer (e.g., 1b: *She was keen on the hops*); and the meaning of "narcotic drug, especially opium" is also recorded from "underground slangs" (meaning 4). At the same time, according to the OED (v.1) the verb *to hop* means "to spring a short way upon the ground or any surface with an elastic or bounding movement, or a succession of such movements: said of persons, animals, and things". The same meaning is also found in the noun derived by the verb by zero-derivation (OED, *hop*, n.2). The two meanings associated with the same word form (*hop* n.1, and *hop* v.1) display a case of homonymy, and therefore do not show any type of semantic relationship. The different meanings of the noun *hop* instead are intuitively connected to one another.

Cognitive linguists interpret polysemous meanings as a radial network that spans around a central prototype, organised in terms of family resemblance relationship, motivated by conceptual mechanisms such as metaphors and metonymy. The set of polysemic senses associated by a single word may be described as a category, whose members are the different senses related to a central prototypical case. Thus, the different senses of the noun *hop* might be described as a result of metaphors and metonymies. For instance, the relationship that exists between the meaning of *hop* (plant) and its product used for beers may be regarded as an example of the conceptual metonymy PRODUCER FOR PRODUCT. Likewise, the semantic relationship holding between *hop* (as in ingredient of the beer) and its meaning in New Zealand English of "beer" itself, may also be regarded as an example of the conceptual metonymy PART FOR WHOLE. The semantic relationship that these readings hold with the meaning of "opium" may be reconstructed on the basis of a conceptual metaphor that connects two separate plants by virtue of their effects on human physiology.

7.3 Novel, conventional, live, dead, and sleeping metaphors

The realisation of a conceptual metaphor may be broadly divided into two categories: novel metaphors and conventional metaphors. Novel metaphors show a higher degree of creativity and arbitrariness. The sentence *that movie gave me diabetes*[13] would probably be considered metaphorical both by naïve speakers and trained linguists. It is motivated by a conceptual metaphor that connects a

---

[13] https://www.reddit.com/r/gifs/comments/a79zab/michael_bay_definitely_knows_how_to_do_this_type/, comment by user sidmark1.

gustatory experience, namely SWEET, to the more abstract experience of LOVE, thus instantiating the conceptual metaphor LOVE IS SWEET. Within this set of mappings, this sentence may be interpreted as describing a film containing too much romance and too many love scenes, to the extent that all this (metaphorical) sweetness provokes diabetes in the viewer. The same conceptual metaphor (LOVE IS SWEET) motivates much more conventional realisations. For instance, standard terms of endearment such as *honey* or *sweetie* are considered to be verbal realisations of this conceptual metaphor. Conventional metaphors are common in language, and they often do not appear to be metaphorical to untrained observers, or even to linguists adopting a different definition of metaphor.

Conventional metaphors have also been referred to as *dead* metaphors: that is, metaphors whose status is not entirely recognisable by speakers in that community (e.g., Lakoff and Johnson 1980; Lakoff and Turner 1989; Allan 2009). For instance, the English word *exacerbate* derives from Latin *exacerbare*. In both languages it refers to the event of making a situation more severe than it was. The root of the Latin verb is the word *acerbus*, an adjective that means *unripe, sour, biting*. The overall semantic structure of the verb *exacerbare* means to increase the level of unripeness and sourness of something, and metaphorically it describes the process of increasing difficulty and severeness of something. From Latin, the verb has transited into English, where it maintains the same meaning. The same path may be identified in a conceptually cognate English verb: *embitter*. While the root of the verb is physiologically different, the semantic transfer of the two words is analogous between the two languages.

Recently, the distinction between live and dead metaphors has been questioned by Müller (2008). In her discussion of dead and conventional metaphors, she argues in favour of a new model of the old dichotomy between old and live metaphors. She proposes a "dynamic category that covers a spectrum ranging from sleeping to waking metaphors" (Müller 2008: 195), where sleeping metaphors present a low activation of metaphoricity, while waking metaphors have a high level of activation of metaphoricity. In her model, "activation" does not refer to the speaker's consciousness. Rather, it refers to activation indicators that may be found in the context of usage of the metaphor. Drawing on previous research (Stibbe 1996; Goatly 1997; Kyratzis 2003), Müller reviews some mechanisms that may be found in speech, through which a dead metaphor may become "deautomatized" (or in more common linguistic jargon, "revitalised"). These include for instance repetition, elaboration, accumulation, and others (Müller 2008: 195).

Müller's claims are supported by empirical evidence coming from various sources. To exemplify, consider her discussion of primary metaphors (Müller 2008:

76–80). In her discussion, Müller combines data from a sequence of gestures with a linguistic analysis. She presents an analysis of a traditionally dead metaphor (German *Depressivität*, 'depressiveness') accompanied by a metaphorical gesture. The noun *Depressivität* is considered to be a dead metaphor, as traces of its metaphoricity may be identified in Latin, where it means *to press down*. The data analysed by Müller were taken from an interview with a young woman who was describing her first romantic relationship, and she says that she felt sad because her partner was depressive. In doing so, she also produced gestures that point downwards, in keeping with the conceptual metaphor SAD IS DOWN, although this conceptual metaphor was not present in speech. Duly, the lexical item *depressive* is motivated by this conceptual metaphor, but the metaphoricity of this adjective is not available to the speaker producing it, as "etymological reconstruction is needed to discern it" (Müller 2008: 78). As the author notes, this supports Lakoff and Turner's (1989) original claim that a conceptual metaphor may still be active, despite its realisations may be dead, as well as her general claim about sleeping metaphors.

The importance of sleeping metaphors should not be underestimated. Although their activation may be not conscious in the minds of speakers, and therefore they may not realise they are in front of a metaphor, Kövecses (2010) warns us that what is more entrenched is also more easily activated, and consequently most salient in our thought. The usage of SWEETNESS in conceptualizing LOVE may be regarded as a case of a highly conventionalised metaphor. Traces of this metaphorical transfer are found in Old English, as in (5), from Cynewulf's *Juliana* (Woolf 1966: 25).

(5) *Đu eart dohtor min seo dyreste ond seo* **sweteste** *in sefan minum*;
    'Thou art my daughter, the dearest and **sweetest** in my heart.' (Kennedy 2000: 4)

There is also linguistic evidence that attests to this usage already in Sumerian, one of the first languages of which we have a written record. This is suggested by excerpts from a love song, in which the lover is described as *honeysweet* (6):

(6) Bridegroom, dear to my heart, goodly is your beauty, **honeysweet.**
    (Kramer 1958: 300)

Despite its conventionality, and its attestation in such an early stage of literacy, this metaphorical link still yields evidence of mental simulation. Many of the metaphorical mechanisms retrieved in English are conventional realisations that have become part of the entrenched, polysemic meaning of gustatory words.

7.4 Polysemy and sensory linguistics

The role of conceptual metaphors and metonymies in motivating polysemy has been long known and explored in cognitive semantics, both from a synchronic and diachronic perspective(e.g., Lakoff and Johnson 1980; Lindner 1981; Johnson 1987; Lakoff 1987; Brugman 1989; Sweetser 1990; Blank 1999). The observations are based on an evaluation of semantic change and evolution from a historical perspective. The data often include etymologies of words in current usage, and the set of metaphorical correspondences that systematically link different portions of human conceptual structure.

Contributions on the lexicon of the senses however very rarely take a diachronic perspective. Noteworthy exceptions to this trend are represented by the recent contributions in the volume *Perception Metaphors* (Speed et al. 2019) by Anderson, Strik Lievers and De Felice, and Steinbech-Eicke, who follow semantic evolutionary trajectories of perceptual words in English, from Latin to Italian, and Hieroglyphic Egyptian respectively. The paucity of contributions with this approach advocate for larger and more consistent investigations undertaking this perspective.

A seminal example of investigation in the polysemy of perception language is Sweetser's analysis of perception verbs and their semantic development in Indo-European languages (Sweetser 1990). She identifies a major metaphorical mechanism that has motivated this change, namely the Mind-As-Body metaphor (Table 14). The set of mappings that she reviews contemplate the five senses and their figurative usages as follows:

Table 14: The Mind-As-Body metaphor, adapted from Sweetser 1990.

Source domain: BODY	→	Target domain: MIND
SIGHT	→	KNOWLEDGE
HEARING	→	HEED, OBEY
TOUCH	→	EMOTIONAL FEELINGS
SMELL	→	BAD CHARACTER, DISLIKEABLE CHARACTERISTICS
TASTE	→	PERSONAL LIKES AND DISLIKES

Sight and hearing are the two senses that are most commonly associated with "higher" qualities of the human beings' intellectual and rational capacities such as knowledge and obedience. The other senses, associated with "lower" bodily functions and abilities (see Paragraph 2.1) seem to have come to structure more personal qualities, such as character, emotion, and preferences. The distinction of the metaphorical elaborations on the senses proposed by Sweetser paved the way for a number of other contributions. For instance, Ibarretxte-Antuñano (1996, 1997, 1999a, 1999b) expands the metaphorical scope of SMELL basing her observations on cross-linguistic data covering English, Spanish, and Basque, and she includes also SUSPECTING, GUESSING, and INVESTIGATING; Trojszczak (2019) reviews the domain of TOUCH in both Polish and English; Bagli (2016, 2017) expands the metaphorical extensions of TASTE.

Sweetser's contribution represents a crucial development in the study of meaning change, especially in the realm of perception. She demonstrates how conceptual metaphors intervene in motivating semantic change, and how these changes produce systematic and conventional realisations of conceptual metaphors in language. A paradigmatic case is the conceptual metaphor KNOWING IS SEEING, which according to Sweetser (1990) has motivated the meaning shift of many Indo-European SEEING verbs that have come to refer to KNOWLEDGE. This is not only found in synchronic meaning extensions, such as *I see what you mean*; but even in more specific and often less transparent cases, in which the metaphorical mechanism may not be as evident. An example of a metaphorically motivated etymology is the English word *wit* (Dancygier and Sweetser 2014), which developed from the Proto Indo-European root **weid-* meaning 'see', which also motivated the English *witness*. While in the latter case the reference to physical seeing is still present, the connection to the perceptual dimension is totally lost in the case of *wit*, which in contemporary English only has a cognitive meaning. Yet, the metaphor that motivated this change is still productive, as it motivates a vast number of metaphorical expressions, such as the creative expressions *political astigmatism*, *theoretical blinders* (Dancygier and Sweetser 2014: 33).

7.5 Primary metaphors and culture

The Mind-As-Body mappings may be considered as being part of a larger theory of correspondences, involving the experiential-correlation aspects of metaphor (Grady 1997a, 1997b; Johnson 1997; see also Müller 2009; Dancygier and Sweetser 2014; for a review). According to this theoretical framework, metaphorical mappings between distant domains in experience are based on simpler mappings, motivated by a direct embodied experience. Conceptual Metaphors that possess this quality are labelled as Primary Metaphors, i.e., metaphors that are motivated by an experiential correlation. Examples of this kind of metaphors are MORE IS UP, POWER IS UP, AFFECTION IS WARMTH. Crucially, one of the metaphors reported by Grady is APPEALING IS TASTY (Grady 1997a: 292), thus correlating gustatory perception to a general state of pleasure. Along these lines, I argue that the primary metonymy motivating more elaborate mappings with sweet is to be found at a more generic level, namely SWEET FOR PLEASANT. The set of correlations that instantiate primary mappings develop early in childhood and are motivated by everyday experiences. Johnson (1997) argues that metaphorical mappings between visual and cognitive events referring to the KNOWING IS SEEING metaphor develop together and are found in speech by young children. He used data from the CHILDES corpus, and retrieved cases such as *See the ducks!*, or *Let's go see what mom's doing* to exemplify the connection between the visual event of seeing and the cognitive activity of knowing.

Primary metaphors are especially productive in the conceptualisation of emotions: for instance, ANGER is pervasively described as HEAT (Kövecses 1986, 1995; Lakoff 1987), and this correlation is based on directly co-occurring physiological events. The experience of anger increases blood pressure (e.g., Ohira et al. 2000) and body heat, and this experiential correlation forms the basis of the conceptual metaphor, which in turn motivates linguistic expressions such as *I was steaming with rage*. As we see in the following chapters, gustatory experiences motivate metaphorical realisations that are mainly correlated in experience. The embodied nature of this correlation may bring to the false idea that the ensuing metaphorical realisations are universal. After all, humans are all members of the species *Homo sapiens* and have similar neural and physiological equipment. It would therefore be logical to assume that the same physical sensations would motivate the same metaphorical realisations. While there are many cases of cross-linguistic correspondences (anger is one of such cases, Kövecses 1986, 1995) there are also counterexamples. Wilkins (1996) and Evans and Wilkins (1998) examined a range of Australian languages and demonstrate that verbs of hearing typically extend metaphorically to structure KNOWLEDGE, as opposed to Indo-European languages that prefer VISION to structure KNOWLEDGE (Viberg 1983; Sweetser 1990). This semantic development path is consonant with cultural characteristics of aboriginal populations, exemplified by "the practice of learning about country, tracks, and routes, and mythological knowledge by hearing them recounted in stories and 'songlines'" (Evans and Wilkins 1998: 51).

Although conceptual metaphors and figurative language are grounded in embodied experience, it would be misleading to affirm that there is a direct, unmediated correlation between the two. Ibarretxte-Antuñano (2013) provides a model to account for the relationship between perception and linguistic output. Building on cross-linguistic analysis of metaphors, she proposes the culture sieve model, according to which physical experiences "sift through" the set of cultural beliefs that are idiosyncratic to a given culture and that are acquired through acculturation of the individual. Crucially, the culture sieve is not just a passive element in the conceptualisation of human embodied experience, rather "it filters those elements that are in accordance with the premises of a given culture, and [. . .] it impregnates the mapping with touches of a culture in contrast with other cultural and social systems" (Ibarretxte-Antuñano 2013: 324). The culture sieve model bridges universal bodily information with the cultural dimension, thus accounting for linguistic variations.

Hence, while the chemical compound QSO_4 interacts with the papillae of *Homo sapiens* following the same universal transduction mechanisms that have been referred to as bitter, the linguistic description of such a sensation might be coded differently in distinct languages, and might develop peculiar metaphorical extensions, in keeping with diverse linguistic and cultural systems. Crosslinguistic data coming from Chinese (Xu 2017) and Hebrew (Gilead et al. 2015) support this claim (see Chapter 1). The emic perspective sponsored in this book is paramount to a description of taste that takes into account the cultural, linguistic, and physiological factors that intervene in the conceptualisation and usage of gustatory terms.

7.6 Mapping taste metaphors with the English thesaurus

As I mentioned, the lexical approach is one of two possible methods to investigate metaphorical elaboration (Kövecses et al. 2019). I followed this approach using material retrieved from the "Mapping Metaphor with the Historical Thesaurus" project (hence MMP). The project, developed at the University of Glasgow, draws on lexicographical material that represents the historical development of English. The aim of my analysis is to provide an account of the role that the sense of taste has had in motivating metaphorical meaning extension in a diachronic study of English.

The guiding principle of the MMP is that two lexemes retrieved in two or more lexical categories in the Historical Thesaurus (Kay et al. 2009) may be motivated by metaphorically driven semantic expansion. The Historical Thesaurus contains nearly 800,000 word senses, taken from the second edition of OED, with the addition of *A Thesaurus of Old English* (Roberts and Kay 1995), thereby encompassing data for over a millennium of the history of English. The researchers in the MMP firstly classified the linguistic items in the Historical Thesaurus in 415 semantically coherent categories, identified with an alphanumeric code. For instance, the lexical category *Weapons and Armour*[14] is coded as Category 3C03. The first number

---

14 In keeping with the MMP usage I capitalise the first letter of the lexical category names, which in the MMP loosely correspond to semantic domains.

corresponds to one of three macro-categories in which each category was grouped. These are: 01 *External World*, 02 *Mental World*, and 03 *Social World*.

After having divided the lexical items in the Historical Thesaurus into different categories, the Glasgow researchers ran queries in the database of word senses to identify lexical overlap between different categories. They compared lexical data in each category with those of other categories. The lexical overlap was manually analysed and coded to determine whether a connection between categories was metaphorical or not. For instance, there is a strong metaphorical link between category 3C03 *Weapons and Armour* and category 1G02 *Drinks and drinking*, exemplified by words such as *pocket-pistol*, which since c1730 may be used to refer to a Container for Liquor. As I mentioned earlier, the linguistic data analysed by the MMP come from the Historical Thesaurus, which in turn is based on the OED. Thus, the MMP website provides intertextual links to retrieve lexicographic information from the dictionary that motivates such metaphorical realisations.

Despite the intensive work, "only a small proportion of the lexical overlap is due to metaphor: the majority is a result of polysemy motivated by processes other than metaphor (such as widening, narrowing, and metonymy), and 'accidental' connections such as homonymy" (Anderson and Bramwell 2014: 43), which they categorised as "noise", and hence not included in the database. The notion of lexical overlap intended in the present book, and by the MMP, is the presence of the same lexical item(s) in two or more distinct categories. The metaphorical links between categories were then classified as "strong", i.e., systematic and numerous metaphorical links between domains; or "weak", i.e., less systematic and more sporadic metaphorical links between domains. The user can browse the MMP displaying data according to three main metaphorical directions: from a selected category to other categories (Source Domain), from another category to a selected category (Target Domain), and "Bidirectional".

7.6.1 Methodology

I retrieved the metaphorical links involving 1I10 *Taste* in the MMP by posing a simple query in the website database. This yielded to 109 categories that involve 1I10 *Taste* (73 categories as Source Domain; 27 categories as Target Domain; and 9 categories with a bidirectional metaphorical link). Notably, the number of categories that function as a target with *Taste* as the source domain is higher than those that map linguistic knowledge onto *Taste* as their target. This may reflect the basic nature and almost instinctual nature of gustatory perception that has led philosophers to a disparagement of taste (Korsmeyer 2002), as well as supporting the directionality of lexical transfer among different sensory modalities in English described by the hierarchy of the senses (e.g., Williams 1976; Bagli 2017; Winter 2019a: 99).

I selected exclusively the categories in which *Taste* was Source Domain, in order to verify the metaphorical elaborations of the lexical items in this category. The data of the MMP are displayed in the lexical categories developed by the researchers and that reflect categories in the Historical Thesaurus. Each category is composed of specific linguistic items, which provide a hypertextual link to the Historical Thesaurus entry that motivates their inclusion. Moreover, the entries in the Historical Thesaurus are further linked to entries with chronology and examples in the OED, thus making it possible to investigate the specific lexicographic entries that motivate inclusion of an item in one category or another.

In the next section, as a result of my in-depth analyses, I propose an organisation of the lexical categories of the MMP into semantic domains that are structured by taste according to the eight metaphors that emerged as motivating the semantic expansion of linguistic items. This analysis offers a broad picture of the role of the semantic domain of taste in motivating lexical overlap across the history of English.

7.6.2 CHARACTER IS TASTE

The general conceptual metaphor CHARACTER IS TASTE motivates lexical overlap between different lexical categories. This conceptual metaphor conceptualises the character of someone as its taste. This metaphor motivates lexical overlap retrieved in distinct categories, which may be grouped in different semantic domains. The first domain, ATTITUDE is illustrated in Table 15.

Table 15: Lexical overlap in ATTITUDE.

Domain	Cat ID	Category Name	Examples
ATTITUDE	1J24	Electromagnetism and atomic physics	flavour
	1O20	Vigorous action and degrees of violence	bitter, sour, sweeten, spicy, peppery
	1O22	Behaviour and conduct	sweet, sweetness, bitterness, bitter, sweetly, honeyed, rancour, unsavoury, embitter
	2D14	Pride	spicy

I labelled the first semantic domain ATTITUDE. The meaning of the lexical items in this domain is motivated by the metaphor CHARACTER IS TASTE. The lexical categories it contains are *Electromagnetism and atomic physics*,[15] *Vigorous action and degrees of violence, Behaviour and conduct*, and *Pride*.

The most emblematic case found in this category is the item *flavour* in *Electromagnetism and atomic physics*. In this context, it refers to a specific characteristic of quarks, the elementary particles that are fundamental constituents of matter. Each quark has a set of different characteristics, one of which has been called *flavour*, and it predicts its behaviour and character along a set of possibilities (Bissi 2016, personal communication). Despite belonging to specialised terminology, this metaphorical meaning expansion of the word *flavour* exemplifies the role of taste in conceptualizing the character of someone or something.

The lexical overlap in *Vigorous action and degrees of violence* is consistent in using different taste types to conceptualise diverse attitudes of individuals. The metaphorical link between this category and *Taste* originates in Old English. An illustrative case is (7), which exemplifies the meaning of the lexical item *spicy* recorded as *slang* between 1828 and 1898, and defined by the OED as "full of spirit, smartness, or 'go'" (OED *spicy*, adj.,6.a):

(7) We had a remarkably **spicy** team out of town. (*Sporting Magazine* N.S. XXI. 324, 1828)

The word *rancour* found in category *Behaviour and conduct* is classified as a taste word with the sensory meaning of "rancidity, rankness, foulness of smell" (OED *rancour*, n., †2), even if according to the OED this is currently obsolete. This word is a borrowing from French, but it originates from Latin *rancor*, which denotes "a stinking smell or flavour, rankness, rancidity" as its first meaning, but it could also be used with the figurative meaning of *anger*. The metaphorical link between rancidity and anger had already developed when the word entered the English vocabulary, to the extent that in the OED the first meaning of the word is "Deeprooted and bitter ill feeling; resentment or animosity, esp. of long standing; an instance of this" (OED *rancour*, n., 1.a), with the first instance dating back to 1380. The perceptual meaning of "Rancidity, rankness; foulness of smell" is recorded only from c1425 to 1658. This metaphorical link is a "dead metaphor", in that the motivation that links the two domains is not transparent and may only be retrieved by etymological research. Nonetheless, the metaphor links a gustatory

---

15 I do not report the codes of each lexical category in running text to make the discussion smoother. However, I do report the Category IDs in the tables.

sensation to a person's attitude, even if the historical development reported by the OED is in the reverse order: from a person's character (1380) to taste (c1425 to 1658). It is likely however that the two meanings entered together in English, and that the 40 years that separate the two attestations do not really signal a subsequent development of the perceptual sense from the psychological sense.

The conceptual metaphor CHARACTER IS TASTE motivates inclusion of the lexical overlap found in categories *Existence and its attributes*, *Similarity*, *Communication and disclosure*, and *Signs and signals*. I labelled this domain ESSENCE (Table 16), because the lexical items refer to the intrinsic qualities of objects as opposed to individuals.

Table 16: Lexical overlap in ESSENCE.

Domain	Cat ID	Category Name	Examples
ESSENCE	1K01	Existence and its attributes	tarage, taste, taste of, savour, flavour, taste
	1P09	Similarity	smatch, tarage, savouring, taste, smack, taste, season of, flavorous, tarage, savouring, taste, smack, taste, season of, flavorous
	3I01	Communication and disclosure	taste
	3I03	Signs and signals	savour, tang

I included the two categories 3I01 and 3I03 because the lexical items *taste*, *savour*, and *tang* refer to the essence of words. For instance, the word *tang* in category 3I03 may be found in linguistic realisations such as (8) from OED (*tang*, n., 6.b):

(8) His speaking-voice.. was sweet, but with a kind of trenchant edge upon it, a genial asperity, that gave it character, **tang**. (H. Harland, *Cardinal's Snuff-box* xv. 122, 1900)

The lexical item *tarage* in 1P09 is of French origin, and it is not in use in Contemporary English. Its meaning is reported in the OED as "taste, flavour; quality, character" (OED †*tarage*, n.1), and its last attestation dates to Middle English. The noun *smack* refers to the special and distinctive taste of something, and the OED reports as its figurative meaning "a trace, tinge, or suggestion *of* something specified" (OED *smack*, n.1,3.a), as in (9):

(9) A **smack** of real earnestness in his tone. (F. C. Burnand, *My time*, xxix 280; 1874)

Taken altogether, the lexical overlap in the two domains of ATTITUDE and ESSENCE is motivated by the metaphor CHARACTER IS TASTE, which is consistent in conceptualizing the character of someone or something as its taste, both at a general level, with lexical items such as *flavour, taste,* and *smack,* and a more specific level such as *spicy, peppery,* and *bitter.*

7.6.3 KNOWING IS TASTING

If we conceptualise the character of someone or something as its taste, then we may be able to appreciate its inner qualities through tasting, which is the metaphorical entailment of KNOWING IS TASTING. This entailment elaborates on the more general metaphor COGNITION IS PERCEPTION (Ibarretxte-Antuñano 2019: 54; Steinbach-Eicke 2019), and motivates the semantic extension of lexical overlap found in the domains of EXPERIENTIAL KNOWLEDGE and GENERAL PERCEPTION.

Table 17 exemplifies the lexical overlap in the domain EXPERIENTIAL KNOWLEDGE found in the lexical categories *Sexual relations, Operation and influence, Perception and cognition, Knowledge and experience,* and *Judgement.*

Table 17: Lexical overlap in EXPERIENTIAL KNOWLEDGE.

DOMAIN	Cat ID	Category Name	Examples
EXPERIENTIAL KNOWLEDGE	1I06	Sexual relations	taste of, taste
	1O01	Operation and influence	taste, attaste, savour, taste of, taste of
	1P13	Exemplification and specificity	spice, taste, savour
	2A07	Perception and cognition	savour, taste
	2A20	Knowledge and experience	taste, taste, taste of, smatch, gust
	2B04	Judgement	taste

The meaning of lexical items in this domain is motivated by the metaphor KNOWING IS TASTING. The role of gustatory experience in conceptualising the act of knowing has been noted in literature by other scholars. More specifically, Ibarretxte-Antuñano suggests that the type of cognition that is metaphorically structured by the different senses depends on which sensory modality is selected as source domain, as "the way we gather information through the senses is not the same and, consequently, the type of information also differs" (2019: 51). According to her account, the type of cognition that both TOUCH and TASTE structure is EXPERIENTIAL COGNITION.

The lexical items in category *Sexual relations* conceptualise sexually knowing someone as tasting them, as in (10):

(10) If you can mak't apparent that you haue **tasted** her in Bed; my hand, And Ring is yours. (W. Shakespeare, *Cymbeline* II. iv. 57; 1623)

This meaning is reported as obsolete by the OED (*taste*, v., 3.b), and it is reported as a specific realisation of the more general meaning "to have experience or knowledge of; to experience, feel" (OED *taste*, v., 3.a), which instead is marked as still alive in Contemporary English. For instance, consider the expression "A taste of Umbria",[16] retrieved from an online review of a restaurant on TripAdvisor. The writer of this online review wanted to convey the message that in this specific restaurant they were able to perceive, experience, and get to know Umbria, as an index of the authenticity of the restaurant. In the lexical overlap, a similar meaning is found in *Exemplification and specificity*, see (11):

(11) My first **taste** of grouse-shooting was a complete success. (A. Morrison, *Dorrington Deed-box* I; 1897)

In (11), the lexical item *taste* is defined as "a slight experience, received or given; a slight show or sample of any condition or quality" (OED *taste*, n.1, †3.c). The usage of the word *taste* to refer to the entire experience of grouse-shooting is motivated by the conceptual metaphor KNOWING IS TASTING. As argued by Ibarretxte-Antuñano (2019), the knowledge structured by gustatory sensations is experiential, as it is based on physical proximity with the object being experienced. The conceptual contiguity between experience and perception is evidenced in the lexical overlap in the domain GENERAL PERCEPTION, which encompasses the lexical categories *Physical sensation* and *Perception and cognition*, illustrated in Table 18. The lexical items found in this domain draw on gustatory vocabulary to conceptualise the entirety of physical sensation and perception. For instance, *lick one's lips* in the Historical Thesaurus is found under the entry "Please/gratify the senses: anticipation of", thus suggesting that the embodied, physical reaction to anticipation of food is

---

[16] https://www.tripadvisor.com/ShowUserReviews-g608939-d1531928-r212268649-Enoteca_L_Alchimista-Montefalco_Province_of_Perugia_Umbria.html, posted by user Binky W, and I concur.

Table 18: Lexical overlap in GENERAL PERCEPTION.

Domain	Cat ID	Category Name	Examples
GENERAL PERCEPTION	1I01	Physical sensation	savour, sweet, sugared, lick one's lips, taste, tastelessness, bitter-sweet
	2A07	Perception and cognition	savour, taste

extended to refer to anticipation of general physical and sensuous pleasure. The lexical item *savour* in *Physical sensation* clarifies the lexical overlap found in the category even further, as it is glossed in the OED as "to enjoy or appreciate fully; to take lingering pleasure or delight in" (*savour*, v., 5.c), as in (12)

(12) He wastes no time **savouring** victory but immediately moves toward his next goal. (*New Yorker*, 6 Dec. 58/3; 2010)

The usage of the verb to savour in (12) is motivated by the conceptual metaphor ENJOYING IS SAVOURING. Arguably, this conceptual metaphor is an entailment of the usage of gustatory verbs to conceptualise experiential cognition: in order to enjoy something, one must experience it first. Likewise, the terms *savour* and *taste* in 2A07 are listed in the Historical Thesaurus under the heading "to perceive". The corresponding OED entry (*savour*, v., †6.b) glosses to "savour" as "to understand, comprehend; to perceive, apprehend". The most recent attestation (13) of this meaning dates to 1659:

(13) In your writings I **savour** a spirit so very distant from my disposition, that I have small hopes that my words will escape your displeasure. (P. Heylin, *Certamen Epistolare* 8; 1659)

The extended meaning of the lexical items reported in the domains of EXPERIENTIAL KNOWLEDGE and GENERAL PERCEPTION are motivated by the conceptual metaphor KNOWING IS TASTING. As discussed in previous chapters, taste was mainly considered as having a lower cognitive value than other sensory modalities that were in turn considered as more prestigious and better candidates for the conceptualisation of knowledge. The usage of gustatory perception to conceptualise KNOWING suggests a more relevant role of the act of tasting in English than it has been held traditionally in philosophy.

7.6.4 INTELLECTUAL ABILITY IS TASTE

Another semantic domain that is structured by the lexicon of *Taste* is INTELLECTUAL ABILITY. Lexical categories that merge in this domain are consistent in conceptualising the intellectual ability of an individual as its taste. Table (19) illustrates the categories *Cleverness, Wisdom, Stupidity, Foolishness, Intellectual weakness, Foolish person*, and their examples.

Table 19: Lexical overlap in INTELLECTUAL ABILITY.

DOMAIN	Cat ID	Category Name	Examples
INTELLECTUAL ABILITY	2A10	Cleverness	salt, causticity
	2A11	Wisdom	savourly, sapient
	2A14	Stupidity	wearish, insipid
	2A15	Foolishness	insipidly, insipidity
	2A16	Intellectual weakness	insipidity
	2A17	Foolish person	insipid, insipidity

The lexical items that form this domain mainly conceptualise the LACK OF AN INDIVIDUAL'S INTELLECTUAL ABILITY as LACK OF TASTE. This metaphorical link is instantiated by the words *insipid, insipidity*, and *wearish* (currently obsolete), and it is exemplified in (14) and (15):

(14) Words and phrases without Sense Tickle the Ears of **insipid** people. (Ld. Delamere, *Wks.* 20; 1694)

(15) If Michaela gets her own show, for her own sake, I hope it's nothing like the stupid and **insipid** "Parks and Recreation" show that Amy Poehler is doing. [COCA; Web 2012]

The word *insipid(ity)* derives from Latin (via French) and it means *tasteless(ness)*: it is the property of a food item whose flavour is very feeble. Likewise, wisdom is conceptualised as savour, as in (16):

(16) The Company and Discourse of such as speak seriously and **savourly** of God, and Religion, and the Concern of Eternity. (*Ministers Advice to his Parish* 30; 1703)

The meaning of the lexical item *savoury* in reference to *wisdom* is dated from 1494 to 1703 in the OED (*savourly*, adv.,†2), and it attests the realisation of the metaphor INTELLECTUAL ABILITY IS TASTE. In Latin, the verb *sapio (sapere)* is polysemous: it refers both to *to taste* and *to have sense*. The same metaphorical link is instantiated also in the related adjectives *sapidus* (tasty) and *sapiens* (rational, sane, wise) (see also: Cavalieri 2014: 23). The metaphorical relationship between TASTE and INTELLIGENCE has developed in Italian as well: besides the Italian verb *sapere* that maintained the same polysemous structure of Latin, there are other realisations such as It. *sciocco*, which means both *stupid* and *insipid*, or more specifically, lacking salt (cfr. It. *pane sciocco*, 'unsalted bread'). Another instantiation may be found in the Italian expressions It. *avere il sale in zucca* (lit. *to have salt in the squash* > 'to have intelligence in the head' > to have common sense). Torres Soler (2020) discusses the usage of Spanish *soso* and English *bland* with similar results. In English, the use of *salt* to conceptualise cleverness is attested by the lexical items in *Cleverness*, where the noun *salt* is glossed as "That which gives life or pungency to discourse or written composition; poignancy of expression; pungent wit" (OED *salt*, n.1, 3.c).

It must be noted that in this case the figurative elaboration does not draw on an adjective of taste, rather on the noun of a mineral commonly used in cooking. Salt is widely used among human cultures, and allegedly it has played a major role in the evolution of human diets and cooking habits (Hladik 2004; Cavalieri 2014). It is a flavour enhancer, as it facilitates dehydration of food and the release of chemical components that make up flavour (Holley 2006). The action of adding salt to food corresponds to enhancing its flavour, and this correspondence is motivated by a physical and embodied metonymy CAUSE FOR RESULT: ADDING SALT FOR ENHANCING TASTE, which in turn combines with the metaphor INTELLIGENCE IS TASTE. Other metaphorical realisations that involve salt as a source domain and refer to the intellectual ability and poignancy of an individual are *the salt of the earth*, from Matthew v.13; *salt of youth*, from Shakespeare's *Merry Wives of Windsor*. Taste, or lack thereof, may be used in English to conceptualise intellectual activity, as testified by the lexical overlap displayed in Table 19.

7.6.5 EMOTIONAL FEELINGS ARE TASTE

The semantic domain of EMOTIONAL FEELINGS may be conceptualised using terms from the domain of TASTE. The lexical categories contained in this domain are: *Contempt, Emotion, Strong emotion and lack of emotion, Excitement, Pleasure, Emotional suffering, Love and friendship,* and *Hatred and hostility*. The lexical overlap found in this domain is consistent in transferring semantic knowledge from individual gustatory sensations to emotional feelings. Each specific taste loosely conceptualises a different feeling. The lexical overlap whose extended meaning is motivated by this metaphor is illustrated in Table 20.

Table 20: Lexical overlap in EMOTIONAL FEELINGS.

DOMAIN	Cat ID	Category Name	Examples
EMOTIONAL FEELINGS	2B08	Contempt	bitter, acid, causticity, gamy
	2D01	Emotion	dulce, sugary, flavour, sweetly, saccharine, saccharinity
	2D02	Strong emotion and lack of emotion	tasteless, tastelessness
	2D03	Excitement	sauce, salt, savour, gusto, haut-goût, piquant, flavorous, spicy, nutty, saltily
	2D05	Pleasure	sweetness, sweet, savoury, bitter-sweet, honeyed, mellifluous, taste, sugary, honeysome, gustful, palatable, saccharine, sugar-candyish
	2D06	Emotional suffering	bitterness, bitter, unsweet, sour, attery/attry, unsavoury, wersh, tasteless, unpalatable, spiceless
	2D08	Love and friendship	sweet, sweetly, palate, sugared, taste, goût, honey-sweet, acquired taste
	2D09	Hatred and hostility	bitterness, unsavoury, sourly, distaste, disgust, mistaste

Adjectives describing *bitter* and *sour* sensations are found in categories such as *Contempt*, *Emotional suffering*, and *Hatred and hostility*; adjectives describing sweetness are mainly found in *Emotion*, *Pleasure*, and *Love and friendship*. Gustatory sensations of saltiness and spiciness conceptualise *Excitement*, while the lexical item *tastelessness* (i.e., a lack of taste) in *Strong emotion and lack of emotion* refers to a lack of emotion. The realisations found in lexical categories *Pleasure*, *Emotional suffering*, and *Love and friendship* originated in Old English, and some of these are still in use in Contemporary English.

The metaphorical conceptualisation of feelings and emotions as taste has been observed by other scholars (e.g., EMOTION IS PERCEPTION, Kövecses 2019). The conceptual mechanisms that motivate this figurative realisation are discussed with reference to intrafield metaphors in Chapter 9. In the data of the

MMP, it is epitomised in the word *flavour* in the category *Emotion*, retrieved in the Historical Thesaurus entry for "Emotion". This confirms a conceptual, metaphorical transfer between the two domains. The lexical items found in these categories may be organised in a set of mappings that transfer gustatory information to the domain of EMOTIONAL FEELINGS, helping structure it. Thus, the mappings of the metaphor EMOTIONAL FEELINGS ARE TASTE are formulated in Table 21:

Table 21: The mappings of EMOTIONAL FEELINGS ARE TASTE.

Source domain: TASTE	→	Target domain: EMOTIONAL FEELINGS
LACK OF TASTE	→	LACK OF EMOTION
BITTER	→	GRIEF
BITTER/ SOUR	→	HATRED
SOUR	→	HOSTILITY
SWEET	→	LOVE
SALTY/ SPICY	→	EXCITEMENT

These mappings suggest that the knowledge transferred from gustatory perceptions to the domain of feelings is not limited to specific emotional values of individual sensations, rather they are structured in a set of correspondences. Individual gustatory perceptions conceptualise different emotional feelings in a network of meanings motivated by the individual mappings. A compelling example is provided by the lexical item *unsweet*, found in category *Emotional suffering*, which is glossed by the OED as "*unpleasant, disagreeable, distasteful*" (OED *unsweet*, adj., 1). This adjective derives through prefixation from the adjective *sweet*, but rather than denying the literal sense of *sweet*, it denies its figurative sense of "pleasant", thus referring to a negative emotional state, as in (17).

(17) Certain terms in the letters. . ., **unsweet** to ladies, began to trouble his mind. (G. Meredith, *Beauchamp's Career*, III. i. 2; 1876)

Other lexical items in this category that refer to unpleasant emotions are *bitter*, *sour*, and *unsavoury*.

Noteworthy examples are the adjectives in the category *Pleasure*: *mellifluous* (from Latin *mel*, Eng. honey), *honeysome*, *sugary*, and *saccharine*, all sharing a positive and pleasant meaning motivated by the conceptual association between sweetness and pleasure, which in turn is based on the embodied value of sugars and perception of sweetness. The large number of adjectives in the semantic domain of sweetness that have come to refer to pleasure in the history of English illustrate how the figurative meaning of sweet as pleasant arises from the embodied metonymy SWEET FOR PLEASANT.

Lastly, the lexical item *piquant* in *Excitement* is glossed as "stimulating or agreeable to the mind or senses; fascinating, charming" (OED *piquant*, adj., 3), as in (18):

(18) Their husbands.. leave home to seek for more agreeable, may I be allowed to use a significant French word, **piquant** society. (M. Wollstonecraft, *Vindic. Rights Woman* iv. 144; 1792)

The occurrence in (18) conceptualises a feeling of excitement and fascination through the lexical item *piquant*. This metaphorical meaning is shared also by lexical items such as *salty* and *spicy*, and it came to refer to *vulgarity* and *coarseness* over the centuries (see Chapter 8).

7.6.6 AESTHETICS IS TASTE

Lexical items in categories *Aesthetics and good taste*, *Tastelessness*, *Fashionableness*, *Beauty and ugliness*, *Will – personal choice*, *Visual arts*, and *Literature* conceptualise beauty and personal choices as taste (Table 22).

Table 22: Lexical overlap in AESTHETICS.

DOMAIN	Cat ID	Category Name	Examples
	2B09	Aesthetics – good taste	sweet, sweetness, gusto, taste, goût
	2B10	Tastelessness	tasteless
AESTHETICS	2B11	Fashionableness	goût, taste
	2B12	Beauty and ugliness	sweet, sugared, sweet, spicy, unsweet
	2E01	Will – personal choice	taste

The conceptual metaphor that motivates the semantic extension of the lexical items in the domain AESTHETICS is perhaps the most widely accepted and studied conceptual metaphor that has TASTE as a source domain, and it is part of the more general the Mind-As-Body metaphor, firstly proposed by Sweetser (1990). This conceptual metaphor motivates the meaning of lexical items such as *taste* glossed as "the fact or condition of liking or preferring something; inclination, liking for" (OED *taste*, n.1, 7.a), or "style or manner exhibiting aesthetic discernment; good or bad aesthetic quality; the style or manner favoured in any age or country" (OED *taste*, n.1, 8.b). Lexical items include borrowing from French, e.g., *gout* or Italian, *gusto*, while a lack of the sense of beauty is conceptualised as *tasteless*, as in (19):

(19) The **tasteless** fashion of an artificial and decaying civilization. (C. Kingsley, *Hypatia*, I. vii. 157; 1853).

The adjective *tasteless* is glossed as "devoid of good taste; of persons, lacking in discrimination, or in critical discernment and appreciation" (OED *tasteless*, adj., 4). According to evolutionary psychologists, the sense of taste probably evolved to allow animals to discriminate between different food choices available in their environment, and to prevent ingestion of potentially toxic or dangerous substances, while carefully selecting the most profitable and nutritious food (Bachmanov and Beauchamp 2007: 390). Similarly, the metaphorical meaning of *taste* refers to discrimination and selection of appropriate embellishment supplies for the daily needs of our culture and social milieu.

7.6.7 VALUE IS SWEET

Out of the eight conceptual metaphors that emerged, there is a separate set of three conceptual metaphors specifically involving SWEET as a Source Domain. The conceptual metaphor VALUE IS SWEET motivates the lexical overlap with categories *Trade and commerce, Money, Leisure and games*, as exemplified in Table 23.

Table 23: Lexical overlap in VALUE.

DOMAIN	Cat ID	Category Name	Examples
	1I07	Drug use	sweet
	1O14	Advantage	sweet, sweet
VALUE	3L01	Trade and commerce	sweetener, sweetening, sweeten
	3L02	Money	sweetly, sweetener
	3M01	Leisure and games	sweetening, sweeten

The lexical overlap in these categories refers to the VALUE of an object as a SWEET taste and MAKING SOMETHING MORE VALUABLE as SWEETENING it. Thus, raising the price of an object by bidding is said to *sweeten* something (20), and the bidder is the *sweetener*; and if someone buys it at a high price, it is paying it *sweetly* (21), in keeping with the action of *sweetening* in card games, which refers to the tactics of increasing the stakes:

(20) 'Safe bidding' or **'sweetening'** at an auction sale was a fraud on the public. (*Daily Chronicle*, 23 Sept. 6/4; 1904)

(21) Everything in this world has to be paid for, and some things **sweetly**. (R. L. Stevenson, *New Arabian Nights*, I. 169; 1882)

I argue that the motivation for this metaphorical link lies in our embodied perception of *sweet* substances as being highly valuable in a nutritious and cultural perspective. The same metaphorical link is maintained in contemporary English (see Chapter 8). The lack of solid linguistic data to establish this metaphor advocates for an investigation of its psycholinguistic reality, which however exceeds the scope of the present investigation. An experimental paradigm similar to that of Schneider et al. (2011) for the metaphor IMPORTANCE IS WEIGHT might be able to elicit the metaphorical link between the two conceptual domains.

7.6.8 HARMONY IS SWEET

Lexical overlap with categories *Social discord and Harmony* and *Music* are consistent in conceptualizing HARMONY as a SWEET substance (Table 24).

Table 24: Lexical overlap in HARMONY.

DOMAIN	Cat ID	Category Name	Examples
HARMONY	3A10	Social discord and Harmony	dulce, sweeten
	3M04	Music	sweet, sweetly, sweetness, sugared, dulce, sour

The conceptualisation of sounds as sweet has been traditionally described as a synaesthetic metaphor. As I mentioned and discuss in more depth later, according to sensory linguistics, the usage of sensory adjectives in one modality to describe perceptual quality in another modality is better accounted for in terms of intrafield metaphors. Yet, the lexical overlap in this domain is found also in non-perceptual lexical categories, such as *Social discord and Harmony*, as exemplified in (22)

(22) The Emperor to **sweeten** the People, restor'd the Confiscated Goods.
    (tr. J. Le Clerc *Mem. Count Teckely* II. 124; 1693)

The meaning of *sweeten* reported in (22) is no longer in use in contemporary English, yet it illustrates the usage of sweetness perception to conceptualise a sense of peace and harmony. Similarly, the search for *dulce* in the OED retrieves different entries, all of which are marked as rare, or obsolete. Disregarding their frequency of usage, the verb *to dulce* is defined as "To make sweet or soft; to mollify, appease" (OED *dulce*, v.), while the adjective *dulce* is defined (beyond its literal meaning of "sweet in taste or smell") as "pleasing to the eye, ear, or feelings" (OED *dulce*, adj., 2), and as "sweetly, harmoniously" (OED *dulce*, †adv.). Similarly, the listing of the verb *to sweeten* under the Historical Thesaurus heading of "appeasing" is motivated by the sense 6.b in the OED (*sweeten*, v.; now rare or obsolete) that is "to make things pleasant for, relieve, comfort, soothe, gratify", thus suggesting a similar mapping of making things harmonious.

The lexical category *Music* contains lexical items relative to sweetness, with the only exception of the adjective *sour*. I argue that the metaphorical mapping that motivates this lexical overlap is DISCORDANCE IS SOUR, which may be considered an entailment of HARMONY IS SWEET. The heading in the Historical Thesaurus that contains the lexical items listed in *Music* is "Melodious/ Harmonious", with the exception of *sour*, which instead is listed under the heading "Out of Tune". Taken all together, the lexical evidence analysed for this category suggests that the overlap may be motivated by the conceptual metaphor HARMONY IS SWEET. I discuss further this metaphorical realisation and its possible embodied motivation in Paragraph 9.5.1.

7.6.9 MITIGATING IS SWEETENING

The conceptual metaphor MITIGATING IS SWEETENING (Table 25) is strongly connected to HARMONY IS SWEET. The idea of mitigation includes different activities that result in making things better and reaching a more favourable state of affairs. The concept of sweetening conceptualises different changes of state in different domains, but it signals a passage from a more negative to a more positive relative position on that scale.

Table 25: Lexical overlap in MITIGATING.

DOMAIN	Cat ID	Category Name	Examples
MITIGATING	2A22	Truth and falsity	sugared, honey, sugary, honeyed, sweet
	2B07	Esteem	honeyed, savour, sugary, sweeten, sweetener
	2D11	Pity and pitilessness	edulcorate
	2F10	Taking and thieving	sweetener
	3F01	Morality and immorality	sweeten, sweetener
	3K02	Industry	sweetening, sweeten
	3K06	Machines	sweetly, sweet

The lexical categories that constitute the semantic domain of MITIGATING are: *Truth and falsity*, *Esteem*, *Pity and pitilessness*, *Taking and thieving*, *Morality and immorality*, *Industry*, and *Machines*. The concept of mitigation is best exemplified with reference to the lexical items found in *Industry* (23), where the word *sweetening* conceptualises the process of refining oil, thus eliminating impurities from rough substances and making it more suitable for further exploitation (OED *sweeten*, v., 8.e).

(23) The lighter distillates, liquid petroleum gas, gasolenes and kerosenes, can be **sweetened** by simple chemical treatments which either remove the sulphur compounds or turn them into harmless and non-smelly forms. (W. G. Roberts *Quest for Oil* (rev. ed.) ix. 92.; 1975)

A similar metaphorical occurrence may be observed in *Taking and thieving*. In this lexical category, the item *sweetener* refers to a person who frauds, and therefore metaphorically makes a situation sweeter by omitting negative details, in order to make it more acceptable (OED *sweetener*, n., 2.a). In other words, in this context a *sweetener* is someone who deceptively mitigates reality to make it easier to be accepted. A similar mapping may be found in expressions such as *sweeten the pill*, i.e., to make something seem less unpleasant (OED *pill*, n.3, 3.b); or in *to edulcorate* in *Pity and pitilessness*. This verb originally comes from Latin (Lat. *edulco*, Eng. 'to sweeten'). It developed in Italian *edulcorare*, which is polysemous between the senses of *to sweeten* and *to mitigate, to embellish*. In English, the literal sense of the verb is currently marked as obsolete by the OED. It now refers to the process of freeing substances from harsh properties (24), "to purify, soften" (OED *edulcorate*, v., 2).

(24) Experiments for **edulcorating** vicious train-oil. (*Gentleman's Mag.* May 225/1; 1762)

Similarly, in chemistry this verb conceptualises the action of freeing from soluble particles by agitation or trituration in water, or by washing on a filter (OED *edulcorate*, v., 3). The specific meaning of this word suggests that despite the lexical realisations, the contexts, and the frequency of usage, the conceptualisation of the process of adding sugar to a substance has been metaphorically transferred to the process of making something purer, more acceptable and less unpleasant, i.e., mitigating.

The conceptual metaphor MITIGATING IS SWEETENING largely motivates the semantic extension of lexical items in the categories *Geological features, Atmosphere and weather*, and *Farming*, illustrated in Table 26.

Table 26: Lexical overlap in NATURE.

Domain	Cat ID	Category Name	Examples
	1A15	Geological features	sour, sweeten, sweeten
NATURE	1A28	Atmosphere and weather	sour, bitter, bitterness
	1G03	Farming	sweeten, sweetener

The meanings of the lexical items in Table 26 refer to natural elements and phenomena, i.e., *soil*, or *weather*. The gustatory sensations that are found in these categories have the specific sense of making the soil fertile (*sweeten*, in 1A15) through a *sweetener*, i.e., "an alkali or similar substance used to neutralise acidity; something which renders soil rich and mellow" (OED *sweetener*, n., 1.b) as in (25):

(25) The plough is.. used with great propriety, as a **sweetener** of the soil.
(C. Vancouver, *Gen. View Agric. Cambr.* 201; 1794)

On the contrary, a land which is not fertile and uncongenial to cultivation may be *sour* (1A15). Furthermore, inclement and especially cold weather may be conceptualised as *bitter* or *sour*. The first attestation of *bitter* in describing coldness reported by the OED (*bitter*, adj., 8) is to be found in Shakespeare's *As You Like It*, although an informal search on EEBO (Early English Books Online) attests to its wide usage also in earlier texts:

(26) Freize, freize, thou **bitter** skie. (W. Shakespeare, *As you like it (1623)*, II. vii. 185; a.1616)

However, the conceptualisation of bitterness as coldness is related to the etymology of *bitter*, and it is discussed at length in Chapter 9. The conceptualisation of *sweetening* as *making fertile* and thus *making something more appealing, more positive* is in keeping with the general metaphorical value of *sweet*, and with the more specific meaning of MITIGATING IS SWEETENING.

7.7 What are the conceptual mechanisms that drive gustatory semantic change in English?

This chapter has investigated the role of gustatory sensations and the semantic domain of gustatory descriptors in motivating semantic change in English. The linguistic data that I discussed represent a classification of the lexicographic material that has been retrieved by the Mapping Metaphor with the Historical Thesaurus project. I organised the lexical categories proposed by the MMP into semantic domains, with the aim of describing conceptual metaphors that could motivate such lexical overlap. The results show eight metaphorical mappings that intervene in structuring semantic change in English.

Taken altogether the data suggest the emergence of the generic metaphor CHARACTER IS TASTE, as exemplified in Table 27. The label in the target domain accounts for applications of this metaphor to a variety of Source Domains, as it may be used to describe the character, or attitude of animate beings as well as metaphorically the essence, or the nature of something. I propose that the mappings of the metaphor CHARACTER IS TASTE reveal the mappings projecting positivity and negativity entailments in relation to TASTE both as an object and as a relation:

Table 27: The CHARACTER IS TASTE metaphor.

	Source: TASTE		*Target:* CHARACTER
a.	TASTE	→	CHARACTER
b.	A PALATABLE TASTE	→	A POSITIVE CHARACTER
c.	AN UNPALATABLE TASTE	→	A NEGATIVE CHARACTER
d.	TASTING	→	KNOWING

Table 27 (continued)

Source: TASTE		Target: CHARACTER
e. TASTING A PALATABLE TASTE	→	HAVING A POSITIVE OPINION
f. TASTING AN UNPALATABLE TASTE	→	HAVING A NEGATIVE OPINION
g. SWEETENING	→	MAKING SOMETHING POSITIVE
h. EMBITTERING	→	MAKING SOMETHING NEGATIVE

Furthermore, the lexicographic data show that gustatory words may be used in English to conceptualise emotional feelings. These metaphorical links involve both generical lexical items (e.g., *flavour*) and more specific taste types (see Chapter 8). The figurative elaborations of gustatory terms span throughout the history of English, driving the semantic expansion of perceptual language. Some lexical items are no longer in use: e.g., *wearish, tarage*; some meanings are obsolete: e.g., *to taste* meaning "sexually knowing someone"; while other meanings originated in Old English and still motivate metaphorical expressions in contemporary English. Some meanings entered English from Latin, where they first evolved in the semantic structure of the language, e.g., *rancour, to edulcorate*. The variety of conceptual metaphors identified in the lexicographic material of the MMP advocates for a reconsideration of the gustatory perception in grounding conceptual mechanisms, as well as a more extensive application of a diachronic approach to the development of figurative elaborations of sensory language. English sponsors an overwhelming written, historical record, which may provide a model to investigate the role of perception and its linguistic representation in motivating language change.

8 The taste of words today

8.1 Introduction

The previous chapter investigated the role of taste and gustatory vocabulary in motivating semantic change in the history of English. The present chapter complements the previous analysis, by identifying and classifying conceptual metaphors and metonymies that motivate polysemous usages of gustatory lexicon in contemporary English, thus answering the question "what do taste words mean when they are used figuratively?". The linguistic material analysed was retrieved through the COCA. I carried out the corpus analysis on a randomly selected sample of occurrences. As mentioned, this methodological approach to the study of metaphor is usage-based and in keeping with contemporary literature in Conceptual Metaphor Theory (Kövecses et al. 2019).

The corpus analysis was limited to the Primary and Secondary Basic Taste Terms. To recall, these items were elicited in an emic perspective through a freelisting task, and by calculating the CSI. Notably, the lexical items *hot* and *delicious* were among the most salient terms in the domain of taste. These however were excluded from the list of BTTs. Although I did not investigate their metaphorical uses, an informal search in the COCA supports the claim that they are not BTTs. The term *hot* may also refer to temperature, and in metaphorical uses it is impossible to disentangle whether the transfer is grounded in gustatory or thermal perception. The sensory linguistics account of perception and the sensorium sponsors a continuous account of perception, nonetheless the present analysis is limited to items that are primarily associated to taste. The term *delicious*, despite certainly being a gustatory term, describes a general quality and it does not convey information on a specific taste type. Therefore, investigating the figurative uses of the word *delicious* would amount to investigating the conceptualisation of an item as "food good to eat", as opposed to the metaphorical value of specific sensations and transduction processes.

8.2 Methodology

The corpus analysis concentrates on the terms *sweet, bitter, sour, salty, spicy,* and *savoury*.[17] The first step of the research was the retrieval of occurrences from the COCA. The only adjective *sweet* yielded 32654 results,[18] a considerable number of occurrences to be manually checked. I decided to analyse 5% of the overall number, that is 1632 occurrences. The same percentage was applied to the rough occurrences of the other terms, to allow for comparable results and percentages. Table 28 reports the quantitative details of the occurrences.

Table 28: Numerical details of occurrences for English BTTs in the COCA.

Item	Total	5%	Literal	Figurative	Percentage of figurative uses
sweet	32654	1632	789	843	51.6%
bitter	10639	532	114	418	78.6%
sour	6320	316	179	137	43.3%
salty	2331	117	96	21	17.9%
spicy	3416	171	154	17	11%
savoury	1535	77	76	1	1.3%

The first column reports the items, the second their total occurrences in the COCA (i.e., before being checked), and the third their number after 5% reduction. The columns Literal and Figurative show the number of occurrences in each category, while the last column reports the percentage of figurative occurrences.

The most frequent item is *sweet* (1632 occurrences), followed by *bitter, sour, salty, spicy* and *savoury*. The frequency rank in the corpus follows almost directly the salience of gustatory adjectives, with the exception of *bitter*, which was ranked fourth in the CSI. The adjective *bitter* is also the most used figuratively in all the corpus: 78.6% of occurrences are used in a non-literal context, while only 21.4% are used literally, i.e., in reference to the taste of something

---

[17] The lexical item *savoury* in American English is spelled as *savory*. I chose to use *savoury* in the discussion of results nonetheless, to maintain consistency with the previous sections of the book.
[18] These data refer to 2017, when they were retrieved. The same search in any future time would yield higher numerical results, considering the constant expansion of the COCA. This analysis offers a synchronic, qualitative picture of significant aspects in the semantic expansion of gustatory terms.

(e.g., *Ciceron's mouth twisted as though he'd bitten into something unexpectedly **bitter**.* FIC 1990).

I occasionally report on some numerical data of frequency of the occurrences, especially when comparison with similar phenomena is useful for the discussion or comprehension of the conceptual elaboration. However, these results should not be intended as having a strict quantitative value: given the dynamicity of construals and meaning creation, I did not want to impart a strict categorisation on the metaphorical elaborations. As such, some of the metaphorical mappings could be considered as belonging to more than one category. For example, a strong tendency to conceptualise women and children as *sweet* emerged from the corpus. Some of these metaphorical realisations have been described in previous literature as the WOMAN AS DESSERTS metaphor (Hines 1999); but they may also be motivated by the conceptual metaphor LOVE IS SWEET, or INNOCENCE IS SWEET. I discussed the three metaphors separately, by providing different examples for each of them. It was often very difficult, if not impossible, to disentangle the realisations. I preferred adopting a dynamic model and I did not perform quantitative operations on specific metaphorical realisations.

At the time of extraction, the COCA contained more than one billion words collected from five different genres: spoken, fiction, popular magazines, newspapers, academic texts. In March 2020, the corpus was updated to contain even more genres, such as TV and Movies subtitles, blogs, and other web pages. The specific source for each of the examples presented is reported in parentheses at the end of the example, using the following abbreviations: SPOK, FIC, MAG, NEWS, ACAD.[19] Each source is complemented by the year of occurrence, to allow for an easier retrieval from the corpus. The examples are reported with a minimum portion of context that is necessary for comprehension. I highlighted the lexical item relevant for the discussion in bold. Lastly, I present my analysis of the data discussing one BTT at a time.

8.3 Sweet

The adjective *sweet* is the most numerous BTT in the COCA. The search for *sweet* yielded 32654 results. I manually analysed 1632 occurrences. Of these, 51.6% (843) were used non-literally. A number of occurrences of *sweet* are part of collocations,

---

[19] I integrated the discussion with examples retrieved later than the original corpus: their source therefore is BLOG, which was not among the sources available when I extracted the original data.

recurrent constructions, and formulaic language, which are nonetheless based on figurative elaborations.

The usage of the adjective *sweet* to conceptualise the semantic domain of LOVE, and related terms of endearment and affection is the most common within the corpus (22% of metaphorical occurrences), and it motivates a variety of conceptualisations that slightly differ from a semantic point of view. These include sex, kindness, cuteness, and personal attributes such as INNOCENCE. The general label LOVE includes a wide array of related concepts which are consistent in conceptualising a positive feeling. The standard usage of SWEET as a source domain for LOVE is in (27–29), where the feeling that develops among two individuals involved in a romantic relationship is described with reference to this taste type.

(27) Love felt real when the good times weren't as **sweet** when she wasn't there. [MAG 1994]

(28) She says it is almost unheard of for a musician to be as **sweet** and loving in real life as their songs suggest. [NEWS 2007]

(29) Life is hard, but love can make it **sweet**. [NEWS 1997]

The occurrences in the target domain of LOVE include also more general feelings of affection between individuals which are not necessarily related to romantic relationships, as in (30–31):

(30) The two beekeepers were **sweet** enough to name the two queens after my daughters, Olive and Zoe. (NEWS 2009)

(31) How **sweet** and wonderful that the police department is offering an apology. (NEWS 2012)

There are also more specific realisations that describe sex as being SWEET, as in (32–34):

(32) [. . .] whispering my undying love, actually coming to tears when we reached our **sweet** climax and lay beside each other, pleasantly exhausted. (FIC 1995)

(33) Itched to pull her dress down to bare the **sweet** darkness of her nipples. (FIC 2008)

(34) [. . .] there was no mystery about the curve of her breasts or the **sweet** little shape of her ass. (FIC 2009)

The general label of love does not exclusively refer to affection between human beings, but it extends also to pets:

(35) He's only a **sweet**, shaggy old mutt but I love him like mad. (FIC 2003)

(36) But there's not a mean bone in his body. He's a very **sweet** dog. (NEWS 1995)

The metaphorical realisations in (35–36) conceptualise the qualities of a pet (a dog, in this case) as *sweet*, in keeping with similar realisations that describe people and the affection for them as *sweet*. The utterances in (37–40) are motivated on the basis of a mapping that connects children and youth as sweet. I argue that this mapping is INNOCENCE IS SWEET, and it is particularly evident in (37):

(37) It gave her a **sweet**, innocent air that contrasted sharply with Autumn's black Goth outfit. (FIC 2011)

(38) A pastel sweater with a **sweet** bow and dirndl skirt are not appropriate for the workplace. (MAG 2005)

(39) Your baby ain't **sweet** like mine. (SPOK 2010)

(40) Like a hatchling, I was imprinted by gentle surroundings and **sweet** whimsy. (MAG 1990)

Alternative construals of the metaphorical meanings might be *naivety* (38, 40), or *cuteness* (39), but they are all consistent in describing a docile, gentle and harmless disposition, that is often associated with children. The same conceptual link motivates the metaphorical collocation in (41), which refers to the cultural practice of celebrating the coming of age on a teenager's sixteenth birthday (especially of girls in the US):

(41) America needs less **Sweet** 16 parents and more people willing to let their kids sacrifice temporary popularity. (NEWS 2006)

The conceptualisation of innocence and gentleness is consistently found at a discourse level in reference to women in a large number of occurrences. Consider the following (42–45):

(42) He'd forgotten how **sweet** she tasted, how soft she was in his arms. (FIC 1990)

(43) There was a rising tide of **sweet** femininity this spring, like lush floral flocks from Erdem, to counter the hard-edged sultriness dominating the runways. (MAG 2010)

(44) I've always thought you gentle, **sweet**, and full of feminine sensibilities. (FIC 2009)

(45) It's as if the pages of a bodice-ripping romance novel have come to life, with unassuming, chiseled young guys and busty, **sweet** young gals [. . .]. (NEWS 2004)

While some of the occurrences (e.g., 42, 44) might be interpreted as referring to love or sexual attraction, others reveal the more specific conceptualisation of feminine qualities as being *sweet*. These examples illustrate what Hines (1999) calls the WOMAN AS DESSERT metaphor. According to Hines, "there is a consistent, widespread, generally unconscious and undocumented metaphor in English equating women-as-sex-objects with desserts" (Hines 1999: 145), motivating both linguistic and behavioural realisations. Examples of the latter would be, for instance, women jumping out of cakes. The analysis proposed by Hines extends to expressions that do not involve the lexical item *sweet* (e.g., *creampuff, cheesecake,* etc.) but they show a well-established tendency and practice to conceptualise women as desirable sex objects with reference to desserts. She recognises the evolution of the metaphor as a blend of different conceptual mappings, stemming from a combination and elaboration on the ubiquitous PEOPLE ARE OBJECTS with ACHIEVING A DESIRED OBJECT IS GETTING SOMETHING TO EAT, with the cultural stereotype that women are sweet. Together, they result in WOMEN ARE SWEET OBJECTS (Hines 1999: 147). The equation of women not just to food, but specifically to peripheral food items motivates further elaboration that point to the derogatory use of such realisations towards women:

> As desserts, women can be bought and sold, eaten, elaborately decorated (as in the use of *frosting* to describe the makeup of beauty pageant contestants), admired for their outward appearance, dismissed as sinful and decadent – or, in the ultimate degradation, simply done without: desserts are optional/inessential, frivolous, perhaps even a waste of time.
> (Hines 1999: 148)

Hines' analysis is compelling in the description of gendered discourse and representations, and she rightly emphasises the sexual and sexist aspect to it. However, data from my corpus analysis suggest that the sexual perspective might be part of a larger complex of metaphorical usages. Consider examples (46) and (47)

(46) she was recently standing behind a **sweet** old lady counting out change [. . .]. (MAG 2013)

(47) To my **sweet** baby girl, it's been ten years now since you were born. (SPOK 1993)

Both examples refer to women, and yet neither have a sexual innuendo. Example (46) describes an old lady as *sweet,* and the usage of this adjective refers to a form of affection and gentleness. Example (47) instead refers to a 10-year-old girl and once again conveys a meaning closer to love and affection. Nonetheless, they both refer to women. The occurrences that explicitly refer to males are strikingly lower: 12 for males as opposed to 88 referring to females. The disparagement in conceptualisation between genders, and the widespread usage to refer to children and youth, suggests an even subtler metaphorisation pattern, based on gender stereotypes in Western society, according to which women are "the gentle sex"[20] and children are to be protected. The conceptualisation of attitudes, behaviours, and dispositions as sweet conceal a gendered stereotype of masculinity as rough and ungentle, as opposed to more sweet attributes, stereotypically associated with women and children. These occurrences may also be regarded as motivated by entailments of the LOVE IS SWEET metaphor. If we consider sex as part of the domain of love, then we may consider these realisations as motivated by the same metaphor: the fact that mainly women are talked about as "sex objects" may reveal the fact that, as Hines (1999) observes, standard English "largely means white, heterosexual, middle-class English" (Hines 1999: 149). The results of the corpus analysis confirm the existence of a continuum that spans from INNOCENCE IS SWEET, to LOVE IS SWEET, through stereotypical conceptualisations of gender.

From a pragmatic point of view, the adjective *sweet* may also be used in vocative constructions that describe the referent as being *sweet*. They invoke directly an individual, as in examples (48–50):

(48) "What was the pizza cutter for?" Nadine asked. "For cutting pizza, **sweet** Nadine". (FIC 2015)

---

20 Anecdotally, consider **Sugar** Kane, the name of Marylin Monroe's character in *Some Like it Hot* (1959), who sings in the ***Sweet*** *Sue and her Society Syncopators*; or the habit of considering *sweet* drinks as more suitable for women.

(49) Good night, **sweet** wife, my love. (SPOK 1990)

(50) Hi, **sweet** boy. How you doing? (SPOK 2001)

These realisations are most commonly found in direct speech, and in reference to women, although (50) directly refers to a *boy*. The usage of *sweet* in epithets and vocative constructions is well attested in English, especially in literary studies (see Busse 2006; Bagli 2016 for a discussion on Shakespeare's usage of vocative constructions involving *sweet*).

A similar class of occurrences is the usage of *sweet* in exclamations (51), possibly as a form of euphemism instead of using swear words, as in (52–53):

(51) That is so **sweet**! (SPOK 2011)

(52) **Sweet** Jesus! (FIC 1998)

(53) [. . .] for Christ's **sweet** fucking sake [. . .]. (FIC 1993)

The most common referent for this type of exclamation is Jesus Christ, as in (52–53), but similar realisations include expressions such as (51), where *sweet* is used as describing a general situation with no specific reference. The usage of *sweet* in exclamations seem to fit with the conceptual metaphor VALUE IS SWEET, which emerged from the lexical data of the MMP. Examples in (54) and (55) instantiate this metaphorical mapping:

(54) It's why SolarCity is fighting. It's a **sweet** deal for them. (NEWS 2015)

(55) [. . .] One thing FONU2 does have is a **sweet** lease on public land. (NEWS 2015)

There are a number of mappings that seem related to the conceptual metaphor VALUE IS SWEET, such as SUCCESS/REWARD IS SWEET (56–58):

(56) the **sweet** taste of success. (SPOK 2010)

(57) he'll find that the rewards are immeasurably **sweet.** (NEWS 2000)

(58) A child can savor the **sweet** opportunity of playing on a level field against his peers, siblings or parents. (NEWS 1992)

Or even the conceptualisation of easiness and functionality as *sweet* (59–61):

(59) The discovery of neutron stars was swift and **sweet**. (MAG 2005)

(60) but lately, that **sweet** efficiency has eroded. (NEWS 2014)

(61) It's a little pocket of palm trees with tropical birds and **sweet**, grippy bouldering. (MAG 2003)

The conceptual metaphor VALUE IS SWEET accounts also for the motivation of the collocation *sweet spot*. It refers to a particularly advantageous or pleasant position. In sports, it refers to "the point on a bat, club, racket, etc., at which it makes most effective contact with the ball" (OED *sweet*, adj. and adv., compound *sweet spot*). Wikipedia reports similar uses in jargons such as Acoustics (focal point between two speakers, where an individual is fully capable of hearing the stereo audio mix the way it was intended to be heard by the mixer); or even in Economics (i.e., the setting of a policy that results in the optimum balance of costs and benefits). The occurrences retrieved in the corpus further elaborate on the concept and yield expressions such as (62) and (63)

(62) The key is to hit these restaurants in the **"sweet spot"** of their cycle of rise and fall. (NEWS 2012)

(63) Each drive delivers either 240GB or 256 GB of storage which is the current **sweet spot** in the balance between price and performance. (MAG 2013)

Finally, a number of occurrences conceptualise a general positive feeling of appreciation and pleasure, as in (64–66).

(64) It was hard, but it was so **sweet** to see him. (SPOK 2012)

(65) Just over a year ago, life seemed **sweet** for the Wilsons. (MAG 1996)

(66) Elsewhere, my brother was bedded down beside his lovely wife, his girls dreaming **sweet** dreams down the hall. (FIC 2005)

I argue that the meaning of the adjective *sweet* in sentences (64–66) is motivated by the conceptual metonymy SWEET FOR PLEASANT. In earlier contributions, I analysed occurrences of this type as motivated by the conceptual metaphor PLEASURE IS SWEET. Such position is maintained by Kövecses (2019), among others. I would like to propose a slightly different analysis, considering physical and biological reaction to exposure to sweet. Ingestion of sugars triggers the reward-mechanism in the human body; it elicits an instinctually positive facial response in infants, even in anencephalic individuals, thus suggesting a strongly embodied and physiological response to the experience of this sensation. Thus, a metonymic explanation seems more accurate to account for the construction of meaning attributed to the adjective *sweet*: the cause (i.e., *sweet*) is the vehicle to access the result (i.e., *pleasure*); instantiating CAUSE FOR RESULT. Such an account subsumes the conceptualisation of the act of perception as an event, in which tasting sweetness and experiencing pleasure happen following a rapid chain of events.

8.4 Bitter

The case of the conceptualisation of bitter is peculiar and different from other taste terms, as this gustatory adjective is used more frequently in its metaphorical meanings than in its literal counterpart. Overall, this taste term mainly intervenes in conceptualizing negative feelings and divisive situations, such as, divorce, fight, and attack. The figurative occurrences however mainly fall into two large groups of conceptual metaphors, namely CONFLICT IS BITTER, and DISAPPOINTMENT IS BITTER.

The largest metaphorical mapping that involves bitterness is the conceptual metaphor CONFLICT IS BITTER. I chose the label conflict as an umbrella term that covers different realisations and more specific concepts that share an idea of friction, anger, hostility, and sometimes even violence between two sides. This whole array of divisive feelings and sensations is conceptualised as bitterness, but there are consistent lexical patterns. One group of such occurrences is *divorce*, as in (67) and (68).

(67) And when people get divorced or break up, they're angry or they're **bitter**, and there's so many emotions. (SPOK 2012)

(68) When he hired me to come to Megiddo, Norris had just finalized a **bitter** divorce. (2009 FIC)

Furthermore, the feelings and emotions that this taste conceptualise often relate more explicitly to *anger* and *revenge*, as in (69–71):

(69) ·I grow hyperbolic, say I'm small-minded and petty, still **bitter** after all these years, calculating acts of mental revenge [. . .]. (FIC 1994)

(70) Benteen was a **bitter**, mean, vindictive, wise and foresighted man. (NEWS 1991)

(71) Some people go through hard times, become angry and **bitter** as a result and stay stuck in that bad place. (MAG 2014)

The physical sensations of bitterness are also often used to describe war related terms (72), which in turn are often used to metaphorically refer to discussions and quarrels, as in examples (73–75):

(72) **Bitter** conflicts in Liberia and Somalia call into question the viability of these states as coherent entities. (ACAD 1992)

(73) The federal government's last attempt to convict Gotti on racketeering charges provoked a **bitter** feud between the FBI and the federal prosecutor. (NEWS 1992)

(74) That is a **bitter** debate going forward. (SPOK 2013)

(75) it became a topic of **bitter** dispute inside the administration. (MAG 2009)

The concept of CONFLICT not only involves feelings evoked by conflictual situations, but it also includes feelings between people (76–77):

(76) To motivate voters, Virginia's **bitter** rivals for governor reached out to the same figure on the weekend before Election Day: President Obama. (NEWS 2013)

(77) **Bitter** enemies, Butt and Hamilton ran against each other for president in 1800. (MAG 2012)

Moving along the continuum of negative emotions, the same gustatory sensation may be used to conceptualise feelings of hatred and meanness (78–79):

(78) found my **bitter** hatred for them changed to loving. (MAG 2012)

(79) and so he grows **bitter**, cynical, and withdrawn. (MAG 2010)

A number of occurrences are consistent in conceptualizing angry and laconic words, comments, and thoughts as bitter, as in (80) and (81):

(80) the **bitter** comments made in the course of prolonged debates. (ACAD 2001)

(81) "He's gone," Mrs. Deene said, her words gratingly **bitter**. (FIC 2012)

The sentence in (81) represents a case in point of the vagueness and dynamicity of meaning creation: the figurative usage of bitterness in such an example may refer to anger, but it may even refer to disappointment. The concept DISAPPOINTMENT is the other large target domain that is conceptualised by bitterness. The occurrences motivated by this mapping are less numerous, but among them there are some instantiations that require further comments. The label of DISAPPOINTMENT includes feelings of regret, loss, defeat, and failure as in the following examples (82–85).

(82) The difference between now and then is a century's worth of **bitter**, disillusioning experience. (MAG 2003)

(83) I, who defied the lackeys of the regime and remained loyal to my homeland and who now have to eat the **bitter** bread of defeat along with all those former lackeys [. . .]. (FIC 1999)

(84) An hour earlier, as the Rams streamed back into the locker room after suffering yet another **bitter**, down-to-the-wire loss [. . .]. (NEWS 2013)

(85) "I have observed presidential candidates who take the loss and become angry, **bitter**, look around for somebody to blame for the failures", he says. (MAG 2009)

A similar conceptualisation to the DISAPPOINTMENT IS BITTER mapping, is the collocation *to the bitter end*, which metaphorically refers to "to the last and direst extremity; to death itself" (OED *bitter*, adj., 2.b). A total of 3% of the analysed occurrences displayed such a pattern (86):

(86) If Saddam persuades his troops to keep fighting till the **bitter end**, the scene of battle will shift to cityscapes that look more like Atlanta (or pre-war Beirut) than like the open desert (NEWS 1991).

According to the OED, the collocation *to the bitter end* does not undoubtedly refer to gustatory sensations, but it may have a different origin. In nautical jargon (OED, *bitter*, n.3), a bit is "one of the strong posts firmly fastened in pairs at the deck or decks of a ship, for fastening cables, belaying ropes, etc.". According to Smith's Seaman Grammar (1627), a "bitter" is the turn of a cable around the Bitts; and in 1867 Smyth, in his *The sailor's word-book* defines this collocation as follows: "A ship is 'brought up to a bitter' when the cable is allowed to run out to that stop. When a chain or rope is paid out to the bitter-end, no more remains to be let go". The OED however regards this etymology as dubious and lists the collocation also in reference to gustatory bitter. Among the occurrences I found, (87) is ambiguous and seems to refer to the homonym bitter (nautics) as opposed to bitter (taste):

(87) A few feet up rope from the **bitter end**, my cramping, white-knuckled hands were doing their best to keep a grip [. . .]. (NEWS 1995)

In both cases the collocation would be metaphorical. If we consider it as deriving from *bitter* in nautical terms, then the rope corresponds to life, and so coming to *the bitter end* metaphorically would refer to the end of life. At the same time, if we considered *bitter* as referring to gustatory terms, it would describe death as bitter, as motivated by the conceptualisations of DISAPPOINTMENT as bitter.

Another realisation of the DISAPPOINTMENT IS BITTER mapping is the usage of bitter in describing reality, as in examples (88) and (89):

(88) I was ready to kind of accept the **bitter** reality that it wasn't going to work. (SPOK 2013)

(89) We have to face that **bitter** reality. (NEWS 1990)

In these occurrences, reality may be described as bitter because it does not correspond to our expectations, and therefore it is disappointing. At the same time, the usage of bitter in (88) and (89) may be consistent with other realisations that use bitter to conceptualise something difficult to accept, thus yielding the conceptual metaphor DIFFICULTY OF ACCEPTANCE IS BITTER. This metaphor mainly motivates collocations with the noun *pill* in (90) and (91):

(90) It's a **bitter pill**, but we had to swallow it [. . .]. (NEWS 1993)

(91) For Dor, the loss of his home province, to which he would never again return, was a particularly **bitter pill** to swallow. (MAG 2007)

The conceptual metaphor DIFFICULTY OF ACCEPTANCE IS BITTER is a cognate with other, well-established conceptual metaphors such as IDEAS ARE FOOD, ACQUIRING IDEAS IS EATING, and ACCEPTING IS SWALLOWING (see EnMetaNet wiki). The conceptual link between bitterness and difficulty of acceptance is old, and it is already found in some of the earliest attestations in the history of Western literature. The Roman poet Lucretius, in his *De Rerum Natura* (1ˢᵗ century BC) uses an extended gustatory metaphor to conceptualise philosophy, poetry, and knowledge (book 1, vv. 937–943; in Ferguson Smith 2001: 28):

> For obviously my technique does not lack a motive. Doctors who try to give the children **foul-tasting wormwood** first coat the rim of the cup with the sweet juice of golden honey; their intention is that the children, unwary at their tender age, will be tricked into applying their lips to the cup and at the same time will drain the **bitter draught of wormwood** – victims of beguilement, but not of betrayal, since by this means they recover strength and health.

According to Lucretius, Epicureanism (the philosophical system that he adhered to, and about which *De Rerum Natura* was written) is a *bitter medicine* (De Rerum Natura I, 931–50, Ferguson Smith 2001: 28–29; IV, 8–25, Ferguson Smith 2001: 100–101). As the doctor would put honey on the rim of a cup containing bitter-tasting wormwood, to make it more palatable and easier to swallow, so the poet would use poetry and musicality to make the ideas contained in it more acceptable. The sophisticated usage of this metaphor is not far from the realisations in (90–91), where a difficult situation is conceptualised as a *bitter pill*, which *has to be swallowed*.

Bitterness also occurs in the conceptualisation and description of *irony* and *mockery*, as in (92) and (93):

(92) But in a **bitter** irony, Gorbachev was more admired abroad than at home. (NEWS 1991)

(93) Many of the workers recount how losing their jobs on that day, with scant possibilities of finding work in the height of an acute economic crisis, made a **bitter** mockery of the direness of their situation. (ACAD 2008)

The OED reports as ultimate origin of the word *irony* (OED, *irony*, n.) the Ancient Greek εἴρων (Eng. 'dissembler'). The connection between this concept and violence may be better sketched if compared to the etymology of the word *sarcasm*, a form of "bitter irony" (OED *sarcasm*), which ultimately derives from Ancient Greek σαρκασμός (sarkasmos), from the cognate verb σαρκάζειν, which means "to tear flesh, gnash the teeth, speak bitterly" (OED *sarcasm*, n.). Sarcastic words and speech are conceptualised as a painful entity, and they share the same root with verbs that unequivocally depict forms of violence and pain. Notably, the conceptual link between irony and pain is found across various Indo-European languages: Fr. *ironie tranchante*, Sp. *ironia cortante*, It. *ironia tagliente*, 'cutting irony'; Fr. *ironie mordante, glaçante*, 'biting, freezing irony'. In English, this conceptual link is instantiated by the dead metonymy BITTER FOR PAINFUL TOUCH and is realised in occurrences such as (92) and (93), (see Chapter 9.5.2).

A last case of figurative uses related to the concept of BITTERNESS are those in which this gustatory sensation is used in constructions based on the event-frame, according to which CHANGE IS MOVEMENT (94–95):

(94) We do not get **bitter** when God teaches us lessons, we get better! (MAG 2001)

(95) But as the years roll by, these government officials repeatedly fail to give Red what he seeks, and so he grows **bitter**, cynical, and withdrawn [. . .]. (MAG 2010)

From a lexical aspectual point of view, these constructions may be defined as inchoative: they describe the initial stage of a transformation that has bitterness as its final stage. The figurative meaning of *bitterness* is consistent with conceptualisations found in other occurrences, and therefore are motivated by the general metaphors discussed: either DISAPPOINTMENT IS BITTER (94) or CONFLICT IS BITTER (95). These occurrences share a similar structure with occurrences found for *sour*, but these are less numerous in the whole corpus.

The concept of BITTERNESS intervenes in the conceptualisation of negative and unpleasant feelings and domains, but the array of negative feelings it conceptualises is vast and it ranges from anger to failure, from death to pain. The figurative meaning of this taste type is consistent with the embodied and hedonic value of the sensation. The general conceptual mechanism that unifies the negative value of *bitter* may be considered to be the metonymy BITTER FOR UNPLEASANT, motivated by the experience of ingesting bitter substances, which elicits a negative embodied response.

8.5 Sour

The figurative uses of *sour* are close to the conceptualisation of bitterness. More specifically, sourness conceptualises a general meaning of stagnation and unpleasantness, but also a hostile disposition towards someone or something, which is generally more violent than the figurative value of bitterness. While bitterness seems to refer to a more permanent feeling of uneasiness and unpleasantness, *sour* conveys a feeling of decay and spoilage. This is often found in inchoative constructions of the type *to go sour* (96), that mark the initial stage of a process that will end in a nasty, negative situation. This usage is similar to the inchoative constructions that have *bitter* as their final stage; but they are more frequent in usage with *sour*. Furthermore, *sour* may be used as a verb by means of zero affixation, as in (97). In the cases in which *sour* is used as a verb, it conceptualises the process of *becoming sour*:

(96) This was the first and only time in my life a date had gone **sour** like this (MAG 1990).

(97) Public attitudes toward higher education will **sour**, and public funding will be in increasingly short supply (MAG 2009).

The source domain for this metaphorical mapping refers to physical processes of deterioration, such as meat and dairy products (which typically go sour when they expire). Therefore, sour is an undesirable, final stage of food that once was edible, desirable, and consumable, but which has gone bad. The conceptual link that motivates this realisation is a metonymy EFFECT FOR CAUSE: SOUR FOR SPOILAGE. Example (98) contains an occurrence that albeit literal, exemplifies the development of the metaphorical meaning from a literal description:

(98) Eventually someone gave her an H_2S[21] detector, which she clipped to her collar whenever she approached a well that had turned **"sour"** enough to be hazardous. (MAG 2013)

This occurrence may be regarded as emblematic of the shift from perceptual sourness to figurative sourness. This is because H_2S may be perceived as sour. At the same time, in the context of drilling that characterises the utterance in (98), it is an entire well that presents high levels of H_2S and it has become *hazardous*.

Some related realisations specifically refer to the Economy (99), conceptualising an economic situation as *sour*. This realisation is related to previous ones because the economy *turns sour* after a prolonged period of crisis:

(99) During good times, such schemes prosper, but as the economy turns **sour**, investors start demanding their money back and the fraudster can't cover it. (NEWS 2009)

---

21 H_2S is Hydrogen sulfide, a natural gas commonly found during drilling and typically having a characteristic foul odour of rotten eggs; it is dangerous: poisonous, corrosive and inflammable.

The gustatory quality of *sour* not only signals the final stage of food that has rotten, but it may also refer to the initial stage of fruit that is not ready to be consumed yet. This physical quality is at the basis of formulaic expressions such as *sour grapes* (100)

(100) Also, O'Brien's **sour grapes** after his failure does not give us any confidence in his counseling mediation skills. (NEWS 2000)

The origins of this metaphorical mapping lie in the popular fable *The fox and the grapes* by ancient Greek writer Æsop. The original expression was *the grapes are sour*, and now it is most commonly referred to just as *sour grapes*; it refers to "a person [who] is heard to disparage something which it is suspected he would be glad to possess if he could" (OED *grape*, n.1, 1.a). Thus, sour is the phase of the gustatory qualities of something that is not as it should be: either because it is in its initial stage (like grapes that are sour before being ripe) or because it is in its final stage (dairy, meat, water is *sour* when it goes bad). While bitterness is a permanent physical attribute (bitter weeds are always bitter), sour represents a phase, a stage in a transformative process, and it describes an undesirable and non-complying characteristic of something. In the majority of cases, this characteristic is food spoilage.

Another common figurative usage of *sour* is exemplified in (101–103):

(101) Then she caught a glimpse of Frankenstein's **sour** expression, and laughed some more. (FIC 1995)

(102) Docter said the character originated from one of his old drawings: an old man with a grouchy, **sour** face and a handful of balloons. (NEWS 2009)

(103) A 90-year-old photograph on the wall of Falk's office shows her in a pince-nez, mouth turned down and a **sour** look on her face. (NEWS 1998)

Examples in (101–103) are consistent in describing an individual's attitude and disposition as *sour*, which in these cases conceptualise a hostile and particularly negative distinctive mark in someone's expression. I identify the metaphorical mapping that motivates these linguistics expressions as A HOSTILE TEMPER IS SOUR. The linguistic realisations of this mapping include the description of expression, face, look, and smirk as *sour*. I grouped the realisations exemplified in (101–103) together, and considered them as motivated by the same mapping, because they all metonymically refer to someone's attitude. The metonymy that motivates these realisations is of the type RESULTS FOR CAUSE: the facial expression stands for the attitude that caused it.

The perception of sour is often found in conceptualisations that figuratively characterise hostility, as in examples (104–105):

(104) Why are you like **sour** milk to me? (FIC 1994)

(105) The **sour** old bastard called everyone by some derisive nickname [. . .]. (FIC 2015)

The metaphoricity of example (104) does not lie in the adjective, which is used literally, rather it is the whole grammatical and syntactic construction that instantiates the metaphor by means of a simile. It illustrates the prototypical source of *sourness*, which is milk and dairy products. Moreover, such realisation shows by means of a comparison the association of a person to a food and their character to its taste. Similarly, example (105) describes an individual as *sour*, and this usage of the adjective and its meaning is reminiscent of the usages of *bitter*. The semantic differences between sour and bitter in this context are minimal, as both conceptualise negative attitudes and feelings; yet, considering the other occurrences of sour and its more ephemeral and transitory nature, I would suggest that *sour* be more offensive and hostile than *bitter*. While *bitter* conceptualises anger and long-standing conflictual situations, *sour* has a more transient and vitriolic nature. Of course, establishing the difference between the two realisations is almost a moot point, and exact differences (if any) should be verified by further research involving native speakers' judgements.

Other realisations which are also similar to the conceptualisations of *bitter* are illustrated in (106–108):

(106) Luke couldn't remember or share. For him the **sour** reality had been a series of illnesses stealing his father's youth away. (FIC 1998)

(107) A **sour** disillusionment is reflected in the streets, where people see no way of resuscitating trade [. . .]. (NEWS 1993)

(108) For Philip, a graduate of the 1976 uprisings now in his mid-thirties, the possibility represents a **sour** irony. (FIC 1992)

The example in (106) is reminiscent of the mapping DIFFICULTY OF ACCEPTANCE IS BITTER; (107) is close to DISAPPOINTMENT IS BITTER, and (108) is a cognate with the realisations of irony and sarcasm as bitterness. I argue that the occurrences exemplified in (106–108) are motivated more by the lexical and semantic association in usage between *sour* and *bitter*, than by distinct mappings related to sourness. The realisations with *sour* for such expressions are limited in number, and their structure almost directly mirrors similar realisations of bitter. Therefore, I argue that more than separate realisations of frequent figurative meanings of sour, these realisations use *sour* instead of *bitter*, in keeping with their conceptual closeness and interchangeability. Although the perception of bitterness and sour are physically distinct (and humans are able to distinguish between the two, see Paragraph 6.3), their linguistic representation and figurative uses share some characteristics that relate to the conceptual confusion.

8.6 Salty

The figurative occurrences of *salty* are less numerous than the other taste types (17.9% of the occurrences analysed), and in general it is the physiological taste term least represented in the COCA. The figurative processes involved in the conceptualisation of this taste word do not show significant variation, as they did for the other taste types. Rather, the 21 figurative occurrences are motivated by the same conceptual mechanism. The most common figurative meaning of *salty* conceptualises rudeness, as in (109) and (110)

(109) To his credit, Munnings did not try to soften his Suffolk accent or change his **salty** language or his raffish style or dress. (MAG 2006)

(110) Yes, it was the same deer – when a **salty** vaquero spreads his hands that wide, holds his fingers that high, and counts six up on a side, we are talking about the same deer. (MAG 1993)

The figurative use of salty to conceptualise rudeness and non-sophistication is glossed by the OED as "piquant, racy" (*salty*, adj., 3), exemplified in (114). Similar usages retrieved in the sample mainly exemplify the meaning of vulgarity, as in (111–113).

(111) "I'm exhausted every night," Mr. Neeson says, plugging his new film near the start of his run in the show, playing the love-smitten stoker opposite Natasha Richardson's **salty** reformed hooker. (NEWS 1993)

(112) I smile, half smile, imagining the weary young sergeant writing the message, hiding his own fear behind **salty** tough-cop cleverness. (FIC 2014)

(113) Above anything, I hope I made the characters of Frank (Harris' **salty** Irishman) and Walter (Duvall's quiet Cuban) as real as possible. (NEWS 1994)

(114) This..only makes the books more **salty**; and we must add, that the **piquancy** is not diminished by [etc.]. (Athenæum 10 Mar. 332/2; 1866)

In (114), the adjective *salty* is paired with the noun *piquancy*, which is defined in its first meaning as "A pleasant or invigorating sharpness or pungency of taste or smell; zest, tang; an appetizing flavour" (OED *piquancy* n., 1), and in its second, figurative meaning as "The quality (in speech, manner, style, etc.) of being stimulating, exciting, or charming; poignancy; bite" (OED *piquancy*, n., 2. a). An example of this meaning is reported in (115):

(115) Some standing jest that may give rellish and **picquancy** to all the other insipid and phlegmatick parts of the discourse. (S. Parker *Reproof Rehearsal Transprosed* 249; 1673)

The adjective *racy* on the other hand originally referred to wine "having a distinctively strong taste or odour; piquant, pungent, or flavourful" (OED *racy*, adj., 1.a), but it also had a meaning of "Of a person or personal attribute: having a distinctive lively or spirited quality" (OED *racy*, adj., 3.a, now obsolete). This meaning developed into 3.c: "of speech, writing, performance, etc.: having a characteristic vigour, liveliness, or piquancy" (OED *racy*, adj., 3.c, first attestation c1817), and only later it evolved into 3.d: "Daring, bold; suggestive, slightly indecent, risqué" (OED *racy*, adj., 3.d). The first attestation for this meaning in the OED dates to 1901 (116):

(116) Women who tell **racy** stories..can rouse a great deal of enthusiasm in a room full of men. (P. Bee *Vagaries of Men* 107; 1901)

The figurative meanings of adjectives *salty, piquant,* and *racy* describe a state of liveliness and excitement, which qualifies as a distinctive attribute of someone or something. The physical capacity of salt to enhance taste is metaphorically transferred to an intensification of personal characteristics that may result as vulgar. This metaphorical correlation elaborates on the conceptual metaphor CHARACTER IS TASTE, and instantiates the entailment BEING VULGAR IS HAVING TOO MUCH TASTE.

There is however also another possible interpretation of the figurative meaning of *salty*. According to the Merriam-Webster dictionary,[22] this meaning originated in reference to sailors, particularly their speech. They had a reputation for "colourful" language, full of character and personality. In the 1930s, it came to mean "explosive anger", and according to the dictionary this was related to fishermen, and their distinctive propensity to cursing. The same etymological link is quoted by the OED, which reports a usage related to *Nautical slang* (*salty*, adj.1, 4), meaning "tough, hard-bitten"; and meaning 5, which is "angry, irritated, hostile". The nautical origin of the usage is evident in (117), where a fisherman is described as *salty*:

(117) Some areas are better than others, and the **salty** fisherman learns to anticipate the hot spots. (NEWS 1996)

In this line of semantic development, the meaning of *salty* is less connected to gustatory perception, than it is to the visual or haptic qualities of objects (or people) covered in salt, as a consequence of their prolonged exposure to this substance during their life in the sea. Duly, there is evidence in the COCA for the metonymic use of *salty* to describe naval objects as in (118) and (119):

(118) the Swift Trawler 42, a modern cruiser that blended **salty**, traditional styling with top-shelf amenities. (MAG 2011)

(119) The tasteful interior is warm, with a "**salty**" ambiance. (MAG 2000)

Unfortunately, there are no definitive data to ascertain whether the meaning of *salty* to describe rudeness, vulgarity, and coarseness in current usage developed from gustatory perception through the metaphor CHARACTER IS TASTE, or through visual or haptic perception in reference to exposure to sea-salt. However, the two distinct lines of semantic development need not exclude one another, rather they may have contributed and reinforced each other, building on perceptual correspondences motivated by real-life experiences and encyclopaedic knowledge, and by taste conceptualisation.

---

[22] https://www.merriam-webster.com/words-at-play/salty-meaning, last accessed 12 August 2020.

8.7 Spicy

The metaphorical conceptualisations of *spicy* are not frequent in the corpus I selected, but they are representative of its usage. The mechanism found in the meaning expansion of spiciness is the metaphor EXCITEMENT IS SPICINESS, which motivates realisations connected to sex (120) and a general feeling of excitement (121):

(120) The Blackstreet video told a "break up and make up" story (as one of the teens labeled it) by juxtaposing saccharin lyrics with **spicy** visuals that encouraged erotic readings. (ACAD 1999)

(121) It's nothing more than a **spicy** bit of gossip, until someone does something stupid. (FIC 2008)

The occurrences in (120) and (121) conceptualise a reference to sex and eroticism as *spicy*. The embodied motivation of this mapping is related to the physical reaction to sexual arousal, which involves increased blood pressure and temperature, in the same fashion as consumption of capsaicin. A similar mapping is related to temperature perception, which motivates the polysemy of *hot* and its usage in conceptualizing sexual arousal, as in (122)

(122) Speaking of **hot** men, Magic Mike XXL hits theaters. (SPOK 2015)

The metaphorical understanding of sexual excitement as spiciness may be considered a primary metaphor, as the correlation between the two concepts is rooted in direct, embodied experience.

Another realisation of the same metaphorical link conveys a more general meaning of liveliness. These realisations are closely connected to the previous one, and motivate occurrences as (123):

(123) What made me a star, I expect, was my own songs like "The lonesome Crow" and "Cropper's Sorrow" and the **spicy** string-ring I could conjure for the more mellow stuff. (FIC 2003)

The motivation behind this realisation is best exemplified in (124), where the item *spicy* is used literally, but the context of the sentence elaborates it in a figurative way.

(124) Steamed crabs had begun to show up as snacks in bars and amusement parks, and soon **spicy** versions were replacing the less lively ones. (NEWS 1996)

In (124), the adjective spicy describes food (i.e., crab snacks), but the spicy version of this food is said to replace the "less lively" version, thus instantiating the conceptual link between SPICINESS and EXCITEMENT. This metaphorical link is consistent in motivating also realisations involving the verb *to spice up* (which however is not part of the corpus), as in (125):

(125) Garden fountains are a great way to **spice up** your garden. (BLOG 2012)

The embodied thermal reaction to spiciness, which is at the basis of the metaphorical usage of SPICINESS to describe sex, is also at the basis of the iconic representation of spiciness as a flame. The connection with flames might also serve as a ground for the conceptualisation of EXCITEMENT and MOVEMENT. Furthermore, this conceptualisation is also found in the domain of food description and perception: a "flat" taste may be enlivened by adding some flavour, e.g., spices, with the result of having a livelier gustatory experience, which in turn is metaphorically extended to other domains as in (125).

8.8 Savoury

The last Basic Taste Term that I investigated is *savoury*. This term did not yield a high number of occurrences, and even less figurative ones. In fact, out of 77 occurrences analysed, only 1 was metaphorical (126):

(126) Many of the fighters motivated to take on the Islamic State are not the most **savoury** of characters [. . .]. (NEWS 2015)

The figurative usage of *savoury* in (126) conceptualises the legal status and attitude of people. The same figurative mechanism motivates the polysemy of the adjective *unsavoury*, as in (127):

(127) The use of heroin on the backstretch lured a number of **unsavoury** characters, mainly addicts hoping to get a fix. (BLOG 2012)

According to the OED, the adjective *unsavoury* has the meaning of "Objectionable on moral grounds; having an unpleasant or disagreeable character or association" (OED *unsavoury*, adj., 4). The sentence in (126), although presents the adjective *savoury*, it contextually realises the same meaning of *unsavoury*. However, *savoury* has also the figurative meaning (now obsolete) of "Renowned for holiness or piety; of saintly repute or memory" (OED *savoury*, adj., 2b). These two uses related to these taste words suggest the existence of a metaphorical link between morality and savoury, thus yielding the conceptual metaphor MORALITY IS SAVOURY. A cognate realisation may be in the figurative conceptualisation of the word *tasty*, which, according to the data from the MMP, instantiates a weak metaphorical link between the category 1I10 *Taste* and category 3E01 *Law*. The adjective *tasty* may be used in mainly US slang to refer to someone who's known by the police and has a criminal record (OED *tasty*, adj., 1.c).

8.9 What do taste words mean when they are used figuratively?

The present chapter presents a corpus analysis of the figurative conceptualisations and meanings of the Basic Taste Terms (BTT) in English that were identified and discussed in Chapter 4. The analysis was carried out using the COCA, one of the largest corpora available for the English language. The first result to be discussed is that the different BTTs do not share the same frequency values, neither in sheer number of occurrences, nor in their metaphorisation rates. The most frequent BTT in the COCA is the item *sweet*, followed by *bitter, sour, salty, spicy* and *savoury*. The term *sweet* also has a high number of metaphorical realisations in comparison to the other BTTs, but the adjective with the highest metaphorisation rate is the BTT *bitter* (78,6%).

The figurative usages of BTTs are largely motivated by the embodied perception and evolutionary value of the single items. The figurative meaning of *sweet* is mainly based on the general conceptual metonymy SWEET FOR PLEASANT, which in turn motivates more specific metaphorical mappings and entailments such as LOVE IS SWEET, and VALUE IS SWEET. Overall, the lexical item *sweet* conceptualises a positive meaning, in keeping with the embodied value of this taste type.

Conversely, the lexical item *bitter* only conceptualises negative feelings and situations, through the conceptual metonymy BITTER FOR UNPLEASANT, which lies at the basis for conceptual metaphors such as CONFLICT IS BITTER, and DISAPPOINTMENT IS BITTER. Similarly, the lexical item *sour* is used as Source Domain in the conceptualisation of states that differ from the expectations, and it draws on prototypical situations in which sourness is present in food, i.e., ripeness of fruit or spoilage of dairy. The figurative mechanisms that involve SOUR as a source domain are largely related to the metonymical elaboration SOUR FOR SPOILAGE, and then metaphorically expand to refer to other domains, such as ECONOMY, and ATTITUDES. The most frequent conceptual metaphor that involves SOUR as a source domain is HOSTILE TEMPER IS SOUR. Notably, some of the metaphorical realisations of *sour* share the same syntactic and semantic structure of metaphorical elaborations of *bitter*, while a small number of conceptual elaborations involving *bitter* share the same syntactic construction that is typically associated with *sour* (i.e., inchoative constructions). I argue that these shared constructions build on the conceptual association between the two taste types.

The BTTs *salty, spicy,* and *savoury* did not yield a wide variety of figurative realisations, but each of them has a figurative value. The term *salty* is used to refer to rudeness and non-refinedness. The semantic development of this figurative meaning may have followed two distinct, yet intertwined trajectories. Despite both possibilities are based in perceptual language, only one of them involves the gustatory metaphor CHARACTER IS TASTE, while the other is based on visual and haptic properties of salt. The figurative elaboration of *spicy* through the metaphor EXCITEMENT IS SPICY is based on embodied experiences. The conceptualisation of *sexual excitement* as SPICY represents a case of primary correlation, motivated by shared embodied responses of the two phenomena, such as increased blood pressure and heat. The other metaphorical realisations of *spicy* conceptualise *liveliness*. This correlation is motivated by the iconic association to fire and flames. Lastly, the only metaphorical occurrence retrieved for *savoury* instantiates a conceptual metaphor that is currently mainly realised with its antonym, mainly *unsavoury*. The polysemy of both lexical items however is based on the conceptual metaphor MORALITY IS TASTE. Other realisations of this metaphor are currently either obsolete (e.g., *savoury* for "saint"), or part of substandard English (e.g., *tasty* for "with a legal record").

It is relevant at this point to keep in mind a punctualisation of the previous chapters' results. Overall, the linguistic data discussed so far show recurrent patterns of conceptual elaboration. Firstly, the concept *sweet* is the most salient item in the lexical domain of TASTE, and it is widely used as source domain in conceptual metaphors that have a positive meaning. Secondly, the continuum between *sour* and *bitter* observed through the categorisation tasks presented earlier is also found at a metaphorical level, as evinced from the figurative elaborations of the two terms. Despite their distinct nature, the two items often serve as source domain for similar target domains, thus reinforcing the claim that the confusion between the two labels in taste recognition tasks is based in the English culture-specific usage of the terms. Crucially, both terms have a general negative meaning, which results from metonymic elaboration. Thirdly, the relationship between *salty* and *spicy* emerging from the sorting tasks may be observed also at a metaphorical level. The semantic path of metaphorical elaboration of *salty* as *rudeness* includes intermediate conceptual steps through piquancy and raciness, which are figuratively used to convey a sense of liveliness and excitement. This same meaning is retained by *spicy*, which is also used to conceptualise sexual arousal. Another taste type that is used in reference to sex is *sweet*, however the connotation of the two types is dramatically different, in keeping with the variety of domains that both these terms construe. Lastly, the adjective *savoury* is only found in one metaphorical occurrence, thus not providing a solid base for any generalization.

Taken all together, the data retrieved through corpus analysis show that the role of gustatory perception in grounding linguistic phenomena is consistent, and it urges for a reconsideration of the sense of taste in contemporary linguistic and philosophical debate. The conceptual metaphors retrieved in contemporary English have been motivating semantic change for many centuries. Notably, some of these metaphors were observed through lexicographic data coming from MMP. The semantic conceptualisations of the various taste types that emerge from corpus data follow embodied patterns of elaboration and are based on the biological role that gustatory perception has played in human evolution. Cross-linguistic data show that this is not always the case: sweetness may have negative meanings, while bitterness may take on positive meanings. In this perspective, the results offer a variegated insight on the relationship between biology, culture, and our cognitive processes.

9 Intrafield metaphors

9.1 Introduction

The issue of metaphorical transfer within perception language has ignited debates and stimulated multiple contributions in recent years and represent a theoretical conundrum for psychologists, philosophers and linguists. Adjectives such as *smooth*, *rough*, and *dry* may be successfully employed to describe taste, but in sensory norms they were predominantly associated to touch (Lynott and Connell 2009). Adjectives such as *sour* and *sweet* may be used to talk about smells, and may also refer to sounds, e.g., *a sour note* or *a sweet voice*.

The usage of lexical items commonly associated to a modality and transferred to another instantiates cases of "Intrafield" metaphors (Matisoff 1978; Vanhove 2008; Speed, O'Meara et al. 2019). Intrafield metaphors are figurative expressions in which the lexical items of both source and target domain belong to one of the five perceptual modalities in folk model systems, i.e., "traditionally" called synaesthetic metaphors. Research in Intrafield metaphor posits relevant issues that need to be investigated. As some scholars have argued (Rakova 2003; Winter 2019a, 2019b) the semantic transfer identified in Intrafield metaphors might be successfully analysed as a literal phenomenon grounded in embodied perception.

In the case of gustatory perception, the account of Intrafield metaphorical transfer needs to be reviewed carefully. As evidenced by the results of the freelisting task, the linguistic elaboration of the sense of taste elicited by native English speakers encompasses adjectives that pertain to different sensory modalities, thus mirroring its multisensoriality. In Chapter 5, I demonstrated how the linguistic representation of the sense of taste includes what physiologists call flavour, and other modalities (Auvray and Spence 2008). In a biological perspective, flavour consists of sensations processed through different sensory modalities, namely gustation, olfaction, and chemesthesis. Gustation per se is responsible for perception of sweet, bitter, sour, salty, and umami stimuli. Olfaction carries information on a larger variety of volatile substances that create what in common parlance are referred to as flavours. The chemesthesis component is responsible for perception of haptic stimuli, such as texture and temperature. Significantly, the lexicon of taste contains also lexical items that have been most strongly associated with the visual modality (e.g., *oily*), and with the auditory modality (i.e., *crunchy*). This suggests that perception is continuous, and that the different senses participate in the linguistic elaboration of taste as a reconstruction of a unique perceptual Gestalt. In this perspective, for example, I interpret the usage of adjectives pertaining to touch in the description of taste as reflecting embodied perceptual experience. For

https://doi.org/10.1515/9783110630404-009

instance, when a speaker describes the taste of something as *smooth* it is because they perceive *smoothness* in their mouths through haptic receptors, which are later reconstructed as a gustatory sensation.

On the other hand, it is worth recalling that I sponsor an emic perspective to the study of taste. The commitment to this approach calls for a distinction between the senses, based on the five senses folk-model: although this model is highly controversial and culture-specific, a description of the usage of these adjectives in a specific language cannot overlook the cultural background in which speakers of given language are immersed. Accordingly, I consider sensory adjectives that describe pain and noxious temperature as integrated in the conceptual domain of TOUCH. I specify however the domain of PAINFUL TOUCH to allow for a more nuanced interpretation. I argue that conceptualisation mechanisms are more evident at the intersection between scientific models and folk-knowledge, thus enabling insights into the nature of our conceptual systems involving the sensory domains.

9.2 The hierarchy of the senses

Intrafield metaphors are linguistic expressions that pair two lexical forms traditionally associated to two distinct perceptual semantic domains. For instance, rough sound, smooth taste, and warm colour. In these pairs, the adjectives are more strongly associated with touch (Lynott and Connell 2009), but they are used in the description of sounds, taste, and colour, respectively. Intrafield expressions are found across the whole spectrum of sensory vocabulary to the extent that arguably they are "a core topic in sensory linguistics" (Winter 2019: 67). Investigations in these expressions are not new in linguistics literature, and different researchers have coined different labels to describe them. Considering the ability of these expressions to cross different sensory modalities, they have been referred to as "multimodal" or "crossmodal" expressions both in linguistics (Bagli 2016; Winter 2019a; Cacciari 2008; Sandford 2019) and in psycholinguistics (Lynott and Connell 2009). More commonly, they have been referred to as synaesthetic metaphors (Ramachandran and Hubbard 2001; Strik Lievers 2016), linguistic synaesthesia (e.g., Holz 2007; Ronga et al. 2012; Whitney 1952), and verbal synaesthesia (Strik Lievers 2015).

Traditional terminology attests to the fact that these expressions bring together lexical items pertaining to different senses. The word synaesthesia derives from Ancient Greek, and it is a combination of *syn* ('together') and *esthesis* ('sensation'): it is "the union of the senses" (Cytowic 1989). In psychology, synaesthesia is understood as a rare phenomenon in which stimulation in one sensory modality triggers perception in another modality (Cytowic 1989; Sagiv and Ward 2006; Martino and Marks 2001; Ramachandran and Hubbard 2001; Simner 2012, among others). Different findings in literature suggest that the phenomenon is systematic, in that a specific perception is usually induced by only one stimulus (Cacciari 2008). Furthermore, Sagiv and Ward (2006) argue that the motivation for synaesthetic experiences lies in our neurobiological structure and in universal mechanisms of perception. This led Ramachandran and Hubbard (2003: 51) to conclude that "the non-arbitrariness both of [neurological] synaesthesia and of metaphor (and their directionality) arise because of constraints imposed by evolution and by neural hardware". Similarly, Cacciari concludes that "metaphorical language is pervaded by cross-modality references that mirror, at a linguistic level, our neural architecture" (2008: 436).

In linguistics, synaesthesia is thought of as a metaphorical process that involves different sensory modalities, through which "a perceptual experience related to one sense is described through lexical means typically associated with a different sense" (Strik Lievers 2015: 69–70). Generally speaking, synaesthetic metaphors are identified as an adjective-noun pair, where the modifying adjective is considered to refer to the source domain and the noun to the target domain (Ronga et al. 2012; Winter 2019a: 68; Sandford 2019). The most striking feature of these expressions is the asymmetry of lexical transfer: the different modalities do not participate equally in structuring one another, rather they are credited to follow a "non-arbitrary" path of lexical transfer. Williams (1976) identified a hierarchy of semantic change in the lexical field of perception adjectives in English. According to his model, lexical transfer between modalities follows specific directions, represented by the arrows in Figure (3).

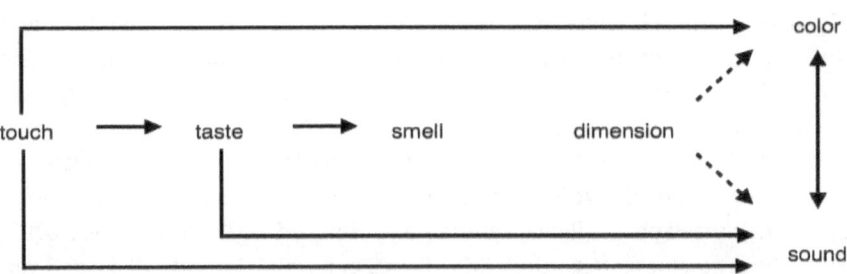

Figure 3: Hierarchy of directionality of semantic transfer. Adapted from Williams 1976.

The hierarchy predicts that there may be synaesthetic realisations such as a *sharp taste* (touch to taste), a *sweet smell* (taste to smell); a *harsh voice* (touch to sound); a *warm colour* (touch to colour), a *sweet sound* (taste to sound), a *loud colour* (sound to colour), and a *bright voice* (colour to sound). Taste can receive lexical items from touch, and may lend its terms to other modalities, such as smell and sound. Alternative directions of transfer are difficult to find, but not impossible (Williams 1976; Cacciari 2008). In fact, in English there seem to be semantic constraints that limit a speaker's expressivity. For instance, it is uncommon to describe tastes as being **bright* or **loud* (but see Sandford 2019 for examples of lexical transfer from sight to taste). The asymmetry in usage described by the hierarchy has been observed also in languages other than English, both Indo-European and non. For instance: Mendelson (1984) on Russian literature; Ronga et al. (2012) on Italian; Strik Lievers (2015) on Italian and English; Erzsébet (1974) and Whitney (1952) on Hungarian; Shen and Gil (2007) on Indonesian; Yu (2003) on Chinese.

Nonetheless, the hierarchy of the senses in lexical transfer has been highly debated for various reasons. First, Williams' hierarchy essentially corresponds to the one proposed by Aristotle (based on the worthiness of the senses, see Chapter 2), thus suggesting that the scientific and cultural background of the researchers may have influenced the interpretation of data. Moreover, research on "synaesthetic metaphors" tacitly assumes that the senses may be singled out in mutually exclusive categories, and hardly ever sponsors a continuous understanding of perception. Lastly, the empirical data on which these analyses are based mainly come from poetry, and they do not include diverse sources of linguistic usage.

Strik Lievers (2015) represents an exception in research on "synaesthetic metaphors", as she reviews the hierarchy with data coming from both English and Italian corpora to establish whether this model holds also in standard language and not only in poetry. Her results confirm the hierarchy, but as she suggests it "must be interpreted in terms of frequency. Backward transfers, such as from colour to taste, are rare (i.e., the number of occurrences is not high for any of the 'backward types') but attested nonetheless" (Strik Lievers 2015: 89). Furthermore, she analyses Süskind's novel *Das Parfum*, which concentrates on the sense of smell: in this particular context the hierarchy of transfer is reversed, with smell being the most frequent Target Domain (see also Popova 2003; Digonnet 2012). This suggests that the asymmetry may be explained in terms of frequency and entrenchment, more than in terms of lexical constraints operating on language. Similarly, Ronga (2016) investigates cases of taste synaesthesia in Italian magazines about wine and food, to assess whether their structure was arbitrary or grounded in physical perception. According to her findings, taste synaesthesias specifically mirror physiological gustatory experiences, and as such they should be considered as motivated by embodied perception. Moreover, she finds that the directionality of transfer changes on the basis of the food type that is described: chocolate descriptions contain more sound to taste synaesthesias than in e.g., tea descriptions, as a result of the auditory component being more prominent in the consumption of chocolate.

Recent research in sensory linguistics is reconsidering the model of the hierarchy of the senses, as it is not sufficient to explain the asymmetrical transfer of lexical items between perceptual modalities. There are numerous factors that contribute to the asymmetry in the sensory lexicon. For instance, words with a higher emotional valence are more frequently used as source domain in intrafield expressions (Winter 2019b), and syntactic constraints operating in English may dictate the order of a sequence of adjectives, thus influencing the order of transfer and its interpretation (e.g., *a loud bitter fat old white man*, Sandford 2019). Finally, iconicity seems to inhibit intrafield expressions (e.g., *squealing colour* is less frequent than *loud colour*; see also Classen 1993; Lupyan and Winter 2018; Emmorrey 2014; Meir 2010 for the blocking effects of iconicity on figurativity), thus suggesting that modalities containing more iconic lexicon are less likely to be transferred to other modalities. A detailed review of the factors motivating the asymmetry exceeds the scope of this book (but see Winter 2019a).

9.3 The sensory linguistics account of "synaesthetic metaphors"

9.3.1 Are they synaesthetic?

Researchers working on linguistic synaesthesia have related this phenomenon to extra-linguistic factors, most commonly referring to cognitive and embodied constraints on the possibilities of language conceptualisation. Nonetheless, they have acknowledged the difference between neurological synaesthesia and linguistic synaesthesia. Recently, Winter (2019a, 2019b) has argued against the usage of the term "synaesthetic", as it is reminiscent of neurological synaesthesia without having any solid base as per the actual connection of the two phenomena. This may lead to theoretical confusion, as a shared terminology suggests shared phenomena. I follow his lead in debunking the usage of the term *synaesthetic* (Winter 2019a: 67–77).

In keeping with earlier research on the topic (Martino and Marks 2001; Spence 2011; Deroy and Spence 2013) Winter distinguishes between "canonical synaesthesia" (the neurological phenomenon) and "crossmodal correspondences", i.e., the correspondence between a stimulus experienced in a modality with another stimulus experienced through a different modality. For instance, sweet stimuli have been repeatedly associated with round forms (e.g., Spence and Gallace 2011; Spence 2011), and lower pitched sounds (Crisinel, Jones, and Spence 2012). Other types of crossmodal correspondence involve the association between high-pitched stimuli and brightness and vice versa, i.e., low-pitched sounds associated with darker colours (Marks 1982). These associations may develop early in childhood through the environment: the repeated exposure to two concurrent events may eventually lead to the correlation of the two stimuli. As a result, they are automatic and very common among individuals, but they are not as vivid as canonical synaesthesia. Most importantly they arise from correlated perceptions in experience, contrary to canonical synaesthesia, which instead connects two sensations that are not environmentally tied. Intrafield metaphors may indeed be motivated by crossmodal correspondences (Stevens and Marks 1965; Marks and Stevens 1966). For instance, Marks (1982) finds a positive correlation between brightness and sneezes (and between dullness and coughs), thus instantiating a crossmodal relation between luminance and pitch and/or loudness, which could serve as the embodied basis for expressions such as *bright/ dark sound*.

A possible criterion to distinguish canonical synaesthesia from Intrafield metaphors may be voluntariness: while canonical synaesthesia is automatic and involuntary, intrafield metaphors may result from creativity of language users. Canonical synaesthesia is experienced by synaesthetes disregarding their will, to the extent that such experience may cause distress to some individuals and may even be the source of ridicule (Cytowic and Eagleman 2009). The automaticity of synaesthesia may be compared to the automaticity of colour vision in non-synaesthetes. It is impossible to stop seeing colour for non-synaesthetes, as much as it is impossible for a synaesthete to stop experiencing concurrent sensations. Obviously, one may argue that language production is the result of a voluntary choice of words (especially in poetic and literary productions), but most theories of language use would contend that the lexical structures found in languages are not a conscious choice. Therefore, voluntariness is not a good criterion to rule out the differences between canonical and linguistic synaesthesia.

Moreover, canonical synaesthesia is characterised by a conscious experience: synaesthetes report to consciously see, for instance, a colour in association with a sound. On the contrary, intrafield metaphors are not always the result of conscious choice by speakers (Whitney 1952; Plümacher 2007; Strik Lievers 2017). Intrafield metaphors typically result from recurrent patterns of conceptualisation between different domains. In addition to this, the mappings of metaphorical transfer involved in intrafield metaphors are substantially different from the perceptual dimensions involved in canonical synaesthesia. Canonical synaesthesia is organised in five different subgroups. In visual synaesthesia colour sensations are triggered by ordinal sequences; particular types of music or sounds induce colour perception; touch or particular emotions trigger colour. In non-visual synaesthesia a smell, sound, touch or taste is triggered (for instance sound to taste, or sight to smell); and sequences are mapped into space (especially numbers have particular spatial locations), (Novich et al. 2011; in Winter 2019a).

Despite the groupings, canonical synaesthesia typically shows idiosyncratic traits (Cytowic and Eagleman 2009; Deroy and Spence 2013). For instance, a common type of synaesthesia is the grapheme-colour association, in which a letter triggers a specific colour sensation, but the same letter is not necessarily perceived as having the same colour for different people. That is, the grapheme "R" may be blue or red depending on the synaesthete (Cytowic and Eagleman 2009). This is in stark contrast to intrafield expressions, for which the most common source and target domains are touch and sound (Day 1996; Strik Lievers 2015). Furthermore, intrafield metaphors involve systematic and highly conventionalised pairings across different domains.

Lastly, although estimates on the distribution of canonical synaesthesia vary among different authors (Ramachandran and Hubbard 2001; Sagiv and Ward 2006; Simner et al. 2006; Simner et al. 2008), they are consistent in suggesting it is an extremely rare phenomenon, to the extent that it is definitionally rare (Grossenbacher and Lovelace 200). Intrafield metaphors are much more common than canonical synaesthesia, according to the accounts in linguistic and literary studies research (e.g., Engstrom 1946). In the domain of TASTE, many intrafield expressions are motivated by its physiology, thus making intrafield metaphors very frequent in the conceptualisation of this sensory domain. The entrenched nature of this realisation, and the salience of these lexical items is at odds with the rarity of canonical synaesthesia. Therefore, I opt for the *intrafield* terminology (as opposed to "synaesthetic"), as it is more apt at capturing the linguistic phenomenon without creating confusion with other psychological phenomena.

9.3.2 Are they metaphorical?

Considering the physiological motivation of many intrafield expressions, their status as a metaphor should be carefully assessed. For instance, when a speaker describes the taste of something as *creamy*, they are describing the haptic component of flavour. As such, the adjective *creamy* may be considered as a literal description of a multisensory experience. On the other hand, usages such as *a sweet voice* are much less clearly based on physiological processes, and therefore require further discussion. In the current account of intrafield metaphors in sensory linguistics, these expressions may not be considered as metaphorical. Winter (2019a, 2019b) is the main proponent of this approach. Before debunking the metaphorical status of intrafield metaphors, he reviews four possible theoretical accounts of intrafield metaphors: they might be analysed as (i) conceptual metaphors; (ii) primary metaphors; (iii) metonymies; or (iv) literal expressions (Winter 2019a: 97). I review the arguments that led him to the claim that "synaesthetic metaphors are neither synaesthetic nor metaphorical" (Winter 2019b).

Winter excludes a metaphorical account for the motivation of intrafield expressions for a number of reasons. Conceptual metaphors, by definition, connect two domains that share different levels of concreteness (e.g., Lakoff 1980; Kövecses 2010; but see Dancygier and Sweetser 2014 for an intersubjectivity account), in a way that intrafield metaphors do not. It is quite strange to ask whether a taste is more or less concrete than a colour: both sensations are equally embodied, and both are equally concrete (Strik Lievers 2016; but see Korsmeyer 2002 for a discussion on the incorporation of proximal senses). Secondly, intrafield metaphors do not instantiate a rich body of knowledge to be mapped across domains: the mappings that are transferred from one domain to the other are less rich and systematic than the mappings identified for other, more established metaphors. For instance, the set of mappings that connects the domains of ARGUMENTS and WAR include expressions of the type *defending their position, being under attack, ideological conflict,* and *communicative strategies* (examples from Dancygier and Sweetser 2014), while the connections between sensory modalities mainly involve individual lexemes and do not map entire portions of a domain onto another.

Another possibility is that intrafield metaphors are cases of primary metaphors. As explained in Chapter 7, a primary metaphor is a special type of conceptual metaphor that stems from direct, embodied correlations between two separate experiences in the environment (Lakoff 1987; Grady 1997a, 1999; Casasanto 2017; Winter and Matlock 2017; Dancygier and Sweetser 2014; among others). Indeed, the embodied crossmodal correlations that intervene in the association of perceptual stimuli between different senses may motivate linguistic intrafield metaphors. These may arise from environmental and psychological correlations, as suggested by many authors (see for example Dirven 1985; Shibuya and Nozawa 2003; Nakamura, Sakamoto and Utsumi 2010). For instance, the distinction between warm and cold colours may be correlated to the fact that entities in nature that are red or orange (e.g., the sun) are also warm, while entities that show an array of blue and grey (e.g., large bodies of water) are cold (Cacciari 2008). Winter however, in keeping with Grady (2005: 1605–1606), excludes primary metaphors as potential candidates to account for intrafield metaphors, because "the target domain of primary metaphors needs to be non-sensory" (Winter 2019a: 86).

Another possible mechanism for the analysis of intrafield expressions could be metonymy. Winter is admittedly in favour of a metonymic analysis (Winter 2019a: 86; see also Barcelona 2008). The strength of a metonymic account lies in the fact that the two perceptual domains involved in the intrafield expression are not seen as complete separate entities, rather as part of a conceptual continuum. For instance, in expressions such as *sweet fragrance*, rather than positing the metaphor TASTE IS SMELL, one can describe such realisations as TASTE FOR SMELL, or in keeping with physiological terminology on flavour, GUSTATION FOR OLFACTION. This analysis of intrafield metaphors sponsors a more fluid conceptualisation of perception, in seeing two sensory modalities being part of a shared continuum. The counterpoint to this analysis, according to Winter, is that this position still underlies a view of two distinct domains (in this case TASTE and SMELL), thus referring to a culturally determined distinction of the human sensorium in the five senses folk model and positing a clear-cut distinction between the different domains.

The last hypothesis is that intrafield metaphors are actually a case of literal language. This radical approach to sensory vocabulary stems from Rakova (2003). Given its centrality in Sensory linguistics and length of discussion, I review it in the next paragraph.

9.3.3 Are they literal?

In her influential book *The Extent of the Literal*, Rakova proposes that the meaning of sensory words is not metaphorical, and that there is no need to recur to figurativity to understand usages such as *sweet smell*; rather, the word *sweet* has already the meaning potential to refer to both taste and smell. In other words, *sweet* is a taste word as much as it is a smell word. Her compelling argument is best exemplified in reference to the synonymity of *hot* and *spicy*.

The adjective *hot* in English may refer both to temperature perception as in *a hot mug*, and to spiciness, as in *a hot pepper*. The relationship between temperature and spiciness may be seen as metaphorical, as the two perceptual dimensions are quite dissimilar in experience and conceptualisation. However, Rakova reviews neurophysiological data to prove that the two dimensions are associated in embodied experience and perception following a non-arbitrary path of meaning expansion.

As discussed earlier, the sensation of spiciness is caused by capsaicin, which is mediated by nociceptors; more specifically, these are TRPV1 receptors (Julius and Basbaum 2001; Basbaum et al. 2009). Crucially, the same receptors are activated when exposed to noxious heat (i.e., temperatures of 43 °C or higher). Thus, capsaicin and heat are mediated by the same receptors. This is also evident in the phenomenological correlation of the two events: when exposed to capsaicin, most people experience a rush of heat and start sweating. This leads Rakova to state that the semantic relationship existing between *hot* and *spicy* is not metaphorical, and it does not arise from correlations of independent events. Rather, it should be considered as literal, correlated by phenomenological characteristics as well as physiological mechanisms.

In addition to this, Winter reviews neurophysiological evidence related to other sensory systems to extend Rakova's analysis to other semantic domains. For instance, touch and sound show interconnections similar to those of taste and smell (e.g., Guest et al. 2002), thus motivating a literal account of expressions such as *rough sound* and *abrasive sound*; and different cases in the two dimensions of nociception (i.e., pain caused by either external or internal stimuli) may be motivated as well through similar analysis. In keeping with Rakova, Winter (2019a, 2019b) argues in favour of a literal interpretation of intrafield metaphors involving two integrated modalities (such as taste and smell integrated in flavour), but this does not deal with the issue of more distant modalities, such as taste and sound. Winter addresses the problem by relying on the emotional valence of sensory words. Particularly, he claims that intrafield expressions such as *sweet sound*, *bitter tears*, or even *sweet love* should be interpreted on the basis of the evaluative meaning of the adjectives. Thus, he concludes that "the phenomenon of synaesthetic metaphors ceases to be metaphorical for two reasons: either there is no need to posit synaesthetic metaphors because the perceptual modalities are highly integrated, or there is no need to posit synaesthetic metaphors because crossmodal uses simply follow from word-inherent evaluative meaning" (Winter 2019a: 96).

9.4 A different proposal

My approach pursues the emic description of taste, which imposes a more attentive evaluation of the theoretical status of intrafield metaphors. On one hand, the multisensoriality of the physical perception of taste has led researchers to formulate a distinction between taste and flavour. In addition to this, research into crossmodal associations has shown an intricate network of correspondences between taste and other modalities. For instance, Ronga states that intrafield metaphors "seem to reproduce the complex set of experiences that can happen in the mouth" (2016: 57). Zellner and Kautz (1990) suggest that the colour of the recipient may influence the expectations about the smell and flavour of the substance. Furthermore, spiciness may be enhanced by auditory stimuli such as high pitch and fast tempo (Wang et al. 2017). Moreover, manipulation of red colouring is used to indicate spicy salsa: the redder the food, the spicier it is expected to taste (Levitan and Shermer 2014). It is also argued that sweet correlates with round shapes, while bitter and sour correlate with more angular, pointy shapes (see Liang et al. 2013; Spence 2012; Velasco et al. 2014; Velasco, Woods, Deroy, and Spence 2015; Velasco et al. 2016). These examples lend evidence to the claim that our multisensory perception of taste is informed and constrained by an embodied neural network.

This however does not necessarily amount to a literal understanding of multisensoriality. Firstly, the relationship between perception and language should always be seen as conceptually mediated (Miller & Johnson Liard 1976; Rakova 2003; Winter 2019a: 88). The mediation that intervenes between perceptual stimuli, concepts, and their realisation in language is the main interest of cognitive linguists, and where conceptualisation processes take place. Secondly, the interest in an emic understanding of the sense of taste urges for a consideration of the five senses folk-model. Although our physiology clearly shows that the senses form a continuum, it is undeniable that English speakers still conceive of the five senses as separate. I argue that this model should not be overlooked when discussing the entrenched semantic mechanisms that regulate sensory lexicon.

The case of integration of the separate sensory modalities of gustation, olfaction, and chemesthesis into the larger perceptual continuum of flavour does not impinge on considering specific lexicon as more strongly associated to specific modalities (Lynott and Connell 2009). This leads to the formulation of the specific metonymy GUSTATION FOR OLFACTION, that is: a lexical item more strongly associated with the gustatory dimension is selected to refer to the olfactory dimension, which is part of the same domain both perceptually (both belong to FLAVOUR) and semantically (they are both part of perception). Winter refuses metonymy as a theoretical model to account for Intrafield metaphors because it underlies a distinction among different modalities, which is not backed up by physiology. I argue instead that the distinction should be maintained when discussing semantic motivation, precisely because the belief-system of native English speakers maintains that the two sensory modalities are separate.

In the case of non-integrated sensory modalities, for instance taste and sound, the evaluative meaning of sensory lexicon may motivate the usage of gustatory adjectives in the description of such modalities. This position is in keeping with Winter. However, I account for the evaluative meaning of gustatory adjectives as emerging from a dynamic conceptualisation construal based on experience. The generally positive meaning associated to *sweet* emerges from an embodied and instinctual response to sugars, which in turn arises from the evolutionary value that this substance has played in our history as a species.

Infants of both human and non-human primates show appreciation for sugars, thus suggesting an immediate hedonic response (Orians 2014). From this experience, the concept of sweetness is abstracted, schematised, bleached out, and eventually reapplied to refer to general pleasantness (Bagli 2016; Kövecses 2019: 338). Therefore, the connection between sweet and pleasure might be better accounted for as a case of metonymy, in which the physical sensation of sweet provides access to its reaction, i.e., pleasure. The resulting metonymy is PHYSICAL SENSATION FOR ITS PHYSIOLOGICAL REACTION, and as such it is a type of CAUSE FOR EFFECT metonymy (see also THE PHYSIOLOGICAL EFFECTS OF AN EMOTION STAND FOR THE EMOTION in Lakoff and Kövecses 1987; Kövecses and Radden 1998; Panther and Thornburg 2000).

The conceptualisation of PLEASURE as SWEET might be thought of as a case of primary correlation. It is illustrative to review the definition provided by Grady of what constitutes a primary metaphor:

> One of the concepts, which will end up being the source concept in a metaphoric pairing, refers to a basic dimension of sensory experience, whether visual, tactile, or in any other modality – heaviness, brightness, forward motion, upright position, etc. [. . .] The other, the target concept, is associated with an equally fundamental element of mental experience, but one not *primarily* associated with a particular sort of sensory impression – effortfulness, happiness, similarity, achievement of a purpose, etc.
>
> (2005: 1605–1606) [emphasis mine]

Although Grady's formulation explicitly refers to metaphors, I argue that the same primary correlation between concepts may also be extended to metonymy. Thus, figurative expressions involving gustatory adjectives as source domain may successfully be accounted for as primary metonymies and primary metaphors that motivate the structuring of a target concept through the lexicon of taste. Furthermore, I want to highlight that the concepts of pleasure and displeasure are "fundamental element of mental experience", but "not primarily associated with a particular sort of impression", thus qualifying for potential target domains in a primary metonymy.

At a closer look, the metonymic account of lexical transfer between sensory modalities may be extended also to Rakova's argument about the *spicy-hot* association. In the unfolding of her argument, Rakova lists the terms for spiciness and temperature in other Indo-European languages, which I report in Table 29.

The associations made by the languages reviewed by Rakova between spiciness and related terms to describe it may be broadly classified into two groups, which follow two main conceptualisation paths: the temperature path (English and Latin) and the sharpness path (Italian, Spanish, German, Greek, and Dutch). French appears to have both conceptual mechanisms. In physiological terms, the

Table 29: Indo-European terms to describe spiciness, adapted from Rakova 2003: 39.

Ancient Greek	hot (of taste) = δριμvs (the temperature term for 'hot' is θερμos); δριμvs = I. piercing, sharp, keen II. Said of things which affect the eyes or taste.
Latin	hot (of flavours) = *feruidus* (the first temperature term for 'hot' is *calidus*; *feruidus* = (1) intensely hot, boiling, burning; . . . (5) hot to the taste
Italian	hot (of food) = *piccante* (the temperature term for 'hot' is *caldo*); *piccante*= (a) spicy, hot, (b) risqué, racy
Spanish	hot (to taste) = *picante* (the temperature term for 'hot' is *caliente*); *picante* = (a) hot, peppery, highly seasoned (b) *fig.* remark: sharp, stinging, cutting
French	hot (to taste) = *cuisant, piquant* (the temperature term for 'hot' is *chaud*; *cuisant*= hot (pepper); smarting, burning (pain); *piquant* = (a) prickly, biting, cutting; (b) hot, pungent
German	hot (to taste) = *scharf* (the temperature for 'hot' is *heiß*); *scharf*= (a) sharp (biting, cutting); (b) hot, highly seasoned
Dutch	hot (hot spices) = *scherpe* (the temperature terms for 'hot' are *heet, warm*); *scherpe* = sharp; hot (spices)
Russian	hot= *ostryj* (the temperature terms for 'hot' are *gorjačij, žarkij*); *ostryj*= sharp; (*ostryj sous*= piquant sauce)

two paths of nociception may be referred to as the thermal path and the mechanical path (Basbaum et al. 2009). The observation of these two paths leads Rakova to the identification of *sharp* as being "the general term which subsumes" (Rakova 2003: 40) all the mechanically noxious terms. This claim is confirmed by physiological research: the receptor TRPV1 is found in both Ab and C primary afferents that respond both to thermal and mechanical pain, thus adding a further piece of evidence, according to Rakova, to the literalness of the hot-sharp-spicy continuum.

Recent findings based on iconic representations of spiciness suggest that spiky flames are better indices for spiciness, as opposed to rounded flames (that seem to be better indicators for *roasted*) for Spanish speakers, (Gil Pérez et al. 2019). Considering that the temperature realisation for spiciness does not seem to be lexicalised in Spanish, and yet it serves as an index of spiciness, one could speculate that the same findings may be extended to English. In any event, the non-linguistic realisation of spiciness as both *flames* and *spikes* suggests that the conceptualisation of perception of capsaicin does not rely on either *flames* nor *spikes*, but on the more general concept of PAINFUL TOUCH, which in turn may be accessed either through adjectives describing thermal or mechanical pain. In this line then different languages would select alternative construals to lexically encode spiciness sensations. Romance languages seem to prefer mechanical pain, even if alternative expressions in non-standard Italian involving thermal pain are also possible (e.g. *questa salsa brucia!* – 'this sauce burns!', to code spiciness). Furthermore, Table 13 in Chapter 6 reports the categorisation of lexical items *tangy* and *pungent*. Both terms refer to noxious perception: *tang* is defined as "a projecting pointed part of an instrument" (OED *tang*, n.1, 1), see Chapter 4.3 on source-based language), and *pungent* derives from Latin *pungens*, Eng. 'sharp, prickly' (OED *pungent*, adj.; see Paragraph 6.5.4). Duly, native speakers of English categorised both lexemes in the categories of Spicy. Thus, to sum up: the conceptualisation of spiciness relies on terms of nociception, and both noxious concepts (i.e., thermal and mechanical) seem to be available to speakers (in Spanish, Italian, and English). Thus, when a speaker is faced with a spicy taste, they may choose between two possible linguistic realisations of the same perception. Each of these realisations may be described as an EFFECT FOR CAUSE metonymy, thus giving rise to the metonymy PAINFUL TOUCH FOR SPICINESS.

This theoretical proposal emerges from an attentive review of both theoretical contributions and linguistic data elicited from corpus analysis, which are presented in the next paragraph.

9.5 Intrafield expressions with taste as source domain

The linguistic data retrieved through corpus analysis on the COCA and discussed in Chapter 8 contained occurrences which I classified as Intrafield. The data presented here therefore result from the same methodology described in Chapter 8 and were manually analysed to identify the type of conceptual mechanisms that motivate their usage. Most of the BTTs (both Primary and Secondary) involved in the corpus analysis display cases of Intrafield transfer, with the exceptions of *savoury* and *salty*. The most common transfer is from TASTE to SMELL (48%), followed by HEARING (30%, only in *sweet*), and TOUCH (19%, mainly in *bitter*).

9.5.1 Sweet

The intrafield transfer of SWEET represents roughly 17% of the entire occurrences for *sweet*. The two modalities that *sweet* mainly applies to are smell and sound, but there are also a few occurrences in which *sweet* describes sight (n = 2), touch (n = 9) as in (128–130):

(128) Mary found herself glaring up at the skylight, the **sweet** blue heaven behind it. (FIC 1996)

(129) She picked up the matches. The small box was **sweet** in her hands. (FIC 2013)

(130) The char of the grilled tomatoes in this soup finds a complement in the **sweet** heat of mint and jalapeno. (NEWS 1997)

Although the occurrences in (128–130) refer to the sensory modalities of sight and touch, the meaning conceptualised by *sweet* is not much different from other conceptualisations found in other domains. The usage in (128) conceptualises the *blue heaven* as being *sweet* by relying on the general positive meaning of *sweet*. The occurrence in (129) instead characterises the haptic sensation of a box of matches in the girl's hands as *sweet*, but the meaning it conceptualises is that of pleasantness. Both realisations are motivated by the general metonymy SWEET FOR PLEASANT. The occurrence in (130) helps conceptualise the spiciness produced by the peppers as more pleasant than it could be expected, thus relying on the mapping MITIGATING IS SWEETENING.

The occurrences of *sweet* to describe hearing all conceptualise a pleasant quality of the sound being described, but they also have more specific meanings. The most common mechanism found in the domain of HEARING is the conceptual metaphor HARMONY IS SWEET: it mainly applies to sounds as in (131–133), but it is also found in other conceptual domains.

(131) Their secret weapon was leaping from **sweet** to screamin' (which Kurt Cobain admitted to boosting). (MAG 2003)

(132) But the **sweet** harmony was all around, as everyone lingered over the last notes of "Silent Night", in a song-born joy that joined us all. (FIC 1997)

(133) Her laugh had a pleasant musicality, a **sweet** viola with bell overtones. (FIC 2002)

The conceptual metaphor HARMONY IS SWEET is supported by lexicographic investigation through the MMP (lexical overlap with categories *Social discord and Harmony; Music*). There are a number of crossmodal associations that provide embodied motivation for the metaphorical understanding of harmony as sweet. In musical theory, "harmonic changes are understood as movements from one key (e.g., C major) to the next (e.g., G major)" (Julich 2019: 167), which are mapped along a circular line typically referred to as the circle of fifths. Harmony therefore may be visually represented as a circle of different keys. The crossmodal association of SWEETNESS with ROUNDNESS was first observed by the ancient Greek philosopher Heraclitus and was recently confirmed in a set of psychological experiments (Velasco et al. 2015; see also Spence 2012). Furthermore, research in crossmodal psychology suggests that sweetness may be associated to non-words such as *maluma* (Crisinel, Jones, and Spence 2012), which in turn is associated with round shapes (e.g., O'Boyle and Tarte 1980). Evidence emerging from crossmodal associations lend support to the primary metaphor HARMONY IS SWEET, which motivates a number of both intrafield and standard realisations.

Some of the occurrences in the Intrafield group that conceptualise hearing as *sweet* may also be motivated by the metaphor LOVE IS SWEET (134–135):

(134) "There may be hope for you", she says very softly, her voice **sweet** as honey. (FIC 2005)

(135) The **sweet**, familiar notes of laughter. A woman's. A child's. (FIC 2011)

The quality of the sounds being described in (134) and (135), more than being harmonious, seem to be loaded with love and affection towards the hearer. Duly, the taste term *sweet* is conceptualised in these occurrences as an attribute of love and affection, thus relying on the common conceptual metaphor LOVE IS SWEET.

The intrafield occurrences in the domain of SMELL are slightly more numerous. The standard case of occurrence of *sweet* in the domain of SMELL is exemplified in (136) and (137):

(136) Nearby Mexican ferns grow at the feet of tall trees, and the small white blooms of Mexican Osmanthus fill the air with **sweet** fragrance. (NEWS 1998)

(137) New machines designed to release sprays based on citronella oil or geraniol, another plant-derived repellent with a **sweet**, rosy odor, also are available. (MAG 2003)

In (136), the adjective *sweet* is used to describe the smell of devilwood (*Cartrema americana*, formerly known as *Osmanthus americanus*) which produces white flowers with a strong fragrance; while in (137) it describes the fragrance of geraniol, a natural chemical often used as insect repellent. I argue that the usage of the adjective *sweet* to describe smell is the result of the metonymic process GUSTATION FOR OLFACTION, in keeping with the continuous nature of perception, and with its emic and culturally based representation.

A less frequent but consistent group of occurrences in the Intrafield label conceptualises a smell as *sweet*, but with a negative value as in (138–140).

(138) The tent reeked of the sickly **sweet** smell of human decomposition. (ACAD 2009)

(139) You took your place in the line and breathed the **sweet**, gritty exhaust of traffic. (FIC 1990)

(140) Splash! A **sweet**, rotten-fruit odor burst forth. (FIC 2004)

While the occurrence in (138) present the adverb "sickly" or "sickeningly", thus contextually emphasizing and construing the negative quality of the overall perception, the occurrences in (139) and (140) clearly use *sweet* as a descriptive item. There is no reference to its usual positive meaning, thus suggesting that the frequent positive meaning of *sweet* results from a dynamic conceptualisation process, and that it is not automatically activated in language.

9.5.2 Bitter

Only one occurrence of *bitter* refers to smell (141), in keeping with other realisations that report taste terms to describe smells sensations. Interestingly, the same referent (i.e., *exhaust*) has also been described as *sweet* (139).

(141) Veronica drew in a deep breath, savoring the spicy-sweet scent of flowers and citrus trees mingled with **bitter** exhaust fumes. (FIC 2013)

The majority of intrafield occurrences of *bitter* refer to coldness, which is frequently coded in Indo-European languages with reference to adjectives that describe PAINFUL TOUCH, as in Table 30:

Table 30: Adjectives to describe coldness in Italian, French, Spanish and German.

Italian	freddo pungente ('stinging, biting cold')
French	froid mordant ('biting cold')
Spanish	frio cortante ('cutting cold')
German	bissig Kalt ('biting cold')

There is a common conceptualisation pattern across languages that consistently construes thermal stimuli in the cold spectrum by using terms that refer to painful events, be it *bites* (German and French), *cuts* (Spanish), or *stings* (Italian). The usage of *bitter* in reference to coldness is unique to English, and it is related to the conflation of painful touch and bitterness in Proto-Germanic *bîtan*, which developed also in words such as *biting* (Buck 1949: 1033; OED *bitter* adj. and n.). This diachronic pattern is reflected also in other languages: Strik Lievers and De Felice (2019: 92) note how the evolution of It. *aspro* from Latin *asper* (Eng. 'sour') follows a trajectory that goes from "sharp, stinging" to its current gustatory meaning; Buck (1949) reports that the Ancient Greek term for *bitter* was πικρός *(pikros)*, Eng. 'prickly' (Buck 1949). Furthermore, the association between bitter and painful touch is testified by family resemblances discussed in Chapter 6. Unlike the case of *hot* and *spiciness* the conflation between *pain* and *bitterness* is not based on shared neural pathways however. It is rather based on the shared negative evaluation of both experiences in embodied and facial responses (see Paragraph 2.4).

Thus, it follows that the simultaneous reaction to different stimuli may represent the embodied basis for the development of conceptual associations between *painful touch* and *bitterness*. This is reflected in the lexical development and semantic evolution of words for *bitter* in different Indo-European languages, including English, from words to describe noxious perception. I argue that the conceptual mechanism that motivates the association between these two experiences is BITTER FOR PAINFUL TOUCH. The same metonymy intervenes in the motivation of occurrences such as *bitter irony* and *bitter jokes* (see Paragraph 8.4). The relationship between the two concepts is metonymical because the sensations that the two domains represent arise simultaneously and dynamically in experience. Furthermore, it should be stressed that although recent psychological literature distinguishes the sense of nociception from the sense of touch, this distinction does not hold in the history of English. The adjective *biting* refers to perception of pain on the skin, thus most likely imposing the construal of a haptic sensation. We may even elaborate further on the semantic development of *bitter* from Proto-Germanic *bîtan*, by posing the metonymy TOUCH FOR TASTE, in which touch is the vehicle to access the target domain of TASTE. This path of lexico-semantic development was first distinguished by Alcmaeon of Croton (see Paragraph 2.1), who considered taste as a type of touch.

9.5.3 Sour

The intrafield occurrences of sour almost uniquely refer to smells. Consider for example the occurrences in (142–144):

(142) The smell was terrible, **sour** as vinegar. (FIC 2011)

(143) There was a smell like **sour** milk. (MAG 1996)

(144) She opened the refrigerator and a **sour** smell floated into the kitchen. (FIC 2003)

The occurrences in (142–144) describe the physical quality of a smell as being *sour*. The usage of gustatory adjectives to describe smell in this case are motivated by the conceptual metonymy GUSTATION FOR OLFACTION, thus mirroring similar mechanisms for the other taste types. While the adjective sour is used descriptively in (142–144), the usage of *sour breath* in (145) is metaphorical, but it relies on a conceptual mechanism that intervenes also in standard metaphorical occurrences:

(145) Every sitcom family at that time was uniformly white and well off, complacent, clean-cut, clean-mouthed and untouched by the **sour** breath of reality. (NEWS 2008)

The metaphorical expression *sour breath of reality* is consistent with previously analysed realisations in which *sour* is used to conceptualise DIFFICULT THINGS TO ACCEPT. The adjective *sour* is also found in occurrences that describe sounds, as exemplified in (146):

(146) But if too much of your dialogue goes nowhere, if your characters talk a lot but say nothing, your fiction is destined to hit a **sour note.** (ACAD 2009)

The realisation in (146) may be considered as motivated by the general negative meaning of the adjective *sour*, which may be used to conceptualise unpleasantness (Lehrer 1978: 121). While the negative evaluation of the expression in (146) is undeniable, when it is compared to the occurrence in (147) a more nuanced motivation emerges:

(147) Something **sweet** in the music had suddenly gone **sour**. (FIC 2002)

The occurrences in (146) and (147) are motivated by DISCORDANCE IS SOUR, an entailment of the primary metaphor HARMONY IS SWEET.

The adjective *sour* is found in intrafield occurrences that refer to smell and hearing. While the realisations for smell are mainly descriptive, most of them are motivated by the metonymy GUSTATION FOR OLFACTION. In the description of sounds, *sour* instantiates the metaphor DISCORDANCE IS SOUR, and the general embodied metonymy SOUR FOR UNPLEASANT, which underlies the lexical figurative meaning of the adjective *sour*. Crucially, this conceptual metaphor may be considered as an elaboration of the metaphor HARMONY IS SWEET.

9.5.4 Spicy

The intrafield occurrences of *spicy* refer to smell, as in (148) and (149):

(148) The lotion has a **spicy** scent. (MAG 1998)

(149) Pungent **spicy** smells and soothing tones of sitar music combined with candles flickering on pink tablecloths [. . .]. (FIC 1997)

As discussed in Paragraph 4.3, the gustatory term *spicy* may be successfully analysed as a source-based adjective. As such, it metonymically refers to the source of sensation (*spices* in this case) to refer to the sensation it produces, via the metonymy SOURCE OF SENSATION FOR THE SENSATION. In the case of intrafield occurrences, the usage of *spicy* may be interpreted as drawing on the same source, albeit perceived via a different modality. Thus, I argue that it is metonymical with respect to its source, following an analogous mechanism to the construction of the meaning in its gustatory usage. However, it is used literally in the description of smell as it draws on the olfactory properties of spices, and not necessarily on its gustatory meaning. This is supported by the occurrences in (148) and (149) in which the adjective *spicy* is used to describe the qualities of smells.

9.6 How do we conceptualise taste to talk about the other senses?

The linguistic data presented in this chapter report intrafield metaphorical expressions involving the BTTs in English. Although this label is not new in linguistic description, it has experienced renewed popularity in recent accounts of the traditionally called "synaesthetic" metaphors in cognitive and sensory linguistics. The modality that is most consistently structured through gustatory items is smell: the occurrences in which gustatory adjectives describe smell represent 48% of the entire intrafield metaphorical transfer in these data. The other modalities that are most frequently described using gustatory adjectives is sound, and lastly touch. Only a limited number of occurrences refer to sight.

In keeping with the continuous representation of perception sponsored in this book, and as evidenced by the linguistic elaboration of the sense of taste, I interpret intrafield occurrences in which taste describes smell as being motivated by the metonymy GUSTATION FOR OLFACTION. The linguistic construal of TASTE as a continuous dimension and semantic domain, and the highly integrated nature of gustatory and olfactory stimuli in flavour suggests that the two perceptions may often emerge together, if not simultaneously. Thus, linguistic labels associated to taste are routinely used in language to provide access to perception of smell. This results in a conventional usage of taste words to describe smell, with no evaluative component being construed. In some occurrences, the adjective *sweet* refers to negative experiences. Yet, our cultural consideration of the two as separate entities suggests a construal of distinctiveness, in keeping with Western philosophical tradition and folk-knowledge.

Overall, gustatory items are consistently used to refer to either positive or negative evaluations, both in standard and intrafield metaphors. Their evaluative meaning is motivated by their embodied value in the dietary habits of our species throughout our evolution. Sweet substances correspond to sugars, a valuable source of readily processable energy, thus providing a strongly embodied motivation for their conceptualisation as positive through the metonymy SWEET FOR PLEASANT. Conversely, both *sour* and *bitter* stimuli elicit a negative response, as they potentially signal dangerous and toxic substances in the food we ingest. Consequently, their negative evaluative meaning is motivated by the metonymy BITTER FOR UNPLEASANT and SOUR FOR UNPLEASANT.

There are cases in which a more nuanced motivation emerges. The usage of GUSTATORY items to describe HEARING relies on conceptual metaphors that motivate occurrences also in other contexts, such as LOVE IS SWEET, HARMONY IS SWEET, and DISCORDANCE IS SOUR. The conceptual metaphor LOVE IS SWEET is perhaps one of the most documented outside sensory linguistics, and it has been observed as influencing behavioural choices in recent neuro-psychological literature. The metaphor HARMONY IS SWEET may be motivated by crossmodal associations that connect sweet to round shapes, which in turn may be associated to the concept of harmony. Lastly, the entailment DISCORDANCE IS SOUR motivates linguistic realisations that describe sounds as sour.

A notable case is the description of cold thermal perception as bitterness. The semantic potential of *bitter* includes *cold* by virtue of a common linguistic ancestor that coded both touch (better accounted as pain in contemporary accounts of perception) and bitterness (Proto-Germanic *bîtan*). The development of words for bitterness from noxious haptic stimuli is widely documented in Indo-European languages, but the mapping between bitterness and cold is unique to English. The shared concept between the two sensations may have arisen from a shared facial and hedonic response to the two stimuli. Although there is no neural connection between perception of bitterness and perception of cold, considering the association of the two stimuli in experience I argue that the semantic overlap between bitterness and coldness be motivated by the metonymy BITTER FOR PAINFUL TOUCH.

The linguistic evidence of intrafield metaphors from the COCA lend support to a reconsideration of the mechanism of intrafield metaphors and metonymies. These may be divided into two main categories on the basis on the integration of the sensory modalities involved in physiology. Thus, in the case of the different components of flavour, the conceptual mechanisms that motivate the usage of gustatory words to refer to olfaction is metonymical. This is most frequent with *sweet* and *sour*. In the case of less-integrated modality, intrafield metaphors may be accounted for on the basis of conceptual metaphors that are also observed to motivate other realisations that have not been traditionally considered as intrafield. In the case of spiciness, there is no need to posit a figurative connection, considering the morphological structure and the semantic motivation of the adjective. Taken altogether, this evidence suggests that the label "Intrafield metaphors" is a useful analytical tool to distinguish in a typological perspective a set of metaphorical occurrences from others, but that the semantic mechanisms that motivate these realisations are not different than other mechanisms found in other domains.

10 Conclusions

This book set off with the specific objective of exploring the role of the physical sense of taste in motivating conceptual processes in English. The analyses that I carried out are set against the background of Cognitive Linguistics theories, the methodologies adopted vary and originate in neighbouring disciplines. Each of them maintains a usage-based approach to the description of linguistic phenomena, in keeping with this tradition. The reasons that motivated the choice of this topic of investigation lie in the scant attention given in linguistic literature to gustatory sensations in motivating figurative thought and language. The sense of taste has been regarded for centuries as an inferior sense, and this disparagement is the cause of such a lack of scientific and rigorous investigation. Taste is believed to be a subjective sense that may not yield true knowledge of the world. Furthermore, it is often believed that there is a dearth of words to specifically describe gustatory perception. The analyses exposed in this book present a different picture, and advocate a reconsideration of the sense of taste in contemporary linguistic debate by offering compelling insights on the dynamic relationship between language and perception.

The starting point of my investigation was an elicitation of the words that describe taste in English. To do so, I asked native speakers of English to produce as many words as possible that could describe taste, applying the procedure called *freelisting*. This methodology is more often adopted in cognitive anthropology than it is in linguistics. Freelistings fit particularly well with the need of describing a linguistic category. Anthropologists use this method to explore salient aspects in cultural domains, while linguists may use it to explore salient elements in a semantic domain. The results of freelistings were necessarily further elaborated through the Cognitive Salience Index: an algorithm through which a researcher may organise the elicited internal elements of a category (or a domain) according to their salience. We may imagine a semantic domain as a sharp mountain. The most salient words lie at the peak of the mountain, but as we progress towards the peak, we realise it is not just one point: rather, the highest point lies in a continuum with other points that share a similar altitude. Likewise, in a semantic domain there are some words that lie at the peak: these are the most salient words, i.e., the words that come first to mind, that better represents the domain, and are most commonly used. From the peak towards the foot of the domain there are a number of different words that may not be uniquely associated with the domain, rather they may start being part of a different "mountain".

The English words that lie at the peak of the semantic domain of taste are *sweet, sour, bitter, salty, spicy, hot,* and *savoury*. These words only partially correspond to the taste types identified by physiologists (sweet, sour, bitter, salty, and umami), and contain at least one word (*hot*) that is most commonly associated with temperature perception, rather than taste per se. This should not surprise us. Psychologists and physiologists who carry out research in the area of perception studies have noted for a long time that what people routinely refer to as taste is in fact better accounted for as *flavour*. That is, a multisensory perception that involves stimuli (and words to describe them) transmitted by a complex network of neural pathways that include gustation, retronasal olfaction, and chemesthesis. The words elicited through the free-listing technique contain also auditory and visual descriptors, thus confirming results of research in perceptual psychology on the interplay between different modalities. However, the difference between taste and flavour is specified at a specific, technical level, while in common parlance the two terms are almost synonyms.

10.1 The words of taste

In order to assess the multisensoriality of the lexicon of taste, I compared the results of the freelisting with the norms elicited by Lynott and Connell (2009). These norms represent a useful tool for researchers working in psycholinguistics and dealing with perception, as they provide a measure of the unique association of an item with a given perceptual dimension. Results of this comparison urge for reconsideration of the vocabulary of taste, showing that this semantic domain is highly multisensory and that it contains an array of adjectives that may be used to code perceptual qualities of an object. However, it must also be noted that this vocabulary is largely built following the construction SOURCE+Y: e.g., *creamy*, *oily*. This construction instantiates a metonymic conceptualisation, according to which the source of the sensation is used to describe its perceptual properties. The SOURCE+Y construction is highly productive in English, but it is not fully informative, and it does not rule out referential ambiguity.

For instance, if we describe the taste of something as **asparagusy*, we may immediately recognise that the source of this descriptive word is an *asparagus*, thus guiding an interpretation of the type *something that tastes like asparagus*. Yet, such an interpretation is ambiguous in many ways. First, if someone has never tasted an asparagus this expression is completely opaque, as the source of the perception is not available to the speaker. Secondly, it is not clear what this adjective refers to: does *asparagusy* refer to the metallic taste of the food, does it refer to the crispy consistency, or maybe to the bitter pungency? The taste words following this construction may therefore lead to confusion and referential ambiguity, but not necessarily. For instance, adjectives such as *salty*, *savoury*, and *spicy* follow this construction as well, and yet their meaning is highly entrenched and conventionalised, thus ruling out the ambiguity of less salient items such as *creamy*, or *oily*, where two distinct facets of meaning may be alternatively accessed depending on context.

Other key information provided by the results of the Cognitive Salience Index is the confirmation of the BTTs in English. Previous literature has often identified BTTs with the basic transduction processes, and this demonstrated to be a predominantly correct assumption. However, the linguistic data elicited through the freelisting suggest that there might also be other taste terms that may be considered as basic, and that according to existing accounts on the nature of Basic Terms we may further distinguish between Primary BTTs (*sweet, sour, bitter,* and *salty*) and Secondary BTTs (*spicy* and *savoury*). I distinguished between Primary and Secondary BTTs on the basis of the criteria that each of them fulfils. These criteria are mainly linguistic, but they also include physiological motivation.

The vocabulary of taste appears to be variegated and it includes sensory adjectives coming from different sensory modalities, thus arguing in favour of the multisensorial nature of the lexicon of perception. Considering this multisensoriality and the ambiguity of source-based language, I investigated the internal composition of the semantic domain of taste through two categorisation tasks, reported in Chapter 6. The first task involved only the most salient items in the domain, while the second included the different terms elicited through the freelisting task. The most salient items in the domain have been consistently associated one with the other, following patterns that have also been observed in other languages, i.e., *sour-bitter*; *salty-savoury, spicy-hot*. The items *sweet* and *delicious* are not strongly associated, and this confirms the general nature of *delicious*. The unique nature of *sweet* –the only adjective in the domain of taste with a clear positive meaning– corresponds to an unequivocally positive physical reaction associated to the perception of sweetness.

The association between sour and bitterness has been previously noted in physiological literature. It has been demonstrated that this was not due to confusion in perception, since participants in taste-recognition studies have proved to be able to discriminate between the two stimuli. Rather, it seems that such confusion may arise in the ability of correctly labelling one sensation or the other. These claims are supported by the results reported in Paragraph 6.4, where native English speakers consistently associated the two concepts, even without having access to the physical counterpart. Therefore, I argue that the association between the two is based in language and on a conceptual level and does not necessarily arise from physical perception.

On the other hand, the conflation between *salty* and *savoury* may be motivated by physiological reasons. The substance that typically elicits saltiness is common table salt (NaCl). It is a flavour enhancer, as it helps volatile particles in the food reach the nose. Thus, more salt in the food elicits more savour. Moreover, experiments on taste recognition suggest that English speakers tend to classify as *salty* stimuli that are categorised as *glutamic* or *umami* by Chinese and Japanese speakers respectively. Furthermore, other languages (such as Italian) show the tendency to describe umami sensations as *saporito*, Eng. 'savoury', thus confirming this association pattern cross-linguistically.

The third noticeable pattern in the association of taste terms is between *spicy* and *hot*. These two terms may be considered synonyms, as both refer to perception of capsaicin by the trigeminal nerve. Nonetheless, *hot* is also a temperature term. Its usage to refer to spiciness has often been considered as a result of polysemy, motivated by metaphor. Recently, this account has been challenged on the basis of neurophysiological data that show how the human body physically interprets exposure to capsaicin as thermal pain, thus motivating the usage of *hot* to refer to *spicy*. This is evidenced also by the results of the association patterns, that show how English speakers consistently chose to group together these two terms. However, I argue that the relationship between spiciness and hot is metonymic, and the same conceptual mechanism underlies the motivation of other phenomena of semantic expansion in sensory language.

The second categorisation task unravels the semantic relationships between lexical items in the domain of taste by means of family resemblance networks. I carried out both the task and the analyses through the online software OptimalSort and recruited native speakers through the online service Amazon Turk. I asked participants to group the items elicited through the freelisting task in different categories that had been previously assessed by pre-tests. The possible categories reflected the BTTs, plus Texture, Mouthfeel, and General Descriptors. Results show an intricate network of sense relationships and further confirm the association between sour and bitter, but also show a conflation pattern between salty-umami-spicy. The lexicon of taste may be successfully organised in a family resemblance network, with some of the items that are associated to more than one category (for instance, *tart* is present both in sour and sweet). The presence of the same items in more than one category may also be explained considering the referential ambiguity of source-based language. Adjectives such as *meaty* appear both in *umami* and *texture*. The meaning of this adjective may vary depending on the facet that is accessed. It is likely that the categorisation of *meaty* in the category *umami* is motivated by the construal of the meaning as "something *tastes* like meat". Alternatively, the same adjective may be found in the category *texture*, thus licensing the interpretation of "something *feels* like meat", tapping into the haptic sensory experiences in the mouth. Taken all together, the data reviewed in Chapter 6 suggest that the semantic network that structures the semantic domain of TASTE is informed by our perceptual knowledge, thus confirming a close relationship between our bodies and the verbal conceptualisation of experiences. Nonetheless, the category with the majority of items is General Descriptors. It is an unspecified category that refers to descriptors at a higher level, thus not describing a specific taste sensation, rather general properties of objects in the gustatory dimension (e.g., *delicious*, *tasty*, and *yummy*).

10.2 What are the conceptual mechanisms that drive the figurative usage of taste words?

The list of lexical items that emerged in the description of the category of taste serves as the basis for the second section of the book, where I explore the semantic elaboration of these terms through the conceptual mechanisms of metaphor and metonymy. There are two main methodologies to retrieve data for the investigation of figurative language in Cognitive Linguistics: the lexicographic and the corpus analysis approach. Chapter 7 reports the results of the first approach, by reviewing data coming from the Mapping Metaphor with the English Thesaurus project. Furthermore, the nature of the data allows for a diachronic analysis of the mechanisms of meaning expansion.

Linguists working on well-documented languages such as English may rely on abundant data, compiled in thesauri, dictionaries, and centuries of usage of the language. These uses are inseparable from the cultural contexts that produced them: this includes literature, philosophy, and the development of scientific knowledge. At the same time, they are motivated by the embodied nature of the lexicon under scrutiny: for instance, the concept of LOVE has been consistently construed and described in terms of sweetness, from the earliest forms of written records in Mesopotamia to current instantiations. In the specific case of the conceptual metaphor LOVE IS SWEET, the relationship between these two concepts has been also proved through empirical experiments, thus further confirming the role of this metaphor in conceptualizing emotions such as kindness, innocence, and affection.

The diachronic approach to these data reveals that metaphorical meanings may develop independently in a linguistic system, but that they may also be borrowed from other languages. The history of English semantic extension shows that some items (for instance, *rancour*) entered English already loaded with a metaphorical meaning that had developed in Latin, and later in French. This gives rise to different realisations and dates of attestation. However, the metaphorical link that has survived through different linguistic systems suggest that the metaphorical relationship between the senses is deep-rooted, and it represents a case of a 'dead metaphor'. The lexicographic data also suggest a general mapping that may motivate the use of taste words in English. Contrary to popular misconceptions of taste, gustatory sensations may be employed to conceptualise the process of reaching experiential knowledge, but also intelligence, the character of someone or something, and aesthetics. Furthermore, positive and pleasant qualities are expressed with palatable tastes, while negative qualities are described with unpalatable tastes. The data retrieved through the MMP show that gustatory perception may intervene in motivating semantic change in a diachronic perspective. Crucially, there have been only sporadic contributions to the description of sensory language in a diachronic perspective, but the data urge for more research undertaking this approach.

Some of the lexical items in the MMP are no longer in use, while other meanings have become obsolete. Nonetheless, most of the conceptual metaphors analysed in Chapter 7 are still active and motivate semantic expansion in contemporary English, as evidenced by corpus analysis in Chapters 8 and 9. This methodology allows the researcher to retrieve data with a usage-based perspective, in line with the general approach of the book. I checked the occurrences of the BTTs in the corpus, and manually isolated their metaphorical occurrences. The lexical item *sweet* elicits the largest number of occurrences, and *bitter* is used in metaphorical occurrences more frequently than the other BTTs. Furthermore, most of these items are used to describe perception experienced through other sensory modalities. In previous literature (including my own published research), this type of expression has been labelled *synaesthetic metaphors*. However, recent contributions to the topic show the inconsistency of such a theoretical construct and prefer calling them Intrafield metaphors.

The conceptual metaphors retrieved in the COCA show an elaborate network of meanings, and it is often impossible to distinguish between one or the other. Rather, a dynamic model of meaning construction fits better with the objective of accounting for the conceptualisation of taste. Following, each basic taste term is illustrated through a figure that reports firstly, at the bottom the BTT; the second line represents the generic domain (i.e., pleasant, unpleasant, liveliness); then at the final level are the lexical concepts emerging from the corpus analysis as metaphorically associated with the taste.

For instance Figure (4) illustrates the linguistic realisations of metaphors involving sweet. The metaphor LOVE IS SWEET is placed on a continuum with realisations of INNOCENCE IS SWEET, which in turn may be analysed, on a socio-pragmatic level, as examples of the WOMEN AS DESSERT metaphor (Hines 1999). The relevance of the analysis of expressions such as *sweet old lady* as motivated by this metaphor acquires even more relevance if we consider that sweetness intervenes in the conceptualisation of various human groups, but it is dramatically less frequent in the description of men. I argue that perception of sweetness is particularly associated with feminine characteristics, and that the conceptualisation of manhood resists the adjective *sweet*. Other metaphorical realisations include VALUE IS SWEET, HARMONY IS SWEET, and SUCCESS/REWARD IS SWEET.

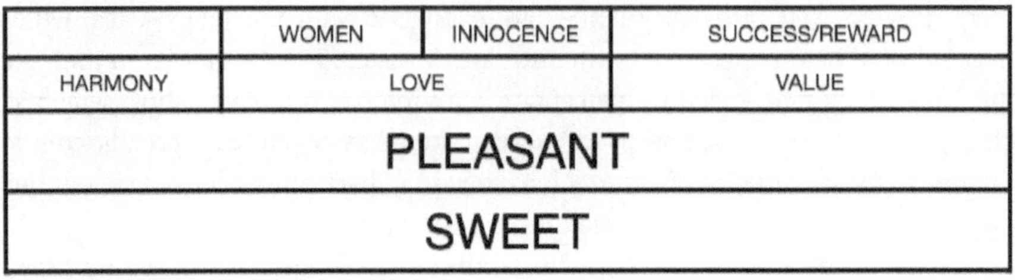

	WOMEN	INNOCENCE	SUCCESS/REWARD
HARMONY	LOVE		VALUE
PLEASANT			
SWEET			

Figure 4: The conceptualisation of sweet.

The adjective *bitter* is mainly used to conceptualise divisive situations and negative feelings (Figure 5), for instance the domains of CONFLICT and DISAPPOINTMENT. For example, bitter is consistently used to describe *divorce, fight, feud,* and also to conceptualise feelings such as anger, contempt, and hatred. Moreover, loss and failure may be described as bitter. These realisations are motivated by the evolutionary role and embodied perception of this taste type. Although it developed to detect toxicity, humans acquired a taste for it and included in their diets, both for hedonic and medicinal purposes. I argue that the practice of swallowing something bitter but necessary may motivate linguistic realisations such as *bitter truth*. Although the connection between "drinking a bitter medicine" and "accepting reality" might be distant in the experience of contemporary English, the lexicon stores encyclopaedic knowledge that surfaces in our conceptualisations and elaborations. Lastly, *bitter* may also be used in the conceptualisation of pain as attested in the semantic evolution of the adjectives that describe this taste type across Indo-European languages.

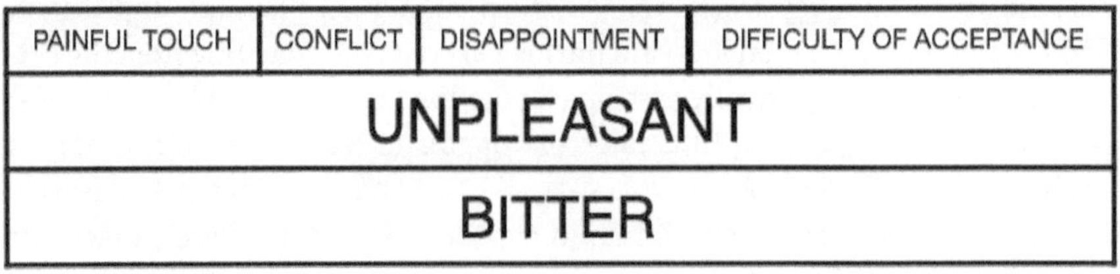

PAINFUL TOUCH	CONFLICT	DISAPPOINTMENT	DIFFICULTY OF ACCEPTANCE
UNPLEASANT			
BITTER			

Figure 5: The conceptualisation of bitter.

The adjective *sour* is used in similar ways to *bitter*, but it conveys a more severe and sudden condition (see Figure 6). It is often used in constructions that may be analysed in the event frame, motivated by conceptual metaphors such as CHANGE IS MOTION (e.g., *our relationship went **sour***). I argue that the conceptual mechanism that motivates these realisations is the SOUR FOR SPOILAGE metonymy. In this case, conceptual metonymy seems a better model to account for this meaning expansion on the basis of the embodied nature of this lexicon. Other metaphorical realisations include HOSTILE TEMPER IS SOUR, and DISCORDANCE IS SOUR. Finally, there is a group of metaphorical realisations involving *sour* that are reminiscent of mappings in which *bitter* seems more frequently used, thus suggesting a further case of overlapping between the two concepts at a metaphorical level.

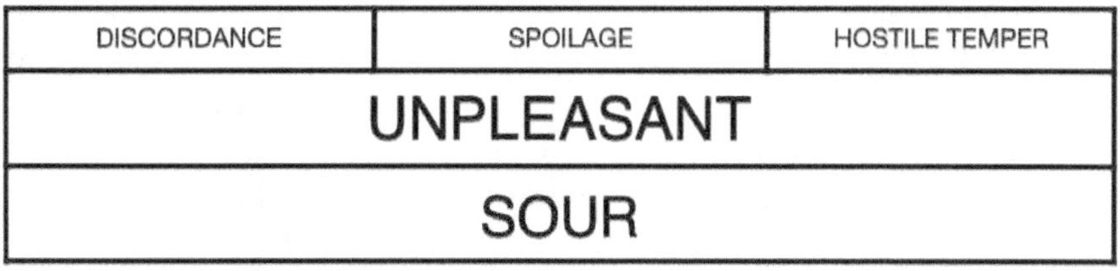

DISCORDANCE	SPOILAGE	HOSTILE TEMPER
UNPLEASANT		
SOUR		

Figure 6: The conceptualisation of sour.

The last group of occurrences is less numerous, but it still offers relevant insights into the nature of the conceptualisation of taste sensations. The adjective *salty* appears in realisations that conceptualise RUDENESS, as in *salty language*. The motivation for this metaphorical realisation lies in the history of English, and in the association between saltiness, spiciness, and piquancy, which is then metaphorically extended to refer to the distinct lively taste of someone (see Figure 7), in keeping with the general conceptual metaphor CHARACTER IS TASTE. The adjective *spicy* is found in occurrences in which it describes sexual excitement (e.g., *a spicy encounter*). The motivational basis of this metaphor is deeply embodied, and it may be considered a primary metaphor: both sexual arousal and spiciness elicit a bodily reaction in terms of heat and vascular dilatation. The generic domain that is conceptualised through spiciness is EXCITEMENT. This is better exemplified with reference to the verb *to spice up* something, that is: to make it more exciting and appealing.

Finally, the adjective *savoury* was not frequently used metaphorically, and a better example may be given with reference to the item *unsavoury*: e.g., *unsavoury characters*, used to define "objectionable" people on moral grounds (OED).

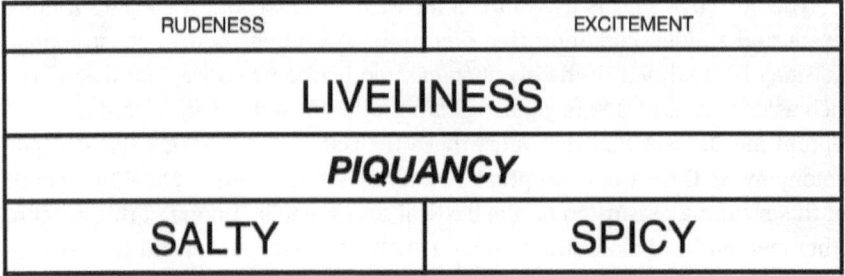

Figure 7: The conceptualisation of salty and spicy.

The metaphorical and metonymic elaborations of the lexicon of taste show a complex set of meaning relations. In some cases, the evolutionary role is overridden by cultural practices and usages, which result in language specific elaborations. More often, these elaborations mirror the physical, evolutionary, and embodied value of taste types. This deep level of embodiment perhaps is best exemplified with the general meaning that assume the adjectives *sweet* and *bitter*, namely positive and negative, by virtue of the conceptual metonymy SWEET FOR PLEASANT and BITTER FOR UNPLEASANT. I argue that the meaning of these adjectives may be accounted for as the result of a metonymy mainly because the process of perception is continuous: exposure to sweet tastants elicits an almost immediate hedonically positive response. Likewise, bitter produces a negative response. Nonetheless, it is a response: be it physiological, unconscious, and instinctual. It is not physically built-in the stimuli, and this distinction seems to be mirrored in language. Analysis of occurrences of *sweet* describing scents shows that this adjective may be used in a descriptive way to denote negative perceptual stimuli, thus suggesting a distinction between the descriptive and evaluative usage of the lexical item *sweet*. Thus, these conceptual metonymies represent the general conceptual mechanism that motivates meaning creation for SWEET and BITTER. They intervene in conceptualisation before the other mechanisms described, thus structuring the polysemy of these two gustatory words.

10.3 Intrafield metaphors reassessed

Finally, Chapter 9 specifically deals with Intrafield metaphors. After having reviewed their theoretical status in recent contributions on the topic, I illustrate the occurrences retrieved for the various BTTs. The adjective *sweet* is found in association with smell and hearing; bitter is found in occurrences with touch and smell; sour intervenes in the description of smell and hearing; and spicy only with smell. The contribution of each gustatory quality to the conceptualisation of perceptual domains is in keeping with their conceptualisations found in other domains. The perceptual domain that is most often conceptualised through TASTE is SMELL. These two modalities are closely associated, and their lexicon often overlaps. Moreover, recent account in physiology show that gustation, olfaction and chemesthesis are part of the same perceptual continuum, which physiologists refer to as flavour, but which is linguistically labelled as taste. Nonetheless, in keeping with the emic commitment to the description of taste, I integrate the cultural set of beliefs of English speakers into the description of the semantic processes that regulate the figurative usage of gustatory vocabulary. This leads to the reconsideration of intrafield metaphors as cases of metonymy, and I argue that the usage of taste adjectives to describe smells is motivated by GUSTATION FOR OLFACTION, in line with a continuous construal of the perceptual event. Figure 8 illustrates the intersection between language and perception. The bottom line reports the conceptual domain of TASTE. The top line lists the six BTTs, which are used in language to access different dimensions of the domain as described by physiology. Thus, distinct BTTs are indicative of the physiological underlying dimension. The adjective spicy is associated with the sensation of chemesthesis. The terms *savoury*, *salty*, *bitter*, *sweet*, and *sour* are associated to gustation, whereas only *bitter*, *sweet* and *sour* are associated to olfaction.

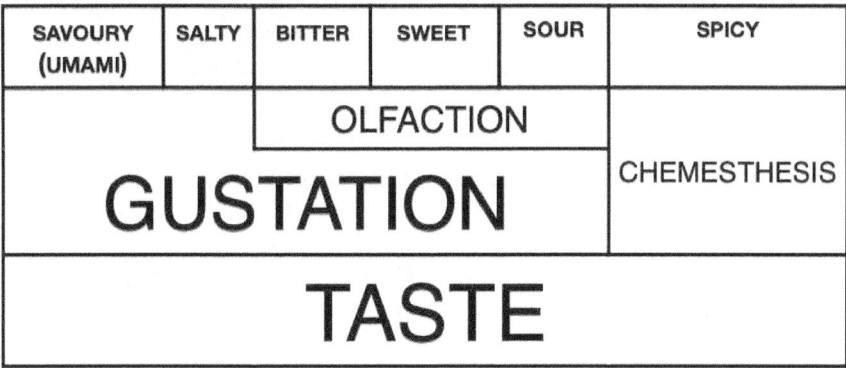

Figure 8: Language and perception in TASTE.

The overlap between gustatory lexicon and audition is structured by conceptual metaphors retrieved in non-perceptual domains, and they are grounded in embodied experiences thus supporting a modal view of meaning representation. The conceptual metaphor LOVE IS SWEET has been assessed through experimental protocols, and there is indirect evidence for the primary metaphor HARMONY

IS SWEET. Experiments in crossmodal psychology suggest that sweet is associated to round shapes, and in music theory harmony is often conceptualised as a circle. Coupled together, these pieces of evidence suggest a conceptualisation of the domain of HARMONY as SWEETNESS. Interestingly, discordant sounds may be described as *sour*, thus showcasing an entailment of the same metaphor using an unpleasant gustatory sensation to conceptualise an unpleasant sound: DISCORDANCE IS SOUR.

The most intriguing case of intrafield expressions is perhaps the lexical overlap between bitterness and coldness. Temperature perception is subsumed in haptic perception, and it is mediated by chemesthesis in flavour, as demonstrated by the lexical items in the free task, and also by the case of *spicy* and *hot*. The case of bitterness however is different because gustatory stimuli intervene in conceptualizing temperature. The adjective *bitter* may be used to describe thermal noxious stimuli in the cold spectrum. The reason behind this conceptual link is to be found in etymology. I argue that these realisations are motivated by the conceptual metonymy BITTER FOR PAINFUL TOUCH, and that facial and hedonic reactions to bitterness perception represent the embodied ground for the development of such a link.

The emotional valence and evaluative meaning of adjectives such as *sweet* might be interpreted as being part of the lexical representation of the word, with no need to posit conceptual mechanisms that elaborate on their semantic potential. While valence and hedonics undoubtedly play a crucial role in the creation of meaning of gustatory adjectives, the richness and variety of senses analysed in this book argue for a more nuanced view. Furthermore, the occurrences of *sweet* as a descriptive item suggest that this adjective may also be used descriptively, and that its positive evaluative meaning is the result of conceptualisation mechanisms such as metaphor and metonymy.

10.4 What can gustatory perceptions tell us about the nature of our minds and conceptual systems?

Taken all together, the evidence in this book points to a revaluation of the role of gustatory perception in motivating conceptual processes. Far from being vestigial and irrelevant, taste is shown to intervene in English in the description of emotional feelings, preferences, and knowledge, to name but a few. This investigation contributes to our knowledge of the interaction between the senses and the mind by showing how the lexicon of taste mirrors perceptual processes and neural pathways. Languages really are "windows on the senses" (Majid and Levinson 2011: 7), and our conceptualisation patterns are revealing of the human capacity of making meaning out of daily mundane experiences. The relationship between perception and language that emerges from the analyses reported in the book is highly dynamic. On one hand, linguistic usage and recurrent conceptualisation patterns override perception, thus influencing the ability to correctly name and recognise distinct gustatory stimuli in English. On the other hand, the linguistic domain of TASTE mirrors the complexity of physical perception and reconstruction of a unique Gestalt of the gustatory experience. Moreover, the categorisation patterns of gustatory language are related to physiological associations that are also observed in other languages, thus providing further support to the hypothesis that linguistic phenomena are grounded in embodied cognition. The figurative elaboration of different tastes is motivated by specific embodied reactions that have evolved across millennia of biological evolution. I do not consider the conceptual mechanisms observed in the description of taste in English as universal. Cross-linguistic data suggest that the creation of meaning based on distinct tastes varies, thus displaying the multifaceted ways in which languages organise, interpret, and conceptualise the same physical experience.

Furthermore, this book offers a methodological protocol for rigorous investigation of the relationship between language and perception, by unravelling both the internal organisation of the semantic domain of gustatory lexicon, and by exploring metaphorical usages of this lexicon in common parlance. The strict usage-based approach allows for an understanding of the role of taste in English in the linguistic practices of non-specialists, thus offering a comprehensive picture of the intersection between the body, mind, and language. Moreover, the evolutionary perspective taken in the book offers new insights into our conceptual systems, positing a close relationship between cognition and its bodily basis. It highlights how evolution and our ecological niches may inform and sometimes even constrain our representation of the world through the stimuli we have selected throughout the millennia and the ways in which our cultural systems have organised them.

The data and the arguments proposed to interpret them may be useful and applied in different disciplines and areas of expertise. Researchers working in sensory linguistics may find a thorough account of an under-represented area in the semantic space in an otherwise largely represented linguistic system. The diffusion of English represents a unique opportunity to verify hypotheses on meaning extension, considering the large amount of data that has been recorded throughout its history. The exploitation of the Mapping Metaphor Project represents another methodological tool available for the researcher to explore the lexicographic record of metaphorical instantiations.

The validation of the experimental protocol of the freelistings and Cognitive Salience Index represents a verified tool for the description of a semantic domain in an emic perspective, thus keeping the researcher's arbitrariness to a minimum. An accurate description of the linguistic realisation of the different sensory domains is paramount for cross-cultural investigations and to grasp a general understanding of the role of perception in cognition. The insights coming from this line of research could prove useful in the development of new technologies in the area of Artificial Intelligence, where there is a constant increase in the realisation of more performative machines that may interface with humans at different levels of interaction.

Secondly, the results discussed in the previous chapters may be applied in the description of food by researchers working in various disciplines. Researchers working in the food industry may benefit from the insights of the categorisation task, by identifying lexical items that have high salience and by recognizing the ambiguity of certain adjectives. This may enable them to develop more accurate communication strategies to convey important information about health and the physical qualities of food. Moreover, advertisers and communication strategists may find useful details regarding the conceptualisation and possible meanings of sensory language, thus exploiting this knowledge for a more effective presentation of content and ideas.

There are still many areas of investigation that require further understanding. Research in sensory linguistics is just at its dawn. In order to gain a more comprehensive picture of the interaction between perception, language, and culture we need data coming from other languages with the most diverse phylogenetic, cultural, and even environmental backgrounds. Data should be collected following a common methodology to allow for comparisons between linguistic systems. The investigations on diverse lexicons of perception should be extended also to their metaphorical and metonymic conceptualisations to ascertain the boundaries between embodied motivation and cultural elaboration. There are only scant, yet promising, attempts to describe cross-cultural variation in meaning expansion. We could benefit from more complete and thorough accounts. Investigations in the cross-cultural dimension should be carried out also in the discipline of World Englishes. This could contribute to an understanding of how culinary practices and ecological niches influence linguistic systems. Possible influences on the lexicon of perception coming from indigenous languages may also suggest socio-linguistic models of interaction and reveal patterns of political and cultural power structures. Is perception linguistically encoded following Western models of organisation, or is its representation formulated on the basis of non-Western systems? In other words, do (often hegemonic) linguistic policies rule over the bodies, or do bodies modify language in those contexts?

In a more philosophical line of inquiry, the relationship between literacy and perception should be investigated. The results of the freelisting task, as well as leading arguments in sensory linguistics on the continuity of the senses, argue for a reconsideration of the five-sense folk model. Yet, this folk model has been passed down generation after generation, and it is currently being taught in schools and kindergartens as a means of gaining consciousness of the body. How does this explicit teaching influence our conceptualisation of the senses? To what extent have these languages changed with the advent of literacy? In Italy, the last speakers of regional languages and dialects are dying out, and most of them have received only minor formal education. Their diets and lifestyles are often radically different to those of contemporary Italians. Their languages of perception should be described, so as to possibly monitor the influence of literacy and explicit instructions on the organisation of perception and conceptualisation. Specific perceptual qualities of objects might be coded in new and unexpected ways for Western folk-models.

Lastly, the research presented in this book has largely benefitted from previous research in psychology labs on mechanisms of grounding thought in sensorimotor processes, and it has observed and posited others. Further investigations in psycholinguistics, psychology, and evolutionary anthropology are essential to verify some of the claims made and elicited through observation of semantic phenomena. Some of the metaphorical links that have been proposed could be verified by implementing existing protocols. An understanding of the mechanisms through which our minds ground abstract thinking in perception may confirm or contradict the metaphors and metonymies proposed in this analysis. Nonetheless, they would shed light on the nature of our meaning making capacities that has adapted to our world over millennia of evolution and offer new perspectives on the tastes we've lived by.

References

Ahn, Ahreem, Dongwon Min. 2019. How Sweetness Plays Sweetly in Persuasion. *Japanese Psychological Association*. doi.org/10.1111/jpr.12260.

Allan, Kathryn. 2009. An Inquest into Metaphor Death: Exploring the Loss of Literal Senses of Conceptual Metaphors. *Journal of Cognitive Semiotics* 5 (1–2), 291–311.

Anderson, John R. 1983. *The architecture of cognition*. Cambridge, MA: Harvard University Press.

Anderson, Wendy. 2019. Perception metaphors in English. A bird's eye view. In Laura J. Speed, Carolyn O'Meara, Lila San Roque & Asifa Majid (eds.), *Perception Metaphors*, 65–83. Amsterdam/ Philadelphia: John Benjamins.

Anderson, Wendy & Ellen Bramwell. 2014. Of anoraks and oysters: metaphors of social communication in the Historical Thesaurus. *Opening New Lines of Communication in Applied Linguistics: Proceedings of the 46th BAAL Annual Meeting*, 41–52.

Ankerstein, Carrie A. & Gerardine M. Pereira. 2013. Talking about taste. Starved for words. In Cornelia Gerhardt, Maximiliane Frobenius & Susanne Ley (eds.), *Culinary Linguistics: The Chef's Special*. Amsterdam/ Philadelphia: John Benjamins.

Antinucci, Marco and Davide Risso. 2017. A Matter of Taste: Lineage-Specific Loss of Function of Taste Receptor Genes in Vertebrates. *Frontiers in Molecular Biosciences*, 4 (81). https://doi:10.3389/fmolb.2017.00081

Auvray, Malika & Charles Spence. 2008. The multisensory perception of flavor. *Consciousness and Cognition*, 17 (3), 1016–1031. https://doi.org/10.1016/j.concog.2007.06.005 (last accessed 21 September 2020).

Bachmanov, Alexander A. & Gary K. Beauchamp. 2007. Taste receptor genes. *Annual Review of Nutrition* 27, 389–414. https://doi.org/10.1146/annurev.nutr.26.061505.111329 (last accessed 21 September 2020).

Bachmanov, Alexander A., Natalia P. Bosak, Cailu Lin, Ichiro Matsumoto, Makoto Ohmoto, Danielle R. Reed, Theodore M. Nelson. 2014. Genetics of Taste Receptors. *Current Pharmaceutical Design*, 20 (16). doi: 10.2174/13816128113199990566 (last accessed 21 September 2020).

Backhouse, Andrew E. 1994. *The Lexical Field of Taste: A Semantic Study of Japanese Taste Terms*. Cambridge, UK: Cambridge University Press.

Baldwin, Maude W., Yasuka Toda, Tomoya Nakagita, Mary J. O'Connell, Kirk C. Klasing, Takumi Misaka, Scott V. Edwards, Stephen D. Liberles. 2014. Evolution of sweet taste perception in hummingbirds by transformation of the ancestral umami receptor. *Science* 345, 929–933. doi: 10.1126/science.1255097 (last accessed 21 September 2020).

Bagli, Marco. 2016. "Shaking off so good a wife and so sweet a lady": Shakespeare's use of taste words. *Journal of Literary Semantics*, 45, 141–159. doi.org/10.1515/jls-2016-0010 (last accessed 29 April 2021).

Bagli, Marco. 2017. Tastes we've lived by. Taste metaphors in English. In Annalisa Baicchi & Alexandra Bagasheva (eds.), *Figurative Language we live by: the cognitive underpinnings and mechanisms of figurativity in language*. Textus, Issue XXX, Vol. 1, 33–48. doi: 10.7370/87664.

Bagli, Marco. 2018. Defining Taste in English Informant Categorization. In Annalisa Baicchi, Rémi Digonnet, & Jodi L. Sandford (eds.), *Sensory Perceptions in Language, Embodiment and Epistemology*, 155–175. Cham (Switzerland): Springer. https://doi.org/10.1007/978-3-319-91277-6_9.

Barcelona, Antonio (ed.). 2003. *Metaphor and Metonymy at the Crossroads: A Cognitive Perspective*. Berlin/ New York: De Gruyter Mouton.

Barcelona, Antonio. 2008. Metonymy is not just a lexical phenomenon: On the operation of metonymy in grammar and discourse. In Christina Alm-Arvius, Nils-Lennart Johannesson & David C. Minugh (eds.), *Selected Papers from the 2008 Stockholm Metaphor Festival*, 3–42. Stockholm: Stockholm University Press.

Barlow, Michael & Suzanne Kemmer (eds.). 2000. *Usage Based Models of Language*. Stanford, CA: CSLI Publications.

Barrós-Loscertales, Alfonso, Julio Gonzáles, Friedemann Pulvermüller, Noelia Ventura-Campos, Juan Carlso Bustamante, Víctor Costumero, María Antonia Parcet, & César Ávila. 2012. Reading Salt Activates Gustatory Brain Regions: fMRI Evidence for Semantic Grounding in a Novel Sensory Modality. *Cerebral Cortex*, 22 (11), 2554–2563. https://doi.org/10.1093/cercor/bhr324.

Barsalou, Lawrence W. 1999. Perceptual symbol systems. *Brain and Behavioural Sciences* 22: 577–660.

Barsalou, Lawrence W. 2003. Situated simulation in the human conceptual system. *Language and Cognitive Processes*, 18, 513–562.

Barsalou, Lawrence W. 2009. Simulation, situated conceptualisation, and prediction. *Philosophical Transactions of the Royal Society, B: Biological Sciences*, 364, 1281–1289.

Barsalou, Lawrence W. 2016. On Staying Grounded and Avoiding Quixotic Dead Ends. *Psychonomic Bulletin & Review*. 23, 1122–1142. https://doi.org/10.3758/s13423-016-1028-3 (last accessed 29 April 2021).

Basbaum, Allan I., Diana M. Bautista, Grégory Scherrer & David Julius. 2009. Cellular and Molecular Mechanisms of Pain. *Cell* 139 (2), 267–284. https://doi.org/10.1016/j.cell.2009.09.028 (last accessed 21 September 2020).

Battig, William F. & William E. Montague. 1969. Category norms of verbal items in 56 categories A replication and extension of the Connecticut category norms. *Journal of Experimental Psychology*, 80 (3, pt.2), 1–46. https://doi.org/10.1037/h0027577 (last accessed 22 September 2020).

Bayliss, Elizabeth A., John F. Steiner, Douglas H. Fernald, Lori A. Crane and Deborah S. Main. 2003. Descriptions of Barriers to Self-Care by Persons with Comorbid Chronic Diseases. *The Annals of Family Medicine*, 1 (1): 15–21. DOI: https://doi.org/10.1370/afm.4

Beauchamp,. Gary K. 2009. Sensory and receptor responses to umami: an overview of pioneering work. *American Journal of Clinical Nutrition* 90 (3):723S–727S.

Beare, John I. 1906. *Greek theories of elementary cognition from Alcmaeon to Aristotle*. Oxford: Clarendon Press.

Bernard, Harvey Russel. 2011. *Research methods in anthropology: qualitative and quantitative approaches*. Lanham: Altamira/Rowman & Littlefield.

Bergen, Benjamin. 2015. Embodiment. In Ewa Dąbrowska & Dagmar Divjak (eds.), *Handbook of Cognitive Linguistics*, 10–30. Berlin/ Boston: De Gruyter Mouton.

Berlin, Brent & Paul Kay. 1969. *Basic Colour Terms. Their Universality and Evolution*. Berkeley: University of California Press.

Berlin, Brent. 1978. Ethnobiological classification. In Eleanor Rosch and Barbara B. Lloyd (eds.), *Cognition and categorization*, 9–26. Hillsdale, NJ: Lawrence Erlbaum.

Berlin, Brent, Dennis E. Breedlove, & Peter H. Raven. 1973. General principles of classification and nomenclature in folk biology. *American Anthropologist* 75: 214–42.
Berlin, Brent, Dennis E. Breedlove, and Peter H. Raven. 1974. *Principles of Tzeltal plant classification*. New York: Academic Press.
Biggam, Carole P. 1997. *Blue in Old English: An Interdisciplinary Semantic Study*. Amsterdam/Atlanta, GA: Brill-Rodopi.
Biggam, Carole P. 2012. *The Semantics of Colour: A Historical Approach*. Cambridge, UK: Cambridge University Press.
Bissi, Agnese. 2016. The meaning of "flavour" when talking about quarks. *Personal Communication*.
Blank, Andreas. 1999. Why do new meanings occur? A cognitive typology of the motivations for lexical semantic change. In Andreas Blank & Peter Koch (eds.), *Historical Semantics and Cognition*, 61–89. Berlin: De Gruyter Mouton.
Borgatti, Stephen. 1990. Using ANTHROPAC To Investigate a Cultural Domain. *Cultural Anthropology Methods Newsletter*, 2 (1), 8. https://doi.org/10.1177/1525822X9000200106 (last accessed 23 September 2020).
Boulay, Thibaut. 2018. Tastes of wine: sensorial wine analysis in ancient Greece. In Rudolph Kelli C. (ed.), *Taste and the ancient senses*, 197–211. New York & London: Routledge.
Breslin, Paul A. S. 2013. An Evolutionary Perspective on Food and Human Taste. *Current Biology*, 23 (9), 409–418. http://dx.doi.org/10.1016/j.cub.2013.04.010
Breslin, Paul A. S. & Alan C. Spector. 2008. Mammalia taste perception. *Current Biology* 18 (4), 148–155.
Brett, J. 1994. Medicinal Plant Selection Criteria among the Tzeltal Maya of Highland Chiapas, Mexico. San Francisco: University of California at San Francisco dissertation.
Brillat-Savarin, Jean-Anthelme. 1949 [1825]. *The Physiology of Taste, or Meditations on Transcendental Gastronomy*, translated by M. F. K. Fisher. New York: Heritage Press.
Brown, Roger. 1958. How shall a thing be called? *Psychological Review* 65 (1): 14–21.
Brown, Roger. 1965. *Social psychology*. New York: Free Press.
Brown, Penelope. 2011. Color me Bitter: Crossmodal Compounding in Tzeltal Perception Words. *Senses and Society* (6) 1, 105–116. https://doi.org/10.2752/174589311X12893982233957 (last accessed 24 September 2020).
Browning, Sharon R., Brian L. Browning, Ying Zhou, Serena Tucci, Joshua M. Akey. 2018. Analysis of Human Sequence Data Reveals Two Pulses of Archaic Denisovan Admixture. *Cell*, 173 (1), p. 53–61. doi.org/10.1016/j.cell.2018.02.031 (last accessed 15 September 2020).
Brewer, Devon. 1995. Cognitive indicators of knowledge in semantic domains. *Journal of Quantitative Anthropology* 5, 107–128.
Brugman, Claudia. 1989. *The Story of Over: Polysemy, Semantics, and the Structure of the Lexicon*. New York: Garland.
Brysbaert, Marc, Amy B. Warriner, Victor Kuperman. 2014. Concreteness ratings for 40 thousand generally known English word lemmas. *Behavior Research Methods*, 46 (3), 904–911. https://doi.org/10.3758/s13428-013-0403-5 (last accessed 23 September 2020).
Buccini, Anthony F. 2013. Linguistics and Food Studies: structural and historical connections. In Ken Albala (ed.), *Routledge International Handbook of Food Studies*. New York: Routledge. 146–158.
Buck, Carl Darling. 1949. *A Dictionary of Selected Synonyms in the Principal Indo-European languages*. Chicago & London: The University of Chicago Press.

Busse, Beatrix. 2006. *Vocative Constructions in the Language of Shakespeare*. Amsterdam: John Benjamins.
Caballero, Rosario. 2007. Manner-of-motion verbs in wine description. *Journal of Pragmatics*, 39 (12), 2095–2114.
Caballero, Rosario & Iraide Ibarretxte-Antuñano. 2014. Ways of perceiving, moving, and thinking: Revindicating culture in conceptual metaphor research. *Cognitive semiotics*, V, 268–290.
Caballero, Rosario & Carita Paradis. 2015. Making sense of sensory perceptions across languages and cultures. *Functions of Language*, 22, 1–19. https://doi.org/10.1075/fol.22.1.01cab (last accessed 29 April 2021).
Cacciari, Cristina. 2008. Crossing the Senses in Metaphorical Language. In Raymond W. Giibs Jr. (ed.), *The Cambridge Handbook of Metaphor and Thought*. Cambridge, UK: Cambridge University Press, 425–443
Cairncross, S. E., & L. B. Sjöström. 1950. Flavor profiles – A new approach to flavor problems. *Food technology* 4 (8), 308–311.
Cameron, Lynne. 2003. *Metaphor in educational discourse*. London: Continuum
Carstens, E., Mirela Iodi Carstens, Jean-Marc Dessirier, Michael O'Mahony, Christopher T. Simons, Makoto Sudo, & Sakoto Sudo. 2002. It hurts so good: Oral irritation by spices and carbonated drinks and the underlying neural mechanisms. *Food Quality and Preference*, 13 (7–8), 431–443.
Casasanto, Daniel. 2017. The hierarchical structure of mental metaphors. In Beate Hampe (ed.), *Metaphor: Embodied cognition and discourse*, pp. 46–61. Cambridge, UK: Cambridge University Press.
Casagrande, David G. 2000. Human Taste Cognition in Tzeltal Maya Medicinal Plant Use. *Journal of Ecological Anthropology* 4 (1), 57–69. http://dx.doi.org/10.5038/2162-4593.4.1.3 (last accessed 24 September 2020).
Casson, Ronald W. 1997. Color shift: evolution of English color terms from brightness to hue. In C. L. Hardin & Luisa Maffi (eds.), *Color categories in thought and language*, 224–239. Cambridge, UK: Cambridge University Press.
Caterina, Michael J., Mark A. Schumacher, Makoto Tominaga, Tobias A. Rosen, Jon D. Levine, & David Julius. 1997. The capsaicin receptor: A heat-activated ion channel in the pain pathway. *Nature*, 389, 816–824.
Caul, Jean F. 1957. The Profile method of Flavor Analysis. *Advances in Food Research*, 7 (1), 1–40. https://doi.org/10.1016/S0065-2628(08)60245-1 (last accessed 24 September 2020).
Cavalieri, Rosalia. 2011. *Gusto: l'intelligenza del palato*. Bari-Roma: Laterza.
Cavalieri, Rosalia. 2014. *E l'uomo inventò i sapori. Storia naturale del gusto*. Rastignano: il Mulino.
Chamberlain, Alexander Francis. 1903. Primitive Taste-words. *The American Journal of Psychology*, 14 (3/4), 146–153.
Chan, Kai Qin, Eddie M. W. Tong, Deborah H. Tan & Alethea H. Q. Koh. 2013. What do love and jealousy taste like? *Emotion*, 13 (6), 1142–1149. https://doi.org/10.1037/a0033758 (last accessed 25 September 2020).
Chen, Meng, Caroline E. A. Strömberg & Gregory P. Wilson. 2019. Assembly of modern mammal community structure driven by Late Cretaceous dental evolution, rise of flowering plants, and dinosaur demise. In *Proceedings of the National Academy of*

Sciences of the United States of America, 116 (20), 9931–9940. https://doi.org/10.1073/pnas.1820863116 (last accessed 21 September 2020).

Chollet, Sylvie, Dominique Valentin, & Hervé Abdi. 2014. Free Sorting Task. In Paula Varela & Gastron Ares (eds.), *Novel Techniques in Sensory Characterization and Consumer Profiling*, 207–228. Boca Raton: CRC Press.

Chu, Simon & John J. Downes. 2000. Odour-evoked Autobiographical Memories: Psychological Investigations of Proustian Phenomena. *Chemical Senses* 25 (1), 111–116. https://doi.org/10.1093/chemse/25.1.111 (last accessed 29 April 2021)

Citron, Francesca M. M. & Adele E. Goldberg. 2014. Metaphorical sentences are more emotionally engaging than their literal counterparts. *Journal of Cognitive Neuroscience*, 26 (11), 2585–2595. doi: 10.1162/jocn_a_00654 (last accessed 29 April 2021).

Citron, Francesca M. M., Jeremie Güsten, Mora Michaelis, Adele E. Goldberg. 2016. Conventional metaphors in longer passages evoke affective brain response. *Neuroimage*, 139: 218–230. doi: 10.1016/j.neuroimage.2016.06.020 (last accessed 29 April 2021).

Clark, Herbert H. 2003. Pointing and placing. In Sotari Kita (ed.), *Pointing: Where Language, Culture, and Cognition Meet*, 243–268. Hillsdale: Erlbaum.

Classen, Constance. 1993. *Worlds of sense: Exploring the senses in history and across cultures*. London: Routledge.

Coleman, Linda & Paul Kay. 1981. Prototype semantcs: the English word *lie*. *Language* 57 (1), 26–44.

Craig, Arthur D. Bud. 2003. A new view of pain as a homeostatic emotion. *Trends in Neurosciences*, 26 (6), 303–307. https://doi.org/10.1016/S0166-2236(03)00123-1 (last accessed 21 September 2020).

Croft, William, & D. Alan Cruse. 2004. *Cognitive linguistics*. Cambridge, UK: Cambridge University Press.

Crojimans, Ilja & Asifa Majid. 2016. Not All Flavor Expertise Is Equal: The Language of Wine and Coffee Experts. *PLOS ONE*, 11 (6), e0155845. https://doi.org/10.1371/journal.pone.0155845 (last accessed 23 September 2020).

Crisinel, Anne-Sylvie, Sophie Jones & Charles Spence. 2012. 'The Sweet Taste of Maluma': Crossmodal Associations Between Tastes and Words. *Chemosensory Perception* 5, 266–273. https://doi.org/10.1007/s12078-012-9133-9 (last access 24 September 2020).

Cutting, James E. 2008. Criteria for basic tastes and other sensory primaries. *Behavioral and Brain Sciences*, 31 (1), 77–78. https://doi.org/10.1017/S0140525X08003373 (last accessed 22 September 2020).

Cytowic, Richard. 1989. *Synesthesia: A Union of the Senses*. Cambridge, MA: MIT Press.

Cytowic, Richard & Eagleman David. 2009. *Wednesday is indigo blue: Discovering the brain of synesthesia*. Cambridge, MA: MIT Press.

Dąbrowska, Ewa. 2012. Different speakers, different grammars: Individual differences in native language attainment. *Linguistic Approaches to Bilingualism*, 2 (3), 219–253. http://dx.doi.org/10.1075/lab.2.3.01dab (last accessed 23 September 2020).

Dąbrowska, Ewa. 2016. Cognitive Linguistics' seven deadly sins. *Cognitive Linguistics*, 27 (4), 479–491. https://doi.org/10.1515/cog-2016-0059 (last accessed 25 September 2020).

Dąbrowska, Ewa & Dagmar Divjak. 2015. Introduction. In Ewa Dąbrowska & Dagmar Divjak (eds.), *Handbook of Cognitive Linguistics*, 1–9. Berlin/ Boston: De Gruyter Mouton.

Dacremont, C. 1995. Spectral Composition of Eating Sounds Generated By Crispy, Crunchy and Crackly Foods. *Journal of Texture Studies*, 26 (1), 27–43. https://doi.org/10.1111/j.1745-4603.1995.tb00782.x (last accessed 23 September 2020).

Dancygier, Barbara & Eve Sweetser. 2014. *Figurative language*. Cambridge, UK: Cambridge University Press.
Davies, Mark. 2008. The Corpus of Contemporary American English: 450 million words, 1990-present. Available online at http://corpus.byu.edu/coca.
Day, Sean. 1996. Synaesthesia and synaesthetic metaphors. *Psyche*, 2 (32), 1–16.
Dedrick, Don. 2005. Explanation and Color-Naming Research. *Cross-Cultural Research*, 39 (2), 111–133. https://doi.org/10.1177/1069397104273627 (last accessed 22 September 2020).
Delwiche, Jeannine. 2004. The impact of perceptual interactions on perceived flavor. *Food Quality and Preference* 15, 137–146.
Deroy, Ophelia & Charles Spence. 2013. Why we are not all synesthetes (not even weakly so). *Psychonomic Bulletin & Review*, 20, 643–664. https://doi.org/10.3758/s13423-013-0387-2 (last accessed 29 September 2020).
Diederich, Catherine. 2015. *Sensory Adjectives in the Discourse of Food. A frame-semantic approach to language and perception*. Amsterdam / New York: John Benjamins.
Digonnet, Rémi. 2012. Odeur et secret dans *Smell* de Radhika Jha et *Perfume* de Patrick Süskind, in Marquié Hélène, Préher Gérald (eds.), *Le secret vol. 1, Résonances*. Paris: Presses Universitaire de Paris VIII, 205–224.
Dijksterhuis, Garmt, Hannemieke Luyten, Rene de Wijk & Jos Mojet. 2007. A new sensory vocabulary for crisp and crunchy dry model foods. *Food Quality and Preference* 18, 37–50. https://doi.org/10.1016/j.foodqual.2005.07.012 (last accessed 29 April 2021).
Dingemanse, Mark. 2012. Advances in the cross-linguistic study of ideophones. *Language and Linguistics Compass*, 6 (10), 654–672. https://doi.org/10.1002/lnc3.361 (last accessed 23 September 2020).
Dirven, René. 1985. Metaphor as a basic means for extending the lexicon. In Wolf Paprotté & René Dirven (eds.), *The Ubiquity of Metaphor: Metaphor in Language and Thought*, 85–119. Amsterdam: John Benjamins.
Divjak, Dagmar & Catherine L. Caldwell-Harris. 2015. Frequency and entrenchment. In Ewa Dąbrowska & Dagmar Divjak (eds.), *Handbook of Cognitive Linguistics*, 53–75. Berlin/Boston: De Gruyter Mouton.
Doty, Richard L., Jonathan H. Chen, Jane Overend. 2017. Taste Quality Confusions: Influences of Age, Smoking, OTC Taster Status, and other Subject Characteristics. *Perception*, 46 (3–4), 257–267. https://doi.org/10.1177/0301006616685577 (last accessed 29 April 2021).
Downing, Pamela A. 1977. On "Basic Levels" and the Categorization of Objects in English Discourse. *Proceedings of the 3rd Annual Meeting of the Berkeley Linguistics Society*, 475–487. https://doi.org/10.3765/bls.v3i0.2256 (last accessed 29 April 2021).
Dupire, Marguerite. 1987. Des Goûts et des odeurs: classification et universaux. *L'Homme* 27 (4): 5–25.
Emmorrey, Karen. 2014. Iconicity as structure mapping. *Philosophical Transactions of the Royal Society of London B: Biological Sciences*, 369, 20130301. http://dx.doi.org/10.1098/rstb.2013.0301 (last accessed 29 September 2020).
Engstrom, A. G. 1946. In defence of synaesthesia in literature. *Philological Quarterly* 25, 1–19.
Erickson, Robert P. & Ellen Covey. 1980. On the singularity of taste sensations: What is a taste primary? *Physiology & Behavior*, 25 (4), 527–533. https://doi.org/10.1016/0031-9384(80)90117-1 (last accessed 22 September 2020).

Erickson, Robert P. 1982. Studies on the Perception of Taste: Do Primaries Exist? *Physiology & Behavior*, 28 (1), 57–62. https://doi.org/10.1016/0031-9384(82)90102-0 (last accessed 22 September 2020).
Erickson, Robert P. 2008. A study of the science of taste: On the origins and influence of the core ideas. *Behavioral and Brain Sciences*, 31 (1), 59–105. https://doi.org/10.1017/S0140525X08003348 (last accessed 22 September 2020).
Erzsébet, P. Dombi. Synaesthesia and poetry. *Poetics*, 3 (5), 23–44. https://doi.org/10.1016/0304-422X(74)90021-7 (last accessed 29 September 2020).
Evans, Vyvyan. 2007. *A glossary of Cognitive Linguistics*. Edinburgh: Edinburgh University Press.
Evans, Vyvyan. 2015. *The Crucible of Language*. Cambridge, UK: Cambridge University Press.
Evans, Nicholas, and David Wilkins. 1998. The knowing ear: an Australian test of universal claims about the semantic structure of sensory verbs and their extension into the domain of cognition. *Arbeitspapiere von Institut für Sprachwissenschaft, Universität zu Köln (Neue Folge)* 32. Cologne: Institut für Sprachwissenschaft.
Feldman, Jerome. 2006. *From Molecules to Metaphors: A Neural Theory of Language*. Boston, MA: MIT Press.
Ferguson Smith, Martin [Lucretius], 2001 [1969]. *On the Nature of Things*. Indianapolis: Hackett Publishing Company.
Fiks, Alexander G., Angela Gefen, Cayce C. Hughes, Kenya F. Hunter, Frances K. Barg. 2011. Using freelisting to understand shared decision making in ADHD: Parents' and pediatricians' perspectives. *Patient Education and Counseling*, 84 (2): 236–244.https://doi.org/10.1016/j.pec.2010.07.035 84 (2): 236–244.
Forceville, Charles. 2006. Non-verbal and multimodal metaphor in a cognitivist framework: Agendas for research. In Gitte Kristiansen, Michel Achard, René Dirven & Francisco J. Ruiz de Mendoza Ibáñez, *Cognitive Linguistics: Current Applications and Future Perspectives*, 379–402. https://doi.org/10.1515/9783110197761.5.379 (last accessed 25 September 2020).
Gatewood, John B. 1983. Loose Talk: Linguistic Competence and Recognition Ability. *American Anthropologist*, 85 (2), 378–387.
Geeraerts, Dirk. 2000. Salience phenomena in the lexicon: A typology. In Liliane Albertazzi (ed.), *Meaning and cognition*, 125–136. Amsterdam: John Benjamins.
Geeraerts, Dirk. 2010. *Theories of Lexical Semantics*. Oxford: Oxford University Press.
Gerhardt, Cornelia, Maximiliane Frobenius, Susanne Ley (eds.). 2013. *Culinary Linguistics. The Chef's special*. Amsterdam / Philadelphia. John Benjamins. https://doi.org/10.1075/clu.10 (last accessed 21 September 2020).
Ghyselinck, Mandy, Roel Custers & Marc Brysbaert. 2004. The Effect of Age of Acquisition in Visual Word Processing: Further Evidence for the Semantic Hypothesis. *Journal of Experimental Psychology: Learning, Memory, and Cognition*, 30 (2), 550–554. https://doi.org/10.1037/0278-7393.30.2.550 (last accessed 23 September 2020).
Gibbs, Raymond W. Jr. 2005. *Embodiment and cognitive science*. Cambridge, UK: Cambridge University Press. https://doi.org/10.1017/CBO9780511805844.
Gibbs, Raymond W. Jr. 2007. Why cognitive linguists should care more about empirical methods. In Monica Gonzalez-Marquez, Irene Mittelberg, Seana Coulson, & Michael J. Spivey (eds.), *Methods in Cognitive Linguistics*, 2–18. Amsterdam/ Philadelphia: John Benjamins. https://doi.org/10.1075/hcp.18 (last accessed 22 September 2020).
Gil-Pérez, Ignacio, Rubén Rebollar, Iván Lidón, Javier Martín, Hans C. M. van Trijp, Betina Piqueras-Fiszman. 2019. Hot or not? Conveying sensory information on food packaging

through the spiciness-shape correspondence. *Food Quality and Preference*, 71, 197–208. https://doi.org/10.1016/j.foodqual.2018.07.009 (last accessed 29 April 2021).

Gilead, Michael, Orian Gal, Marin Polak, & Yael Cholow (2015). The role of nature and nurture in conceptual metaphors: The case of gustatory priming. *Social Psychology*, 46 (3), 167–173. https://doi.org/10.1027/1864-9335/a000238 (last accessed 29 April 2021).

Gilchrist, Hart D., Brandon L. Allard, Donald A. Simone. 1996. Enhanced withdrawal responses to heat and mechanical stimuli following intraplantar injection of capsaicin in rats. *Pain*, 67(1),179–188. doi.org/10.1016/0304-3959(96)03104-1.

Goatly, Andrew. 1997. *The Language of Metaphor*. London: Routledge

Goffman, Erving. 1978. Response Cries. *Language* 54 (4), 787–815.

Golin, Lisa. 2001. The Taste and Smell of Taban Kenyah (Kenyah Medicine): An Exploration of Chemosensory Selection Criteria for Medicinal Plants among the Kenyah Leppo Ke of East Kalimantan, Borneo, Indonesia. Manoa, University of Hawaii dissertation.

Grady, Joseph. 1997a. *Foundations of meaning: Primary metaphors and primary scenes*. Berkeley, CA: University of California at Berkeley dissertation. Retrieved from http://escholarship.org/uc/item/3g9427m2.

Grady, Joseph. 1997b. Theories are buildings revisited. *Cognitive Linguistics* 8, 267–290.

Grady, Joseph. 1999. A typology of motivation for conceptual metaphor: correlation vs. resemblance. In Raymond W. Gibbs Jr. & Gerard Steen (eds.), *Metaphors in Cognitive Linguistics*, 79–100. Amsterdam: John Benjamins.

Grady, Joseph. 2005. Primary metaphors as inputs to conceptual integration. *Journal of Pragmatics*. 37: 1595–1614. doi:10.1016/j.pragma.2004.03.012

Gray, Kurt. 2012. The Power of Good Intentions: Perceived Benevolence Soothes Pain, Increases Pleasure, and Improves Taste. *Social Psychological and Personality Science* 3 (5), 639–645. https://doi.org/10.1177/1948550611433470 (last accessed 29 September 2020).

Gregson, R. A. M. & A. F. H. Baker. 1973. Sourness and Bitterness: Confusions over sequences of taste judgements. *British Journal of Psychology* 64 (1), 71–76. https://doi.org/10.1111/j.2044-8295.1973.tb01328.x (last accessed 24 September 2020).

Gries, Stephan Th. & Dagmar S. Divjak. 2010. Quantitative approaches in usage-based Cognitive Semantics: Myths, erroneous assumptions, and a proposal. In Dylan Glynn & Kerstin Fischer (eds.), *Quantitative methods in cognitive semantics: corpus-driven approaches*, 333–353. Berlin/ New York: De Gruyter Mouton.

Grill, Harvey J & Ralph Norgren. 1978. Neurological tests and behavioral deficits in chronic thalamic and chronic decerebrate rats. *Brain Research* 143 (2), 299–312. https://doi.org/10.1016/0006-8993(78)90570-X (last accessed 25 March 2021).

Grondelaers, Stefan, Dirk Speelman & Dirk Geeraerts. 2007. Lexical Variation and Change. In Dirk Geeraerts & Herbert Cuyckens (eds.), *The Oxford Handbook of Cognitive Linguistics*, 988–1011. Oxford: Oxford University Press.

Grossenbacher, Peter G. & Christopher T. Lovelace. 2001. Mechanisms of synesthesia: cognitive and physiological constraints. *Trends in Cognitive Sciences*, 5 (1), 36–41. https://doi.org/10.1016/S1364-6613(00)01571-0

Guest, Steve, Caroline Catmur, Donna Lloyd & Charles Spence. 2002. Audiotactile interactions in roughness perception. *Experimental Brain Research* 146, 161–171. https://doi.org/10.1007/s00221-002-1164-z (last accessed 29 April 2021).

Hardcastle, Valerie G. 2015. Perception of Pain. In Mohan Matthen (ed.), *The Oxford Handbook of Philosophy of Perception*, 530–541. Oxford: Oxford University Press.

Harnad, Steven. 1990. The symbol grounding problem. *Physica* 42, 335–346.
Harris, Marvin. 1968. *The Rise of Anthropological Theory*. Walnut Creek: AltaMira.
Heider, Eleanor R. 1971. Focal colors and the development of color names. *Developmental Psychology*, 4 (3), 447–455. https://doi.org/10.1037/h0030955 (last accessed 22 September 2020).
Hellekant, Goran & Yuzo Ninomiya. 1991. On the taste of umami in chimpanzee. *Physiology & Behavior*, 49 (5), 927–934. https://doi.org/10.1016/0031-9384(91)90205-3 (last accessed 21 September 2020).
Hines, Caitlin. 1999. Rebaking the Pie. The WOMAN AS DESSERT Metaphor. In Mary Bucholtz, A. C. Liang, Laurel A. Sutton, *Reinventing Identities: The Gendered Self in Discourse*, 145–162.
Hladik, Claude Marcel & Patrick Pasquet. 2004. Origine et évolution des perceptions gustatives chez les primates non humains et chez l'homme. *Primatologie*, 6, 193–211.
Hladik, Claude Marcel, Sabrina Krief, Bruno Simmen, Patrick Pasquet. 2010. Le goût n'est pas le propre de l'homme. *La Recherche: l'actualité des sciences, société d'éditions scientifiques* (443), 64–67. hal-00610023.
Holley, André. 2006. *Le cerveau gourmand*. Torino: Bollati Boringhieri.
Holz, Peter. 2007. Cognition, olfaction and linguistic creativity: Linguistic synesthesia as poetic device in cologne advertisement. In Martina Plümacher & Peter Holz (eds.), *Speaking of Colors and Odors*, 185–202.
Howes, David. 2013. Postscript to Sensuous Cognition: The language of the senses. In Rosario Caballero, Javier E. Díaz-Vera (eds.), *Sensuous Cognition. Explorations Into Human Sentience: Imagination, (E)motion and Perception*, 293–300. Berlin: De Gruyter Mouton.
Howes, David (ed.) 1991. *The varieties of sensory experience: A sourcebook in the anthropology of the senses*. Toronto: University of Toronto Press.
Huffman, Michael A. & Mohamedi Seifu. 1989. Observations on the illness and consumption of a possibly medicinal plant *Vernonia amygdalina* (DEL.), by a wild chimpanzee in the Mahale Mountains National Park, Tanzania. *Primates* 30, 51–63. https://doi.org/10.1007/BF02381210 (last accessed 21 September 2020).
Ibarretxte-Antuñano, Iraide. 1996. Semantic extensions in the sense of smell. *Anuario del Seminario de Filología Vasca 'Julio de Urquijo'* XXX (2), 631–643.
Ibarretxte-Antuñano, Iraide. 1997. Smelling and Perception: A Cross-Linguistic Study. *Cuadernos de Filología Inglesa* 612, 113–121.
Ibarretxte-Antuñano, Iraide. 1999a. Polysemy and metaphor in perception verbs: A cross-linguistic study. Edinburgh: University of Edinburgh dissertation.
Ibarretxte-Antuñano, Iraide. 1999b. Metaphorical mappings in the sense of smell. In Ronald W. Gibbs Jr. & Gerard J. Steen (eds.), *Metaphor in Cognitive Linguistics*, 29–45. Amsterdam: John Benjamins.
Ibarretxte-Antuñano, Iraide. 2008. Vision metaphors for the intellect: Are they really cross-linguistic?, *Atlantis*, 30, 15–33.
Ibarretxte-Antuñano, Iraide. 2013. The relationship between conceptual metaphor and culture. *Intercultural Pragmatics*, 10 (2), 315–339.
Ibarretxte-Antuñano, Iraide. 2019. Perception metaphors in Cognitive Linguistics. In Laura J. Speed, Carolyn O'Meara, Lila San Roque & Asifa Majid (eds.), *Perception Metaphors*, 43–64. Amsterdam/ Philadelphia: John Benjamins.
Ikeda, Kikunae. 2002 [1909]. New Seasonings. *Chemical Senses* 27 (9), 847–849. https://doi.org/10.1093/chemse/27.9.847 (last accessed 21 September 2020).

Ishii, Rie & Michael O'Mahony. 1987a. Defining a Taste by a Single Standard: Aspects of Salty and Umami Tastes. *Journal of Food Science*, 52 (5), 1405–1409.
Ishii, Rie & Michael O'Mahony. 1987b. Taste sorting and naming: can taste concepts be misrepresented by traditional psychophysical labelling systems? *Chemical Senses*, 12 (1), 37–51.
Ishii, Rie & Michael O'Mahony. 1990. Group taste concept measurement: verbal and physical definition of the umami taste concept for Japanese and Americans. *Journal of Sensory Studies* 4 (1990), 215–227. https://doi.org/10.1111/j.1745-459X.1990.tb00473.x (last accessed 24 September 2020).
Johnson, Mark. 1987. *The Body in the Mind: The Bodily Basis of Meaning, Imagination and Reason*. Chicago: University of Chicago Press.
Johnson, Christopher. 1997. Metaphor vs. conflation in the acquisition of polysemy: the case of see. In Masako K. Hiraga, Chris Sinha and Sherman Wilcox (eds.), *Cultural, typological and psychological perspectives in cognitive linguistics*, 155-170. Amsterdam: John Benjamins.
Julich, Nina. 2019. Why do we understand music as moving? In Laura J. Speed, Carolyn O'Meara, Lila San Roque & Asifa Majid (eds.), *Perception Metaphors*, 165–184. Amsterdam/ Philadelphia: John Benjamins.
Julius, David & Allan I. Basbaum. 2001. Molecular mechanisms of nociception. *Nature* 413 (6852), 203–210. doi: 10.1038/35093019 (last accessed 29 September 2020).
Jurafsky, Dan. 2014. *The Language of Food: A Linguist Reads the Menu*. New York-London: W. W. Norton.
Kai Qin Chan, Eddie M. W. Tong, Deborah H. Tan, & Alethea H. Q. Koh. (2013). What do love and jealousy taste like? Emotion, 13(6), 1142–1149. doi: 10.1037/a0033758.
Kawai, Masao. 1965. Newly-acquired Pre-cultural Behavior of the Natural Troop of Japanese Monkeys on Koshima Islet. *Primate* 6 (1), 1–30.
Kay, Paul, Brent Berlin, Luisa Maffi, William R. Merrifield & Richard Cook. 2009. *The World Color Survey*. Stanford: Stanford University Press.
Kay, Christian, Jane Roberts, Michael Samuels & Irene Wotherspoon (eds.). 2009. *Historical Thesaurus of the Oxford English Dictionary*. Oxford: Oxford University Press.
Keegan, Caél M. 2018. *Lana and Lilly Wachowski*. Urbana: University of Illinois Press.
Kennedy, Charles W. 2000. *Juliana*. Cambridge, Ontario: In parentheses Publication.
Kempton, Willett. 1981. *The Folk Classification of Ceramics. A Study of Cognitive Prototypes*. New York: Academic Press.
Kikuchi, Senichiro, Fumio Kubota, Koichi Nisijima, Sumio Washiya, & Satoshi Kato. 2005. Cerebral activation focusing on strong tasting food: A functional magnetic resonance imaging study. *NeuroReport*, 16 (3), 281–283. doi:10.1097/00001756-200502280-00016.
Klein, Amanda H., Mirela Iodi Carstens & Earl Carstens. 2013. Eugenol and carvacrol induce temporally desensitizing patterns of oral irritation and enhance innocuous warmth and noxious heat sensation on the tongue. *Pain*, 154 (10), 2078–2087. doi: 10.1016/j.pain.2013.06.025 (last accessed 29 April 2021).
Kobayashi, Masayuki, Tetsuya Sasabe, Yoshihito Shigihara, Masaaki Tanaka, & Yasuyoshi Watanabe. 2011. Gustatory imagery reveals functional connectivity from the prefrontal to insular cortices traced with magnetoencephalography. *PLOS ONE*, 6 (7), e21736. https://doi.org/10.1371/journal.pone.0021736 (last accessed 29 April 2021).
Korsmeyer, Carolyn. 2002 [1999]. *Making sense of Taste. Food and Philosophy*. Ithaca & London: Cornell University Press.

Kottak, Conrad P. 2007. *Mirror of Humanity. A concise Introduction to Cultural Anthropology*. Boston: McGraw Hill.
Kövecses, Zoltán. 1986. *Metaphors of Anger, Pride, and Love: A Lexical Approach to the Structure of Concepts*. Amsterdam: John Benjamins.
Kövecses, Zoltán. 1995. Anger: Its language, conceptualization, and physiology in the light of cross-cultural evidence. In John R. Taylor & Robert E- MacLaury, *Language and the Cognitive Construal of the World*, 181–196. Berlin: De Gruyter Mouton. https://doi.org/10.1515/9783110809305.181 (last accessed 25 September 2020).
Kövecses, Zoltán. 2010 [2002]. *Metaphor: A Practical Introduction*. Second edition. Oxford: Oxford University Press.
Kövecses, Zoltán. 2019. Perception and metaphor. In Laura J. Speed, Carolyn O'Meara, Lila San Roque & Asifa Majid (eds.), *Perception Metaphors*, 327–346. Amsterdam/ Philadelphia: John Benjamins.
Kövecses, Zoltán and Günther Radden. 1998. Metonymy: developing a cognitive linguistic view. *Cognitive Linguistics 9* (1): 37–77.
Kövecses, Zoltán, Laura Ambrus, Dániel Hegedűs, Ren Imai & Anna Sobczak. 2019. The lexical vs. Corpus-based method in the study of metaphors. In Marianna Bolognesi, Mario Brdar & Kristina Š. Despot (eds.), *Metaphor and Metonymy in the Digital Age: Theory and methods for building repositories of figurative language*, 149–173. Amsterdam: John Benjamins.
Kramer, Samuel Noah. 1958. *History Begins at Sumer*. London: Thames and Hudson.
Kuipers, Joel C. 1984. Matters of Taste in Weyéwa. *Anthropological Linguistics*, 26 (1), 84–101.
Kuperman, Victor, Hans Stadthagen-Gonzalez & Marc Brysbaert. 2012. Age-of-acquisition ratings for 30,000 English words. *Behavior Research Methods* 44, 978–990. https://doi.org/10.3758/s13428-012-0210-4 (last accessed 22 September 2020).
Kyratzis, Sakis. 2003. A New Metaphor for Metaphor. Evidence for a Single Dynamic Metaphorical Category. Unpublished manuscript. Quoted in Müller, 2009.
Labov, William. 1973. The boundaries of words and their meanings. In Charles J. N. Bailey & Roger W. Shuy (eds.), *New Ways of Analyzing Variation in English*, 340–373. Washington, DC: Georgetown University Press.
Lakoff, George. 1987. *Women, Fire and Dangerous Things*. Chicago: University of Chicago Press.
Lakoff, George & Mark Johnson. 1980. *Metaphors we live by*. Chicago: University of Chicago Press.
Lakoff, George & Mark Johnson. 1999. *Philosophy in the flesh*. New York: Basic Books.
Lakoff, George & Mark Turner. 1989. *More Than Cool Reason: A Field Guide to Poetic Metaphor*. Chicago: University of Chicago Press.
Lakoff, George & Rafael E. Núñez. 2001. *Where Mathematics Comes From*. New York: Basic Books.
Lakoff, George & Zoltán Kövecses. 1987. The cognitive model of anger inherent in American English. In Dorothy Holland & Naomi Quinn (eds.), *Cultural Models in Language and Thought*, 195–221. Cambridge, UK: Cambridge University Press. https://doi.org/10.1017/CBO9780511607660 (last accessed 29 April 2021)
Landau, Mark, Brian P. Meier, Lucas A. Keefer. 2010. A Metaphor-Enriched Social Cognition. *Psychological Bulletin*, 136 (6), 1045–1067. doi: 10.1037/a0020970 (last accessed 29 April 2021).
Lalueza-Fox, Charles, Elena Gigli, Marco de la Rasilla, Javier Fortea & Antonio Rosas. 2009. Bitter taste perception in Neanderthals through the analysis of the TAS2R38 gene. *Biology*

letters 5 (6), 809–811. https://doi.org/10.1098/rsbl.2009.0532 (last accessed 29 April 2021).

Langacker, Ronald W. 1987. *Foundations of cognitive grammar*. Vol. 1, *Theoretical prerequisites*. Stanford, CA: Stanford University Press.

Lapis, Trina J., Michael H. Penner, Juyun Lim. 2016. Humans Can Taste Glucose Oligomers Independent of the hT1R2/hT1R3 Sweet Taste Receptor. *Chemical Senses*, 41 (9), 755–762. https://doi.org/10.1093/chemse/bjw088 (last accessed 29 April 2021).

Lawless, Harry T. & Hildegarde Heymann. 2010. *Sensory Evaluation of Food. Principles and Practices*. New York: Springer.

Lehrer, Adrianne. 1975. Talking about wine. *Language*, (51), 901–923.

Lehrer, Adrianne. 2009 [1983]. *Wine and conversation*. Bloomington: University of Indiana Press.

Levins, Richard & Richard Lewontin. 1985.*The dialectal biologist*. Cambridge, MA: Harvard University Press.

Levinson, Stephen C. & Asifa Majid. 2014. Differential ineffability and the senses. *Mind & Language*, 29 (4). 407–427. https://doi.org/10.1111/mila.12057 (last accessed 23 September 2020).

Leavens, David A., William D. Hopkins, & Kim A. Bard. 2005. Understanding the Point of Chimpanzee Pointing. Epigenesis and Ecological Validity. *Current Directions in Psychological Science*, 14 (4), 185–189. https://doi.org/10.1111/j.0963-7214.2005.00361.x (last accessed 23 September 2020).

Levitan, Carmel A. & Devin Z. Shermer. 2014. Red Hot: The Crossmodal Effect of Color Intensity on Perceived Piquancy. *Multisensory Research*, 27 (3–4), 207–223. https://doi.org/10.1163/22134808-00002457 (last accessed 29 September 2020).

Liang, Pei, Soumyajit Roy, Meng-Ling Chen, Gen-Hua Zhang. 2013. Visual influence of shapes and semantic familiarity on human sweet sensitivity. *Behavioral and Brain Research*, 253, 42–47. https://doi.org/10.1016/j.bbr.2013.07.001 (last accessed 29 September 2020).

Li, Qiang, Yuanting Cui, Rongbing Jin, Hongmei Lang, Hao Yu, Fang Sun, Chengkang He, Tianyi Ma, Yingsha Li, Xunmei Zhou, Daoyan Liu, Hongbo Jia, Xiaowei Chen, & Zhiming Zhu. 2017. Enjoyment of Spicy Flavor Enhances Central Salty-Taste Perception and Reduces Salt Intake and Blood Pressure. *Hypertension* 70 (6), 1291–1299. https://doi.org/10.1161/HYPERTENSIONAHA.117.09950 (last accessed 24 september 2020).

Lim, Hyewon. 2015. The Conceptualization of Taste in Korean. *Language and Linguistics* 66: 323–344.

Lindner, Susan. 1981. *A Lexico-Semantic Analysis of English Verb-Particle Constructions with* Up *and* Out. San Diego: University of California at San Diego dissertation.

Littlemore, Jeannette. 2015. *Metonymy: Hidden Shortcuts in Language, Thought and Communication*. Cambridge, UK: Cambridge University Press.

Lupyan, Gary & Bodo Winter. 2018. Language is more abstract than you think, or, why aren't languages more iconic? *Philosophical Transactions of the Royal Society of London B: Biological Sciences*, 373, 20170137. https://doi.org/10.1098/rstb.2017.0137. (last accessed 29 September 2020)

Lynott, Dermot & Louise Connell. 2009. Modality exclusivity norms for 423 object properties. *Behavior Research Methods* 41 (2), 558–564. https://doi.org/10.3758/BRM.41.2.558 (last accessed 23 September 2020).

Lynott, Dermot & Louise Connell. 2013. Modality exclusivity norms for 400 nouns: The relationship between perceptual experience and surface word form. *Behavior Research methods*, 45, 516–526. https://doi.org/10.3758/s13428-012-0267-0 (last accessed 23 September 2020).

Lyons, John. 1977. *Semantics*. Cambridge, UK: Cambridge University Press.

MacPherson, Fiona (ed.). 2011. *The senses: Classic and contemporary philosophical perspectives*. Oxford: Oxford University Press.

MacPherson, Fiona. 2011. Introduction: Individuating the Senses. In Fiona MacPherson (ed.), *The senses: Classic and contemporary philosophical perspectives*, 3–43. Oxford: Oxford University Press.

Majid, Asifa & Stephen C. Levinson. 2008. Language does provide support for basic tastes. *Behavioral and Brain Sciences*, 31 (1), 86–87. https://doi.org/10.1017/ S0140525X08003476 (last accessed 29 April 2021).

Majid, Asifa & Stephen C. Levinson. 2011. The senses in language and culture. *The Senses and Society*, 6 (1), 5–18. https://doi.org/10.2752/174589311X12893982233551 (last accessed 22 September 2020).

Majid, Asifa & Stephen C. Levinson (eds.). 2011. *The Senses and Society*, 6 (1). https://doi.org/ 10.2752/174589311X12893982233551 (last accessed 22 September 2020).

Majid, Asifa, Niclas Burenhult, Marcus Stensmyt, Josje de Valk, & Bill S. Hansson. 2018. Olfactory language and abstraction across cultures. *Philosophical Transactions of the Royal Society of London B: Biological Sciences*, 373, 20170139. https://doi.org/10.1098/ rstb.2017.0139 (last accessed 23 September 2020).

Majid, Asifa & Niclas Burenhult. 2014. Odors are expressible in language, as long as you speak the right language. *Cognition*, 130, 266–270. doi: 10.1016/j.cognition.2013.11.004 (last accessed 29 April 2021).

Marks, Lawrence E. 1982. Bright sneezes and dark coughs, loud sunlight and soft moonlight. *Journal of Experimental Psychology, Human Perception and Performace*, 8 (2), 15–23.

Marks, Lawrence E. & J. C. Stevens, 1966. Individual brightness functions. *Perception & Psychophysics*, 1, 17–24. https://doi.org/10.3758/BF03207815 (last accessed 29 April 2021).

Martino, Gail & Lawrence E. Marks. 2001. Synesthesia: Strong and Weak. *Current Directions in Psychological Science*, 10 (2), 61–65. https://doi.org/10.1111/1467-8721.00116 (last accessed 29 April 2021).

Mathez-Stiefel, Sarah-Lan, Regine Brandt, Susanne Lachmuth & Stephan Rist. 2012. Are the Young Less Knowledgeable? Local Knowledge of Natural Remedies and Its Transformations in the Andean Highlands. *Human Ecology*, 40: 909–930. doi: 10.1007/ s10745-012-9520-5

Mattisof, James A. 1978. Variational Semantics in Tibeto-Burman: The 'organic' approach to linguistic comparison. *Occasional Papers of the Wolfenden Society on Tibeto-Burman Linguistics*, Volume VI. Philadelphia, PA: Institute for the Study of Human Issues (ISHI).

Matthen, Mohan (ed.). 2015. *The Oxford Handbook of Philosophy of Perception*. Oxford: Oxford University Press.

Matthen, Mohan. 2015. The Individuation of the Senses. In Mohan Matthen (ed.), *The Oxford Handbook of Philosophy of Perception*, 567–585. Oxford: Oxford University Press.

Maturana, Humberto. 1980. Biology of cognition. In Humberto Maturana & Francisco Varela (eds.), *Autopoiesis and cognition: The realisation of the living*, 5–58. Boston: Reidel.

McAuliffe, Wayne K. & Herbert L. Meiselman. 1974. The roles of practice and correction in the categorization of sour and bitter taste qualities. *Perception & Psychophysics* 16 (2), 242–244.

McBurney, Donald H. 1974. Are there primary tastes for man? *Chemical Senses*, 1 (1), 17–28. https://doi.org/10.1093/chemse/1.1.17 (last accessed 22 September 2020).

McNeill, N. B. 1972. Colour and colour terminology. *Journal of Linguistics* 8 (1), 21–33.

McRae, Ken, George S. Cree, Mark S. Seidenberg, & Chris McNorgan. 2005. Semantic feature production norms for a large set of living and nonliving things. *Beahvior Research Methods* 37, 547–559. https://doi.org/10.3758/BF03192726 (last accessed 23 September 2020).

Meier, Brian P., Sara K. Moeller, Miles Riemer-Peltz, & Michael D. Robinson. (2012). Sweet taste preferences and experiences predict pro-social inferences, personalities, and behaviors. *Journal of Personality and Social Psychology*, 102(1), 163–174. https://doi.org/10.1037/a0025253 (last accessed 29 April 2021).

Meilgaard, Morten C., Gail Vance Civille & B. Thomas Carr. 2007. *Sensory Evaluation Techniques*. Boca Raton: CRC Press.

Meir, Irit. 2010. Iconicity and metaphor: Constraints on metaphorical extension of iconic forms. *Language* 86 (4), 865–896.

Meiselman, Herbert L. & Ernest Dzendolet. 1967. Variability in gustatory quality identification. *Perception and Psychophysics*, 2 (11), 496–498.

Mendelson, Danuta. 1984 Synaesthetic Metaphor in the Work of Isaak Babel'. *Russian Literature* 15 (3), 347–362. https://doi.org/10.1016/0304-3479(84)90022-X (last accessed 29 September 2020).

MetaNet Metaphor Wiki. International Computer Science Institute in Berkeley, California. Available at https://metaphor.icsi.berkeley.edu/pub/en/index.php/MetaNet_Metaphor_Wiki

Meyer, Julien. 2008. Typology and acoustic strategies of whistled languages: Phonetic comparison and perceptual cues of whistled vowels. *Journal of the International Phonetic Association* 38, 1, 69–94.

Miller, George A. & Philip N. Johnson-Laird. 1976. *Language and Perception*. Cambridge, MA: Harvard University Press. https://doi.org/10.4159/harvard.9780674421288

Milton, Katharine. 1999. Nutritional characteristics of wild primate foods: do the diets of our closest living relatives have lessons for us? *Nutrition* 15 (6), 488–498.

Milton, Kathraine & Jenness, R. (1987). Ascorbic acid content of neotropical plant parts available to wild monkeys and bats. *Experientia* 43, 339–342.

Morris, Desmond. 1967. *The Naked Ape*. London: Vintage Books.

Moskowitz, Howard R., Jacqueline H. Beckley & Anna V. A. Resurreccion. 2012 [2006]. *Sensory and Consumer Research in Food Product Design and Development*. New York: Wiley-Blackwell.

Mukherjee, Sayantani, Thomas Kramer, & Katina Kulow. 2017. The effect of spicy gustatory sensations on variety-seeking. *Psychology & Marketing*, 34(8), 786–794. https://doi.org/10.1002/mar.21022 (last accessed 29 April 2021).

Müller, Cornelia. 2008. *Metaphors Dead and Alive, Sleeping and Waking. A Dynamic View*. Chicago: University of Chicago Press.

Myers, Charles S. 1904. The Taste-names of primitive peoples. *British Journal of Psychology*, 1 (2), 117–126.

Nakamura, Tetsuaki, Maki Sakamoto, Akira Utsumi. 2010. The Role of Event Knowledge in Comprehending Synesthetic Metaphors. In S. Ohlsson & R. Catrambone (eds.), *Proceedings of the 32nd Annual Conference of the Cognitive Science Society*, 1898–1903. Austin, TX: Cognitive Science Society.

Narukawa, Masataka, Sho Sasaki, Tatsuo Watanabe. 2011. Effect of Capsaicin on Salt Taste Sensitivity in Humans. *Food Science and Technology Research* 17 (2), 167–170. https://doi.org/10.3136/fstr.17.167 (last accessed 24 September 2020).

Novich, Scott David, Sherry Cheng & David Eagleman. 2011. Is synaesthesia one condition or many? A large-scale analysis reveals subgroups. *Journal of Neuropsychology* 5 (2), 353–371.

Nolan, Justin M. 2001. Pursuing the fruits of knowledge: cognitive ethnobotany in Missouri's Little Dixie. *Journal of Ethnobiology* 21 (2): 29–51.

Nolan, Justin M. 2004. *Wild Harvest in the Heartland. Ethnobotany in Missouri's Little Dixie: cognitive ecology in a regional culture*. Lanham: University Press of America.

Núñez, Rafael E. & Eve Sweetser. 2006. With the Future Behind Them: Convergent Evidence From Aymara Language and Gesture in the Crosslinguistic Comparison of Spatial Construals of Time. *Cognitive Science*, 30 (3), 401–450. https://doi.org/10.1207/s15516709cog0000_62 (last accessed 25 September 2020).

Ohira, Tetsuya, Takeshi Tanigawa, Hiroyasu Iso, Tomoko Sankai, Hironori Imano & Takashi Shimamoto. 2000. *Impact of anger expression on blood pressure levels in white-color workers with low-coping behavior*, Environmental Health and Preventive Medicine, 5 (1), 37–42.

Okiyama, Atsushi & Gary K. Beauchamp. 1998. Taste dimensions of monosodium glutamate (MSG) in a food system: role of glutamate in young American subjects. *Physiology & Behavior*, 65 (1), 177–181. https://doi.org/10.1016/S0031-9384(98)00160-7 (last accessed 21 September 2020).

O'Boyle, Michael W. & Robert D. Tarte. 1980. Implications for phonetic symbolism: The relationship between pure tones and geometric figures. *Journal of Psycholinguistic Research* 9, 535–544. https://doi.org/10.1007/BF01068115 (last accessed 29 September 2020).

O'Mahony, Michael. 1990. Cognitive aspects of Difference Testing and Descriptive Analysis: Criterion Variation and Concept Formation. In R. L. McBride & H.J.H. MacFie (eds.), *Psychological Basis of Sensory Evaluation*, 117–139.

O'Mahony, Michael. 1991. Descriptive Analysis and Concept Alignment. In Harry T. Lawless & Barbara P. Klein (eds.), *Sensory Science Theory and Applications in Foods*, 223–267.

O'Mahony, Michael & Carmen Manzano Alba. 1980. Taste descriptions in Spanish and English. *Chemical Senses*, 5 (1), 47–52. https://doi.org/10.1093/chemse/5.1.47 (last accessed 24 September 2020).

O'Mahony, Michael, M. Goldenberg, J. Stedmon, & J. Alford. 1979. Confusion in the use of the taste adjectives 'sour' and 'bitter'. *Chemical Senses and Flavour*, 4 (4), 301–318. https://doi.org/10.1093/chemse/4.4.301 (last accessed 24 September 2020).

O'Mahony, Michael & Rie Ishii. 1986. A comparison of English and Japanese taste languages: Taste descriptive methodology, codability and the *umami* taste. *British Journal of Psychology*, 77, 161–174.

O'Mahony, Michael & Teresa Tsang. 1980. A preliminary comparison of Cantonese and American-English as taste languages. *British Journal of Psychology* (1980), 71, 221–226.

O'Meara, Carolyn, Laura J. Speed, Lila San Roque & Asifa Majid. 2019. Perception metaphors. A view from diversity. In Laura J. Speed, Carolyn O'Meara, Lila San Roque & Asifa Majid (eds.), *Perception Metaphors*, 1–16. Amsterdam/ Philadelphia: John Benjamins.

Orians, Gordon H. 2018. Our Biological Mind in the Modern Verbal World. In Annalisa Baicchi, Rémi Digonnet, & Jodi L. Sandford (eds.), *Sensory Perceptions in Language, Embodiment and Epistemology*, 3–20. Cham (Switzerland): Springer.

Orians, Gordon. 2014. *Snakes, Sunrises and Shakespeare*. Chicago: University of Chicago Press.
Osawa, Yoshimi. 2011. The Perception and Representation of *Umami*: A Study of the Relationship between Taste Sensation, Food Types and Cultural Categories. Canterbury: University of Kent dissertation.
Osawa, Yoshimi & Roy Ellen. 2014. The Cultural Cognition of Taste Term Conflation. *The Senses & Society*, 9 (1), 72–91.
Oxford English Dictionary, Oxford University Press. Available online at https://oed.com. (last accessed 30 April 2021).
Panther, Klaus-Uwe & Linda L. Thornburg. 2000. The effect-for-cause metonymy in English grammar. In Antonio Barcelona (ed.), *Metaphor and Metonymy at the Crossroads: A Cognitive Perspective*, 215–231. Berlin/ New York: De Gruyter Mouton.
Paulas, John. 2018. *Tastes of the extraordinary: flavour lists in Imperial Rome*. In Rudolph Kelli C. (ed.), *Taste and the ancient senses*, 212–227. New York & London: Routledge.
Pérez-Sobrino, Paula. 2017. *Multimodal Metaphor and Metonymy in Advertising*. Amsterdam/ Philadelphia. John Benjamins.
Perry, Lynn K., Marcus Perlman & Gary Lupyan. 2015. Iconicity in English and Spanish and Its Relation to Lexical Category and Age of Acquisition, *PLOS One* 10 (9), e0137147. https://doi.org/10.1371/journal.pone.0137147 (last accessed 23 September 2020).
Pierce, Charles S. 1903. *A Syllabus of Certain Topics of Logic*. Boston: Alfred Mudge & Son.
Pike, Kenneth L. 1967. *Language in Relation to a Unified Theory of the Structure of Human Behavior*. The Hague & Paris, Mouton.
Plato. (1996). *Gorgia*. Italian edition by Giuseppe Zanetto. Bergamo: BUR.
Pliny. *Natural History*. 1951. Translated by W. H. S. Jones. Loeb Classical Library 392. Cambridge, MA: Harvard University Press.
Plümacher, Martina. 2007. Speaking of colors and odors. In Martina Plümacher & Peter Holz (eds.), *Speaking of Colors and Odors*, 61–84. Amsterdam / Philadelphia: John Benjamins.
Popova, Yanna. 2003. 'The fool sees with his nose': metaphoric mappings in the sense of smell in Patrick Süskind's Perfume. *Language and Literature*, 12 (2): 135–151. doi:10.1177/0963947003012002296
Prescott, John. 1999. Flavour as a psychological construct: implications for perceiving and measuring the sensory qualities of foods. *Food Quality and Preference*, 10 (4–5), 349–356. https://doi.org/10.1016/S0950-3293(98)00048-2 (last accessed 21 September 2020).
Prinz, Jesse J. 2006. Is emotion a form of perception? *Canadian Journal of Philosophy*. Volume 36, supplement [volume 32], 137–160. https://doi.org/10.1353/cjp.2007.0035 (last accessed 29 April 2021).
Prkachin, Kenneth. 2009. Assessing pain by facial expression: Facial expression as Nexus. *Pain Research and Management*, 14 (1), 53–58. https://doi.org/10.1155/2009/542964 (last accessed 29 April 2021).
Proos, Mariann. 2019. Polysemy of the Estonian perception verb *nägema* 'to see'. In Laura J. Speed, Carolyn O'Meara, Lila San Roque & Asifa Majid (eds.), *Perception Metaphors*, 231–252. Amsterdam/ Philadelphia: John Benjamins.
Pulman, S. G. 1983. *Word Meaning and Belief*. London: Croom Helm.
Quinlan, Marsha B. 2017. The Freelisting Method. In Pranee Liamputtong (ed.), *Handbook of Research Methods in Health Social Sciences*, 1–16. Singapore: Springer. https://doi.org/10.1007/978-981-10-2779-6_12-1 (last accessed 29 April 2021).

Radden, Günther. 2018. Molly married money. Reflections on conceptual metonymy. In Olga Blanco-Carrión, Antonio Barcelona & Rossella Pannain (eds.), *Conceptual Metonymy: Methodological, theoretical, and descriptive issues*, 161–182. https://doi.org/10.1075/hcp.60.06rad (last accessed 23 September 2020).

Ramachandran, V. S. & E.M. Hubbard. 2001. Synaesthesia – a window into perception, thought and language. *Journal of Consciousness Studies*, 8 (12), 3–34.

Ramachandran, V. S. & E. M. Hubbard. 2003. The Phenomenology of Synaesthesia. *Journal of Consciousness Studies*, 10 (8), 49–57.

Ramsey, Rachel. 2016. Style and substance: What network visualisations of sentence-sorting data can tell us about the senses of polysemous words. Paper presented at 6th UK Cognitive Linguistics Conference, Bangor University, July 2016.

Ramsey, Rachel. 2017. An exemplar-theoretic account of word senses. Newcastle, UK: Northumbria University dissertation. Available at http://nrl.northumbria.ac.uk/35586/ (last accessed 24 September 2020).

Ramscar, Michael & Robert Port. 2015. Categorization (without categories). In Ewa Dąbrowska & Dagmar Divjak (eds.), *Handbook of Cognitive Linguistics*, 75–99. Berlin/ Boston: De Gruyter Mouton.

Rakova, Marina. 2003. *The Extent of the Literal: Metaphor, polysemy and theories of concepts*. New York: Palgrave Macmillan.

Reed, Danielle R. & Antti Knaapila. 2010. Genetics of taste and smell: poisons and pleasures. *Progress in Molecular Biology and Translational Science*, 94, 213–240. https://doi.org/10.1016/B978-0-12-375003-7.00008-X (last accessed 23 September 2020).

Ren, Dongning, Kenneth Tan, Ximena B. Arriaga, & Kai Qin Chan. 2015. Sweet love: The effects of sweet taste experience on romantic perceptions. *Journal of Social and Personal Relationships*, 32(7), 905–921 https://doi.org/10.1177/0265407514554512 (last accessed 29 April 2021).

Rhee, Seongha & Hyun Jung Koo. 2017. Multifaceted gustation. *Terminology. International Journal of Theoretical and Applied Issues in Specialized Communication*, 23(1), 38–65.

Rivers, W. H. R. 1905. Observations on the senses of the Todas. *British Journal of Psychology*, 1 (4), 321–396.

Roberts, Jane & Christian Kay, with Grundy L. 1995. *A thesaurus of Old English*. Amsterdam: Rodopi.

Robinson, J. O. 1970. The Misuse of Taste Names by untrained observers. *British Journal of Psychology*, 61 (3), 375–378. https://doi.org/10.1111/j.2044-8295.1970.tb01254.x (last accessed 24 September 2020).

Romney A. Kimball & Roy Goodwin D'Andrade. 1964. Cognitive aspects of English kin terms. *American Anthropologist*, 66 (3), pt. 2, 146–170.

Ronga, Irene. 2016. Taste synaesthesias: Linguistic features and neurophysiological bases. In Elisabetta Gola and Francesca Ervas (eds.), *Metaphor and communication*, 47–60. Amsterdam: John Benjamins. https://doi.org/10.1075/milcc.5.03ron (last accessed 23 September 2020).

Ronga, Irene, Carla Bazzanella, Ferdinando Rossi & Giandomenico Iannetti. 2012. Linguistic synaesthesia, perceptual synaesthesia, and the interaction between multiple sensory modalities. *Pragmatics & Cognition*, 20 (1), 135–167. https://doi.org/10.1075/pc.20.1.06ron (last accessed 23 September 2020).

Rosch, Eleanor. 1973. On the internal structure of perceptual and semantic categories. In Timothy E. Moore (ed.), *Cognitive development and the acquisition of language*, 111–144. New York: Academic Press.

Rosch, Eleanor. 1975a. Cognitive representations of semantic categories. *Journal of Experimental Psychology: General*, 104 (3), 192–233.

Rosch, Eleanor, 1975b. Universals and cultural specifics in human categorization. In Richard W. Brislin, Stephen Bochner & Walter J. Lonner (eds.), *Cross-cultural Perspectives on Learning*. 177–206. New York: John Wiley.

Rosch, Eleanor. 1976. Structural bases of typicality effects. *Journal of Experimental Psychology: Human Perception and Performance* 2 (4), 491–502.

Rosch, Eleanor, Carolyn B. Mervis, Wayne D. Gray, David M. Johnson, and Penny Boyes-Braem. 1976. Basic objects in natural categories. *Cognitive Psychology* 8 (3), 382–439. https://doi.org/10.1016/0010-0285(76)90013-X (last accessed 22 September 2020).

Rosch, Eleanor. 1978. Principles of categorization. In Eleanor Rosch & Barbara B. Lloyd (eds.), *Cognition and Categorization*, 27–48. Hillsdale: Lawrence Erlbaum.

Rosch, Eleanor & Carolyn B. Mervis. 1975. Family Resemblances: Studies in the Internal Structure of Categories. *Cognitive Psychology* 7 (4), 573–605. https://doi.org/10.1016/0010-0285(75)90024-9 (last accessed 22 September 2020).

Rosenstein, Diana & Harriet Oster. 1988. Differential Facial Responses to Four Basic Tastes in Newborns. *Child Development* 59 (6), 1555–1568.

Rozin, Paul. 1982. "Taste-smell confusions" and the duality of the olfactory sense. *Perception and psychophysics* 31, 397–401. https://doi.org/10.3758/BF03202667 (last accessed 21 September 2020).

Rozin, Paul, Leslie Gruss, Geoffrey Berk. 1979. Reversal of innate aversions: Attempts to induce a preference for chili peppers in rats. *Journal of Comparative and Physiological Psychology*, 93(6), 1001–1014. https://doi.org/10.1037/h0077632 (last accessed 21 September 2020).

Rozin, Paul & Keith Kennel. 1983. Acquired preferences for piquant foods by chimpanzees. *Appetite*, 4 (2), 69–77. https://doi.org/10.1016/S0195-6663(83)80003-8 (last accessed 21 September 2020).

Rouby, Catherine & Moustafa Bensafi. 2002. Is there a hedonic dimension to odors? In Catherine Rouby, Benoist Schall, Danièle Dubois, Rémi Gervais & André Holley, *Olfaction, Taste and Cognition*, 140–159. https://doi.org/10.1017/CBO9780511546389.015 (last accessed 29 April 2021).

Rudolph, Kelli C. 2018. Introduction. In Kelli C. Rudolph (ed.), *Taste and the Ancient Senses*, 1–21. New York & London: Routledge.

Running, Cordelia A., Bruce A. Craig & Richard D. Mattes. 2015. Oleogustus: The Unique Taste of Fat. *Chemical Senses*, 40 (7), 507–516, https://doi.org/10.1093/chemse/bjv036 (last accessed 29 April 2021).

Sagiv, Noam & Jamie Ward. Crossmodal interactions: lessons from synesthesia. *Progress in Brain Research*, 155, 259–271.

Salzinger, Julia. 2020. Tasting the smell: variation in synesthetic expressions. Paper presented at the UK Cognitive Linguistics Conference, University of Birmingham, 27–29 July 2020.

Sambre, Paul. 2009. Fleshing out Language and Intersubjectivity: An Exploration of Merleau-Ponty's Legacy to Cognitive Linguistics. *Cognitive Semiotics*, 4 (1), 189–224 https://doi.org/10.1515/cogsem.2012.4.1.189 (last accessed 29 April 2021).

Sampson, Geoffrey. 1980. *Schools of linguistics*. Stanford: Stanford University Press.
San Gabriel, Ana M. 2015. Taste receptors in the gastro-intestinal system. *Flavour* 4 (14). https://doi.org/10.1186/2044-7248-4-14 (last accessed 21 September 2020).
Sandford, Jodi L. 2012. *Red Clover – Linguaggio e percezione dei colori: uno studio cognitivo applicato alla lingua inglese*. Roma: Aracne Editore.
Sandford, Jodi L. 2016. Color Entrenchment in Middle-School English Speakers: Cognitive Salience Index Applied to Color Listing. *Folklore: Electronic Journal of Folklore* 64, 91–108. http://dx.doi.org/10.7592/FEJF2016.64.sandford.
Sandford, Jodi L., 2017. You are the color of my life: Impact of the positivity bias on figurativity in English. In Annalisa Baicchi & Alexandra Bagasheva (eds.), *Figurative Language We Live by: The cognitive underpinnings and mechanisms of figurativity in language*, Textus 30 (1): 223–239.
Sandford, Jodi L. 2018. Redder than red, and turning redder: color term form and conceptualisation in English, pp. 61–96. In Dorota Gonigroszek (ed.), *Discourses on Colour*, Poland: Uniwersytet Jana Kochanowskiego w Keilcach.
Sandford, Jodi L. 2019. Taste and sight: A corpus analysis of English adjective-noun constructions. In Jodi L. Sandford & Mario Brdar (eds.) *Jezikoslovlje, Linguistics*, 20 (2), 221–254. Osijek (HR): Osijek University Press. https://hrcak.srce.hr/index.php?show=toc&id_broj=18319.
Sandford, Jodi L. 2021 (in press). *The Sense of Color. A Cognitive Linguistics analysis of color words*. Perugia: Aguaplano.
Schaefer, Michael, Anne Reinhardt, Eileen Garbow & Deborah Dressler. 2020. Sweet taste experience improves prosocial intentions and attractiveness ratings. *Psychological Research*. https://doi.org/10.1007/s00426-020-01336-x (last accessed 25 March 2021).
Schmid, Hans-Jörg. 2007. Entrenchment, Salience, and Basic Levels. In Dirk Geeraerts & Hubert Cuyckens (eds.), *The Oxford Handbook of Cognitive Linguistics*, 117–138. Oxford: Oxford University Press.
Schmid, Hans-Jörg & Franziska Günther. 2016. Toward a Unified Socio-Cognitive Framework for Salience in Language. *Frontiers in Psychology*, 7 (1110). https://doi.org/10.3389/fpsyg.2016.01110 (last accessed 12 March 2020).
Schmid, Hans-Jörg. 2020. *The dynamics of the linguistic system. Usage, Conventionalization and Entrenchment*. Oxford: Oxford University Press.
Schneider, Iris K., Bastiaan T. Rutjens, Nils B. Jostmann, & Daniël Lakens. 2011. Weighty Matters: Importance Literally Feels Heavy. *Social Psychological and Personality Science*, 2 (5), 474–478. https://doi.org/10.1177/1948550610397895 (last accessed 29 April 2021).
Schubert, Thomas W. 2005. Your Highness: Vertical Position as Perceptual Symbols of Power. *Journal of Personality and Social Psychology*, 89 (1), 1–21.
Scott, Thomas R., & Carlos R. Plata-Salaman. 1991. Coding of Taste Quality. In Thomas V. Getchell, Linda Bartoshuk, Richard L. Doty, James Byron Snow (eds.), *Smell and Taste in Health Disease*, 345–369. New York: Raven Press.
Semino, Elena. 2008. *Metaphor in Discourse*. Cambridge, UK: Cambridge University Press.
Shen, Yeshayahu & David Gil. 2007. Sweet Fragrances from Indonesia: A Universal Principle Governing Directionality in Synaesthetic Metaphors. In Jan Auracher & Willie van Peer (eds.), *New beginnings in literary studies* (49–71). Newcastle, UK: Cambridge Scholars Publishing.
Shepard Jr., Glenn H. 2004. A Sensory Ecology of Medicinal Plant Therapy in Two Amazonian Societies. *American Anthropologist* 106 (2), 252–266.

Shibuya, Yoshikata & Haime Nozawa. 2003. Constraints on Synaestheisa. *Proceedings of the Twenty-Ninth Annual Meeting of the Berkeley Linguistics Society: General Session and Parasession on Phonetic Sources of Phonological Patterns: Synchronic and Diachronic Explanations*, 403–414.

Si, Kao & Yuwei Jiang. 2017. Bidirectional contrast effects between taste perception and simulation: A simulation-induced adaptation mechanism. *Journal of Consumer Psychology*, 27 (1), 49–58. https://doi.org/10.1016/j.jcps.2016.04.002 (last accessed 29 April 2021).

Simner, Julia. 2012. Defining synaesthesia. *British Journal of Psychology*, 103 (1), 1–15.

Simner, Julia, Jenny Harrold, Harriet Creed, Louise Monro & Louise Foulkes. 2008. Early detection of markers for synaesthesia in childhood populations. *Brain* 132, 57–64.

Simner, Julia, Catherine Mulvenna, Noam Sagiv, Elias Tsakanikos, Sarah A. Witherby, Christine Fraser, Kirsten Scott & Jamie Ward. 2006. Synaesthesia: The prevalence of atypical cross-modal expriences. *Perception* 35, 1024–1033. https://doi.org/10.1068/p5469 (last accessed 29 April 2021).

Smith, Barry C. 2015. The Chemical Senses. In Mohan Matthen (ed.), *The Oxford Handbook of Philosophy of Perception*, 314–353. doi: 10.1093/oxfordhb/9780199600472.013.045 (last accessed 21 September 2020).

Smith, David V. & Mark B. Vogt. 1997. The Neural Code and Integrative Process of Taste. In Gary K. Beauchamp, Linda Bartoshuk (eds.), *Tasting and Smelling*, 25–76. San Diego: Academic Press. https://doi.org/10.1016/B978-012161958-9/50003-8 (last accessed 21 September 2020).

Smith, J. Jerome. 1993. Using ANTRHOPAC 3.5 and a Spreadsheet to Compute a Free-List Salience Index. *Cultural Anthropology Methods Newsletter*, 5 (3), 1–3.

Smith, J. Jerome, Louanna Furbee, Kelly Maynard, Sarah Quick, Larry Ross. 1995. Salience Counts: A Domain Analysis of English Color Terms. *Journal of Linguistic Anthropology*, 5 (2), 203–216. https://doi.org/10.1525/jlin.1995.5.2.203 (last accessed 23 September 2020).

Soler, M, Kumru, H., Vidal, J., Pelayo, R., Tormos, J., Fregni, F., Navarro, X., and Pascual- Leone, A. (2010). Referred sensations and neuropathic pain following spinal cord injury. Pain, 150(1), 192–198. https://doi.org/10.1016/j.pain.2010.04.027 (last accessed 29 April 2021).

Sorabji, Richard. 1971. Aristotle on demarcating the five senses. *The Philosophical Review*, 80 (1), 55–79. https://doi.org/10.2307/2184311 (last accessed 21 September 2020).

Speed, Laura, Esther Papies & Asifa Majid. 2020. Perceptual associations explain attractiveness of healthy and unhealthy food words. Paper presented at the UK Cognitive Linguistics Conference, University of Birmingham, 27–29 July 2020.

Speed, Laura J., Carolyn O'Meara, Lila San Roque & Asifa Majid (eds.). 2019. *Perception Metaphors*. Amsterdam/ Philadelphia: John Benjamins.

Speed, Laura, David P. Vinson & Gabriella Vigliocco. 2015. Representing Meaning. In Ewa Dąbrowska & Dagmar Divjak (eds.), *Handbook of Cognitive Linguistics*, 190–211. Berlin/ Boston: De Gruyter Mouton.

Speed, Laura J. & Asifa Majid. 2017. Dutch modality exclusivity norms: Simulating perceptual modality in space. *Behavior Research Methods*, 49, 2204–2218. https://doi.org/10.3758/s13428-017-0852-3 (last accessed 23 September 2020).

Speed, Laura J. & Asifa Majid. 2019. Grounding language in the neglected senses of touch, taste, and smell. *Cognitive neuropsychology*. https://doi.org/10.1080/02643294.2019.1623188. (last accessed 23 July 2020).

Spence, Charles. 2011. Managing sensory expectations concerning products and brands: Capitalizing on the potential of sound and shape symbolism. *Journal of Consumer Psychology* 22, 37–54. https://doi.org/10.1016/j.jcps.2011.09.004 (last accessed 2 April 2021).

Spence, Charles, Malika Auvray & Barry Smith. 2015. Confusing tastes with flavours. In Dustin Stokes, Mohan Matthen & Stephen Biggs (eds.), *Perception and its modalities*, 247–274. Oxford: Oxford University Press.

Spence, Charles & Alberto Gallace. 2011. Tasting shapes and words. *Food Quality and Preference*, 22 (3), 290–295. https://doi.org/10.1016/j.foodqual.2010.11.005 (last accessed 29 September 2020).

Sprouse, Jon. 2011. A validation of Amazon Mechanical Turk for the collection of acceptability judgements in linguistic theory. *Behavior Research Methods* 43, 155–167. https://doi.org/10.3758/s13428-010-0039-7 (last accessed 24 September 2020).

Stadtlander, Lee M. & Latona D. Murdoch. 2000. Frequency of occurrence and rankings for touch-related adjectives. *Behavior Research Methods, Instruments, & Computers*, 32, 579–587. https://doi.org/10.3758/BF03200831 (last accessed 23 September 2020).

Stec, Kashmiri & Eve Sweetser. 2012. Borobudur and Chartres: Religious Spaces as performative real-space blends. In Rosario Caballero & Javier E. Díaz Vera, *Sensuous Cognition: Explorations into Human Sentience: Imagination, (E)motion and Perception*, 265–292. Berlin: de Gruyter Mouton. https://doi.org/10.1515/9783110300772.265 (last accessed 25 September 2020).

Stefanowitsch, Anatol. 2006. Words and their metaphors. In *Corpus-based Approaches to Metaphor and Metonymy*, Anatol Stefanowitsch and Stefan Th. Gries (eds.), 64–105. Berlin: de Gruyter Mouton.

Steinbach-Eicke, Elisabeth. 2019. Taste metaphors in Hieroglyphic Egyptian. In Laura J. Speed, Carolyn O'Meara, Lila San Roque & Asifa Majid (eds.), *Perception Metaphors*, 145–164. Amsterdam/ Philadelphia: John Benjamins.

Steiner, Jacob E. 1973. The gustofacial response: Observation on normal and anencephalic newborn infants. In James F. Bosma (ed.), *Oral sensation and perception: Development in the fetus and infant: Fourth symposium*, 254–278. Us Government Printing Office, Dhew.

Steiner, Jacob E., Dieter Glaser, Maria E. Hawilo, Kent C. Berridge. 2001. Comparative expression of hedonic impact: affective reactions to taste by human infants and other primates. *Neuroscience and Biobehavioral Reviews* 25, 53–74.

Stevens, Joseph C. & Lawrence E. Marks. 1965. Cross-modality matching of brightness and loudness. *Proceedings of the National Academy of Sciences*, 54 (2), 407–411. https://doi.org/10.1073/pnas.54.2.407

Stibbe, Arran. 1996. *Metaphor and Alternative Conceptions of Illness*. Lancaster: University of Lancaster dissertation.

Stone, Herbert & Joel L. Sidel. 2004. *Sensory Evaluation Practices*. San Diego: Academic Press. https://doi.org/10.1016/B978-0-12-672690-9.X5000-8 (last accessed 24 September 2020).

Strik Lievers, Francesca. 2017. Figures and the senses: Towards a definition of synaesthesia. *Review of Cognitive Linguistics*, 15, 83–101.

Strik Lievers, Francesca. 2015. Synaesthesia. A corpus-based study of cross-modal directionality. *Functions of Language*, 22 (1), 69–95.

Strik Lievers, Francesca. 2016. Synesthetic metaphors in translation. *Studi e Saggi linguistici*, 54, 43–70.

Strik Lievers, Francesca & Irene De Felice. 2019. Metaphors and perception in the lexicon. A diachronic perspective. In Laura J. Speed, Carolyn O'Meara, Lila San Roque & Asifa Majid (eds.), *Perception Metaphors*, 85–104. Amsterdam/ Philadelphia: John Benjamins.
Sutrop, Urmas. 2001. List task and a Cognitive Salience Index. *Field Methods*. 13 (3), 263–276.
Sweetser, Eve. 1990. *From etymology to pragmatics: Metaphorical and cultural aspects of semantic structure*. Cambridge, UK: Cambridge University Press.
Talmy, Leonard. 2007. Foreword. In Monica Gonzalez-Marquez, Irene Mittelberg, Seana Coulson, & Michael J. Spivey (eds.), *Methods in Cognitive Linguistics*, xi–xxi. Amsterdam: John Benjamins. https://doi.org/10.1075/hcp.18 (last accessed 22 September 2020).
Talmy, Leonard. 2018. *Ten Lectures on Cognitive Semantics*. Leiden/ Boston: Brill.
Taylor, John R. 1995 [1989]. *Linguistic Categorization. Prototypes in Linguistic Theory*. Oxford: Clarendon Press.
Tewksbury, Joshua J., & Gary P. Nabhan. 2001. Seed dispersal. Directed deterrence by capsaicin in chilies. *Nature*, 412, 403–404. https://doi.org/10.1038/35086653 (last accessed 29 April 2021).
Thibodeau, Paul H. & Lera Boroditsky. 2011. Metaphors We Think With: The Role of Metaphor in Reasoning. *PLoS ONE* 6 (2), e16782. https://doi.org/10.1371/journal.pone.0016782 (last accessed 25 September 2020).
Tomasello, Michael. 2008. *Origins of Human Communication*. Cambridge, MA: The MIT Press.
Torres Soler, Julio. 2020. La diversidad del lenguaje metafórico: un estudio *picante* de las metáforas de los sabores en español e inglés y su aplicación a la enseñanza de ELE. Alicante: Universidad de Alicante. Unpublished MA thesis.
Totelin, Laurence B. 2018. *Tastes in ancient botany, medicine and science: bitter herbs and sweet honey*. In Rudolph Kelli C. (ed.), *Taste and the ancient senses*, 60–71. New York & London: Routledge.
Trojszczak, Marcin. 2019. Grounding mental metaphors in touch. A corpus-based study of English and Polish. In Laura J. Speed, Carolyn O'Meara, Lila San Roque & Asifa Majid (eds.), *Perception Metaphors*, 209–230. Amsterdam/ Philadelphia: John Benjamins.
Uusküla, Mari & Urmas Sutrop. 2007. Preliminary Study of Basic Colour Terms in Modern Hungarian. *Linguistica Uralica*, 43 (2): 102–123.
Uusküla, Mari. 2007. The Basic Colour Terms of Finnish. *SKY Journal of Linguistics*, 20: 367–397.
Uusküla, Mari. 2008. The Basic Colour Terms of Czech. *Trames*, 12 (1): 3–28. doi: 10.3176/tr.2008.1.01.
Van Doorn, George H., Dianne Wuillemin & Charles Spence. 2014. Does the colour of the mug influence the taste of the coffee? *Flavour* 3 (10). https://doi.org/10.1186/2044-7248-3-10
Vanhove, Martine. 2008. Semantic associations between sensory modalities, prehension and mental perceptions: A crosslinguistic perspective. In Martine Vanhove (ed.), *From polysemy to semantic change: Towards a typology of lexical semantic associations*, 341–370. Amsterdam & Philadelphia: John Benjamins. https://doi.org/10.1075/slcs.106.17van (last accessed 29 April 2021).
Velasco, Carlos, Alejandro Salgado-Montejo, Fernando Marmolejo-Ramos, Charles Spence. 2014. Predictive packaging design: Tasting shapes, typefaces, names, and sounds. *Food Quality and Preference* 34, 88–95. https://doi.org/10.1016/j.foodqual.2013.12.005 (last accessed 29 September 2020).

Velasco, Carlos, Andy T. Woods, Ophelia Deroy & Charles Spence. 2015. Hedonic mediation of the crossmodal correspondence between taste and shape. *Food Quality and Preference* 41, 151–158. http://dx.doi.org/10.1016/j.foodqual.2014.11.010 (last accessed 29 September 2020).

Velasco, Carlos, Andy T. Woods, Olivia Petit, Adrian D. Cheok, Charles Spence. 2016. Crossmodal correspondences between taste and shape, and their implications for product packaging: A review. *Food Quality and Preference* 52, 17–26. https://doi.org/10.1016/j.foodqual.2016.03.005 (last accessed 29 September 2020).

Ventura, Alison K. & John Worobey. 2013. Early Influences on the Development of Food Preferences. *Current Biology* 23, R401–R408. http://dx.doi.org/10.1016/j.cub.2013.02.037 (last accessed 23 September 2020).

Vernot, Benjamin & Joshua M. Akey. 2014. Resurrecting Surviving Neandertal Lineages from Modern Human Genomes. *Science* 343, 1017. doi:10.1126/science.1245938 (last accessed 29 April 2021).

Vickers, Zata M. 1984. Crispness and Crunchiness – A difference in Pitch? *Journal of Texture Studies* 15, 157–163.

Viberg, Åke. 1983. The verbs of perception: a typological study. *Linguistics*, 21 (1), 123–162.

Vincent, Julian F. V. 1998. The Quantification of Crispness. *Journal of the Science of Food and Agriculture*, 78 (2), 162–168. https://doi.org/10.1002/(SICI)1097-0010(199810)78:2<162::AID-JSFA97>3.0.CO;2-3 (last accessed 23 September 2020).

Vinson, David P., & Gabriella Vigliocco. 2008. Semantic feature production norms for a large set of objects and events. *Behavior and Research Methods*, 40, 183–190. https://doi.org/10.3758/BRM.40.1.183 (last accessed 23 September 2020).

Wang, Qian (Janice), Steve Keller & Charles Spence. 2017. Sounds spicy: Enhancing the evaluation of piquancy by means of a customized crossmodally congruent soundtrack. *Food Quality and Preference*, 58, 1–9. https://doi.org/10.1016/j.foodqual.2016.12.014 (last accessed 29 September 2020).

Wang, Xue, Liuna Geng, Jiawen Qin, & Sixie Yao. (2016). The potential relationship between spicy taste and risk seeking. *Judgment and Decision Making*, 11 (6), 547–553.

Warriner, Amy B., Victor Kuperman & Marc Bysbaert. 2013. Norms of valence, arousal, and dominance for 13,915 English lemmas. *Behavioral Research Methods*, 45, 1191–1207. https://doi.org/10.3758/s13428-012-0314-x (last accessed 23 September 2020).

Weller, Susan C. & A. Kimball Romney. 1988. *Systematic data collection*. Newbury Park: Sage.

Whitney, Arthur H. 1952. Synaesthesia in Twentieth-century Hungarian Poetry. *The Slavonic and East European Review* 30 (75), 444–464.

Wilkins, David. 1996. Natural tendencies in semantic change and the search for cognates. In Mark Durie and Malcolm Ross (eds.), *The comparative method revisited: regularity and irregularity in language change*. New York: Oxford University Press, 264–304.

Willander, Johan & Maria Larsson. 2007. Olfaction and emotion: The case of autobiographical memory. *Memory & Cognition*. 35 (7), 1659–1663.

Williams, Lawrence E. & John A. Bargh. 2009. Experiencing Physical Warmth Promotes Interpersonal Warmth. *Science* 322, (5901). 606–607. doi: 10.1126/science.1162548 (last accessed 29 April 2021).

Williams, Joseph M. 1976. Synaesthetic adjectives: A Possible Law of Semantic Change, *Language* 52 (2), 461–478.

Winter, Bodo. 2019a. *Sensory Linguistics: Language, perception and metaphor*. Amsterdam/Philadelphia: John Benjamins.

Winter, Bodo. 2019b. Synaesthetic metaphors are neither synaesthetic nor metaphorical. In Laura J. Speed, Carolyn O'Meara, Lila San Roque & Asifa Majid (eds.), *Perception Metaphors*, 105–126. Amsterdam/ Philadelphia: John Benjamins.

Winter, Bodo & Teenie Matlock. 2017. Primary metaphors are both cultural and embodied. In Beate Hampe (ed.), *Metaphor: Embodied cognition and discourse*, pp. 99–115. Cambridge, UK: Cambridge University Press.

Winter, Bodo, Paula Pérez-Sobrino & Lucien Brown. 2019. The sound of soft alcohol: Crossmodal associations between interjections and liquor. *PLOS ONE*, 14(8): e0220449. https://doi.org/10.1371/journal.pone.0220449 (last accessed 24 September 2020).

Winter, Bodo, Marcus Perlman, Lynn K. Perry, & Gary Lupyan. 2017. Which words are most iconic? Iconicity in English sensory words. In Stefan Hartmann, Michael Pleyer, James Winters & Jordan Zlatev (eds.), *Interaction and Iconicity in the Evolution of Language*, 443–464. https://doi.org/10.1075/is.18.3.07win (last accessed 23 September 2020).

Wittengstein, Ludwig. 1953. *Philosophische Untersuchungen* [Philosophical investigations], translated by G. E. M. Anscombe. Oxford: Blackwell Publisher.

Wnuk, Ewelina & Asifa Majid. 2014. Revisiting the limits of language: The odor lexicon of Maniq. *Cognition*, *131* (1), 125–138. https://doi.org/10.1016/j.cognition.2013.12.008 (last accessed 29 April 2021).

Woolf, Rosemary [Cynewulf]. 1966. *Juliana*. New York: Appleton-Century-Crofts.

Wong, Roderick. 2000. *Motivation: A Biobehavioural Approach*. Cambridge, UK: Cambridge University Press.

Wood, Bernard. 2010. Reconstructing human evolution: Achievements, challenges, and opportunities. *Proceedings of the National Academy of Sciences of the United States of America* 107 (Supplement 2), 8902–8909. https://doi.org/10.1073/pnas.1001649107 (last accessed 29 April 2021).

Wrangham, Richard W. 2010. *Catching fire. How fire made us human*. London: Profile.

Xu, J. 2017. *"That's bitter!" culture specific effects of gustatory experience on judgments of fairness and advancement* (Masters' thesis). Winnipeg: University of Manitoba.

Yoshida, S. 1998. Aji no Ninshiki to Choumi no Ruikei. In S. Yoshida (ed.), *Jinrui no Shoku Bunka*, 369–407. Tokyo: Ajinomoto Shoku no Bunka Centre.

Yoshimura, Ken & Kan Kobayashi. 1997. A comparative morphological study on the tongue and the lingual papillae of some marine mammals – Particularly of four species of odontoceti and zalophus. *Odontology* 85, 385–407. https://doi.org/10.1007/BF03039036 (last accessed 29 April 2021).

Yu, Ning. 2003. Synesthetic metaphors: A cognitive perspective. *Journal of Literary Semantics*, 32 (1), 19–34. https://doi.org/10.1515/jlse.2003.001 (last accessed 29 April 2021).

Zellner, Debra A. & Mary A. Kautz. 1990. Color affects perceived odor intensity. *Journal of Experimental Psychology: Human Perception and Performance*, 16 (2), 391–397. https://doi.org/10.1037/0096-1523.16.2.391 (last accessed 29 April 2021).

Zlatev, Jordan. 2010. Phenomenology and Cognitive Linguistics. In: Schmicking, D., Gallagher, S. (eds.), *Handbook of Phenomenology and Cognitive Sciences*. 415–446. Dordrecht & New York: Springer.

Zwaan Rolf A. & Diane Pecher. 2012. Revisiting Mental Simulation in Language Comprehension: Six Replication Attempts. *PLOS ONE*, *7*, e51382. https://doi.org/10.1371/journal.pone.0051382 (last accessed 29 April 2021).

Index

Algonquian languages 28
amodal view of meaning 5
Ancient Greek language 141, 155, 166, 171
ancient Greek philosophy VIII, 16, 19, 144, 157, 169, 171
arbitrariness of meaning VII
asparagus 6, 34, 36, 43, 62
Aymara language 80

Basic Colour Terms 38
Basque language 106
bitter
– evolution of 25
– figurative meaning 137
– intrafield occurrences 170

capsaicin. see spicy
categorisation 36
– basic level 37
– family resemblances 93, 102
chemesthesis 22, 154
Chinese language 9, 80
ciarruttime 11
COCA 130
cognitive linguistics VIII, 1, 6, 11, 101
Cognitive Salience Index 13, 51
continuous nature of perception. see multisensoriality
cross-cultural variation 9–10, 79, 83, 97, 107, 188
crossmodal correspondences 158, 163, 169
culture sieve model. see cross-cultural variation

dead metaphor. see metaphor (conventional)
distal senses 17
Dutch language 166

embodiment 5
emic approach 35, 45, 47, 61, 155, 164
entrenchment 42, 44, 57
Epicureanism 25, 141
Estonian language 12

facial response 171
family resemblances. see categorisation
five senses model 19, 35, 164, 189
freelisting 44, 46, 50
French language 121, 166, 171

German language 166, 171
gustation 20, 31, 70, 154

hearing 12, 16, 75, 107, 167–168, 172–173
hierarchy of the senses 16, 155
Hieroglyphic Egyptian language 12, 32, 105
Homo neanderthalensis 25
Homo sapiens 1, 7, 23–25, 107–108
hop 62, 101
human food choices 24

iconicity VII, 76, 150, 158
indexicality 63
individual differences in language 47
ineffability 10
intrafield expressions
– metaphors 123, 154
– metonymies 175
– vs literal language 162
– vs metonymy 162
– vs primary metaphors 161
– vs synaesthesia 158
– vs. conceptual metaphor 161
introspection 35, 47, 50, 99
Italian language 10, 80, 117, 121, 124, 166, 171, 189

Jahai language 10
Japanese language 30, 46, 80

Kenyah Leppo' ke language 79
kinaesthesia 19

Latin language 96, 103–105, 111, 117, 119, 124, 166–167, 171
lexical codability 10
linguistic conveyability 10

Macaca fuscata 26
mammalian gustatory perception 21, 24
Maniq language 10
Mapping Metaphor Project 108
Maragoli language 80
Matsigenka language 79
meaning simulation of gustatory words 7
metaphor
– A HOSTILE TEMPER IS SOUR 144
– ACCEPTING IS SWALLOWING 140
– ACHIEVING A DESIRED OBJECT IS GETTING SOMETHING TO EAT 133
– ACQUIRING IDEAS IS EATING 140
– AESTHETICS IS TASTE 120
– AFFECTION IS WARMTH 106
– ANGER IS A HOT FLUID IN A CONTAINER 12
– APPEALING IS TASTY 106
– behavioural effect 8
– BEING VULGAR IS HAVING TOO MUCH TASTE 147
– CHANGE IS MOVEMENT 142
– CHARACTER IS TASTE 110, 126, 147–148, 152
– COGNITION IS PERCEPTION 12, 113
– CONCEPTUAL METAPHOR THEORY 3, 8
– CONFLICT IS BITTER 100, 137
– conventional 103
– DIFFICULT THINGS TO ACCEPT ARE SOUR 172
– DIFFICULTY OF ACCEPTANCE IS BITTER 140, 145
– DISAPPOINTMENT IS BITTER 139, 145
– DISCORDANCE IS SOUR 123, 173
– EMOTION IS PERCEPTION 12–13, 118
– EMOTIONAL FEELING IS TASTING 32
– EMOTIONAL FEELINGS ARE TASTE 117
– ENJOYING IS SAVOURING 115
– EXCITEMENT IS SPICINESS 149
– EXCITEMENT IS SPICY 152
– EXPERIENCING IS TASTING 32
– HARMONY IS SWEET 123, 168–169, 173
– IDEAS ARE FOOD 140
– IMPORTANCE IS WEIGHT 8
– INNOCENCE IS SWEET 132, 134
– INTELLECTUAL ABILITY IS TASTE 116
– INTELLIGENCE IS FLAVOUR 12
– INTIMACY IS WARMTH 8
– KNOWING IS SEEING 12, 106
– KNOWING IS TASTING 12, 32, 113
– LOVE IS SWEET 8–9, 103, 131, 134, 169
– MIND AS BODY 105, 120
– MITIGATING IS SWEETENING 123, 168
– MORALITY IS SAVOURY 151
– MORALITY IS TASTE 152
– MORE IS UP 4, 106
– novel 102
– PEOPLE ARE OBJECTS 133
– PHYSICAL FEELING/ TOUCHING IS TASTING 32
– PLEASURE IS SWEET 136
– POWER IS UP 106
– primary 4, 103, 106–107, 149, 161, 165
– RUDENESS IS SALTY 146
– SAD IS DOWN 104
– SPOILAGE IS SOUR 3
– SUCCESS/REWARD IS SWEET 135
– THE GENERAL ATMOSPHERE OF SOMETHING IS PERCEPTION 12
– VALUE IS SWEET 121, 135
– VARIETY IS THE SPICE OF LIFE 9
– WOMAN AS DESSERT 133
metonymy 4–5
– BITTER FOR PAINFUL TOUCH 142, 171
– BITTER FOR UNPLEASANT 100, 142, 151
– CAUSE FOR RESULT 137
– GUSTATION FOR OLFACTION 162, 164, 169, 172–173
– PAINFUL TOUCH FOR SPICINESS 167
– PHYSICAL SENSATION FOR ITS PHYSIOLOGICAL REACTION 165
– primary 107, 165
– SOUR FOR SPOILAGE 143, 151
– SOUR FOR UNPLEASANT 173
– SOURCE OF SENSATION FOR THE SENSATION 62, 173
– SWEET FOR PLEASANT 107, 120, 136, 151, 168, 174
– THE PHYSIOLOGICAL EFFECTS OF AN EMOTION STAND FOR THE EMOTION 165
– TOUCH FOR TASTE 171
Middle English language 112
modal view of meaning 6, 88
Modality Exclusivity Rate 69
motivation of meaning
– biological 7, 9, 107, 137, 142, 164, 187
– cultural 184
– embodied 93, 96, 106, 153

– evolutionary 7, 184
– experiential 187
multisensoriality 19, 32, 48, 68, 77, 97, 154, 164, 174, 177
– of flavour 20, 22, 68, 73, 163–164

nociception. see pain
norms 49, 68–69, 76

Old English language 104, 118
oleogustus 22
olfaction 23, 73, 154, 167
onomasiology XI

pain 19, 74, 96, 155, 166, 171, 175
Pan troglodytes 27
perceptual Gestalt 22, 68, 154
polysemy 101, 105
proprioception 19
Proto-Germanic language 171, 175
proximal senses 17

quark 111

Russian language 166

salience 40, 42, 44, 54, 57
salty
– evolution of 26
– figurative meaning 146
savoury
– evolution of. see umami
– figurative meaning 150
semantic change 106
semasiology XI, 99
sensory linguistics 11, 48, 68, 128, 158
Serer Ndut language 80
sight. see vision
sleeping metaphor. see metaphor (conventional)
smell. see olfaction
sorting task
– closed 88
– free 83
sound. see hearing

sour
– evolution of 25
– figurative meaning 142
– intrafield occurrences 172
sour-bitter confusion 80, 97, 152
source-based language 10, 34, 58, 62, 66, 95
Spanish language 82, 106, 117, 166, 171
spicy
– evolution of 27
– figurative meaning 149
– intrafield occurrences 173
– not a taste 23
spicy-hot association 162, 166
spreading activation 44
starchy 22
Sumerian language 104
sweet
– evolution of 24
– figurative meaning 130
– intrafield occurrences 167
synaesthetic metaphors 155, 158

taste
– basic terms 40, 42, 56–58, 60, 97–98, 129
– cultural construal 35
– disparagement of VIII, 16
– physiology 20
– Receptor Cells 21
– transduction mechanisms 22
temperature 166
thirst 19
touch 19, 72, 154–155, 167, 171, 175
Tzeltal language 79

umami 22
– evolution of 26
usage-based approach 33–34

vision VIII, 16, 24, 74, 167
vocative constructions 134
voluntariness 159

Weyéwa language 30

Yora language 79

www.ingramcontent.com/pod-product-compliance
Lightning Source LLC
Chambersburg PA
CBHW020229170426
43201CB00007B/367